The Chosen Path

To Vic!

May God Bless You and all
your activities as You
Dance to Life's Music!

— Don Wyun

The Chosen Path

Based on the Life of Elizabeth Van Lew

Donald Paul Wyman, Ph.D.

The Chosen Path
Based on the Life of Elizabeth Van Lew

iUniverse books may be ordered through booksellers or by contacting:

iUniverse
1663 Liberty Drive
Bloomington, IN 47403
www.iuniverse.com
844-349-9409

ISBN: 978-0-5954-6665-8 (sc)
ISBN: 978-0-5959-0960-5 (e)

Print information available on the last page.

iUniverse rev. date: 10/30/2020

Acknowledgements

The Author wishes to thank:

Boston College Professor Emerita Vera Lee for inspiring me to write this book and then supporting me with important advice throughout the project.

Ms. Carole Ann Smith for the countless hours of repeated readings, valuable editorial suggestions, significant content discussions, historical research assistance, encouragement during the critical stages of the manuscript's development, and mostly, her sincere friendship.

The late Mr. Arthur Curley, former President of the Boston Public Library for his substantial research guidance, access to and assistance with viewing rare books and maps.

The New York Public Library Manuscripts and Archives Division, for the use of the "Elizabeth Van Lew Papers, 1862-1901." With special thanks to Mr. Wayne Furman, New York Public Library Administrative Supervisor in the Office of Special Collections for his timely and courteous assistance.

The numerous readers of the manuscript who encouraged me to have the story published.

And, to Ms. Elizabeth Van Lew and the path she chose. Even though she was so dedicated to protecting her accomplices and destroyed secret war-time dispatches that have kept us from knowing the full extent of her sacrifices, contributions, and successes, she did write over 1000 pages of notes that provided significant insight into her persona, motivation, and activities.

Contents

ILLUSTRATIONS

(Drawn by the author)

PREFACE

This novel is based on the true story of a little known, but significant contributor to the military establishment in Washington, and an open benefactor to the Union. prisoners in Richmond during the Civil War—Miss Elizabeth L. Van Lew. Miss Van Lew's efforts were acknowledged at the highest military and political levels in the United States; and, at the same time discounted and vilified by staunch Post-war Confederate loyalists.

To protect her "loyal to the Union" accomplices from similar retribution, Miss Van Lew destroyed important secret military dispatches and correspondence and omitted specific details of her activities from her diary and manuscripts. This novel is based on the facts that are available from her hand-written journal, eye-witness accounts, biographies, and papers of other characters in the novel, along with interviews, genealogical and historical research in Richmond, Philadelphia, New York, Washington, Baltimore, Canton, Williamsburg, and Boston.

The author has made every attempt to tell the story exactly as it happened when all the facts were known, or might plausibly have happened when the facts either were incomplete, conflicting or non-existent. The events and dialogue are based on the documented deeds, true intentions, writings, personality and reputation of Elizabeth Van Lew. Some names were altered or fabricated to protect any living descendents from questioning their ancestor's true loyalty. In order to fill in several gaps in her life, a few characters were added to provide logical transitions from one factual deed to another. However, what will come through are the chances she took and the high price she paid for her loyal service to the Union.

Miss Van Lew's heart chose the path she was compelled to follow—and she paid dearly for that choice. After years of research into her life, the author also felt a compulsion—to chronicle and credit Miss Van Lew's rightful place in American history along with the others that shared in her contributions and sacrifices.

PROLOGUE

It was early on a clear, warm, late spring morning in the year 1911. From the three-story, south-facing, rear portico of the impressive mansion, the entire city of Richmond, Virginia could be seen over the tops of the magnolia, oleander, beech, acacia, apple, pear and fig trees. The trees, forming the base of the view, caused the city to appear to float on a sea of rustling green leaves.

Beyond the city, the glistening James River, swollen high and wide from the recent spring rains, moved swiftly on its journey to the sea. And even beyond, land was clearly visible, though the many miles muted the colors and details. This was the view from Church Hill, one of the highest points in the city of Richmond and one of its most fashionable addresses.

The stately residence, with its Greek Revival embellishments, was surrounded and complemented by the painstakingly created terraced garden. Boxwoods, roses, azaleas, and rhododendrons were carefully arranged around rustic iron seats and a moss-rimmed garden spring. Terraced gravel walkways sloped away from the house down toward the city of Richmond, softening the land's steep descent.

Adjacent to the main house was a large, two-story dwelling and kitchen that had once been home to generations of devoted servants to the mansion's inhabitants. There was also a barn and smokehouse that completed the residence that encompassed an entire city block. Bordered by Twenty Fourth Street on the east, Franklin Street on the south, and Twenty-Third Street on the West. The main entrance facing north was listed as 2311 Grace Street. The mansion was diagonally across the street from St. John's Church where Patrick Henry made his shocking, impassioned, and patriotic "liberty or death" plea in support of his ideals.

The sweet quiet of the residential area was rudely broken by the clatter of machinery and the gruff voices of workmen, "Ready now … let's do it!" the foreman barked at the small band of men who were looking with part pity and part glee at the defenseless mansion. The thunderous sound of a giant, solid steel ball smashing against brick and board echoed with a sickening crash. The first of many blows the well-built, historic landmark would need to reduce it to ruble. Each cruel and vengeful blow chipping away at its existence echoed the insults, threats, and attacks, which had been suffered by the mansion's mistress of sixty years.

A solitary observer stood on the corner of St. John's Church watching the travesty, his snow-white hair and slightly-bent posture signified his advanced years. He stared helplessly at the unnecessary tragedy before him, thinking, "I'm sorry I couldn't save it Elizabeth. How much it meant to both of us."

He was oblivious to the deep-rooted tears of remorse that filled his eyes and trickled down his cheeks as he softly lamented, "I guess it's Richmond's revenge. And all because the School Board, in its infinite wisdom, decided to relocate the Belleview School on the Grace Street side of the property, rather than the Franklin Street side. So unnecessary … they never forgot … nor forgave you. This visible reminder of you had to be erased to pay for the bitter hurt of their not only losing the war, but because you, a native born Richmond, Virginian, aided and abetted their humiliating defeat."

As each damaging blow was administered, his thoughts returned to another time—a better time—long, long ago. As if anticipating the predictable results of the lethal blows to the house, he sighed, "God, how I loved that house. I can remember the first time I ever saw it," and his mind began to flash back to when he was a young man as, unfortunately, only the mind can do.

CHAPTER 1

A Courtship Period

A handsome young man, accompanied by his parents, both of who were no strangers to the residence, stood at the front entrance of 2311 Grace Street. The father had been there on many occasions as family physician, while the mother attended assorted social functions at the home. The son, upon seeing the residence for the first time, was captivated by its splendor, and the impression was a deep and lasting one.

The building had been newly renovated, and the columns and wooden trim gleamed with a coat of fresh white paint. Its walls of stucco had been bleached with Scotch limestone formerly brought over as ballast in pre-Revolutionary ships. The house seemed to be almost human, having the persona of a proper Southern bride on her wedding day, proclaiming, "Well, look at me, I've been preened and fawned over, dressed in my finest attire, and I feel quite splendid!"

The grounds were also tastefully designed and affectionately pampered. The marriage of house and garden had resulted in a grace and style of a magnitude not seen before in the city of Richmond. The twin semi-circular staircases with their decorated iron balustrade railings led up on either side to the porch and main entrance, giving the impression of two arms extended in a gesture of welcome to all who approached.

Van Lew Residence

The family climbed the twelve steps and the father was about to knock when the door swung open. They were greeted and ushered inside with all dignity by an impeccably dressed servant. They stepped into the sixteen-foot wide grand hall, which ran from the front of the house to the rear. The magnificent chandeliers with their hundreds of rainbow producing prisms, rosewood antique furniture, silk-brocade-covered walls adorned with portraits of family ancestors, gleaming, polished floors reflected satin slippers and an assortment of boots and shining spurs. Elegant fireplaces with mantels of imported Carrara marble and solid-brass andirons with ornate escutcheon; all spoke of the time and resources spent on creating an environment where all who entered would feel esteemed and regally hosted.

The house was alive with well-dressed people engaged in animated chatter. Conversations varied from polite to overbearing, and from boastful to romantic and intimate. Here, a politician charmed a potential supporter; there, a military officer in full-dress uniform detailed his considerable exploits while battling the British. Artisans and actors mingled with authors and entrepreneurs and spoke of their vocational passions, while an army of servants with their silver trays of hot hors d'oevres and chilled champagne weave their way through the multicolored fabric of humanity.

"Hello there, Doc!" boomed the genial voice of the host.

"Good evening John," the physician replied with a friendly tone, "I'd like you to meet my son. John Van Lew, this is my son William, Jr."

"Glad to meet you, William. Is this your first time at our home?"

"Yes, Mr. Van Lew. It's magnificent. Everything is in such perfect harmony."

Proud of his creation, the Van Lew patriarch responded to the young man's acknowledgement, "Why thank you, William. Would you like to look around?"

"Very much, sir!"

"Let me see if I can find Elizabeth. Oh, there she is. Liz, can I see you for a moment?" Dutifully, Elizabeth nodded to her father and excused herself from a guest.

As the young woman approached them, William was struck by his first impression of her. Elizabeth was wearing an exquisite, finely fitted, royal blue dress of imported silk and finest Spanish lace, which complemented her fair complexion and bobbing ringlets of golden curls. She glided across the floor with the grace of a dancer. Her sylph-like figure was petite and fragile. It appeared both delicate and sophisticated, befitting a Southern lady of refinement. Yet, there was something commanding in her walk that also hinted of energy, agility, strength and self-assured determination, a Napoleonic woman in appearance and bearing.

"Liz, I'd like you to meet Dr. Parker's son, William. William, this is my daughter Elizabeth."

They exchanged the usual courteous greetings, but William's interest and fascination were stirred. Elizabeth was surprised that she had never met this handsome son of her family doctor. She admired his clean-cut appearance and the sincerity of his friendly, brown eyes.

"Liz, this is William's first time here, and he is interested in seeing more of the house. Would you be kind enough to give him a tour?"

"I'd be delighted. Come with me, William. Let's start outside on the south portico; it has the most wonderful view of our city this time of day." As she spoke, William couldn't take his eyes off her face. Elizabeth was radiant as a result of having just returned from a refreshing visit to the White Sulphur Springs health resort with her family. Her slightly tanned face beamed with the glow of youth and her complexion was flawless. Her clear and sparkling blue eyes appeared to know and assimilate everything at once, and her mouth, even in repose seemed to speak volumes.

Taking his arm, Elizabeth and William threaded their way through the crowd and the oversized doorway. The attractive pair started out on a house tour, little realizing how their lives will intertwine in the eventful years ahead.

William caught his breath at the sunset-enriched scene before him and thought, "This place is unbelievable. Just when you feel you've seen it all, you see something else that makes it even more exquisite!"

Their lofty and commanding view of the city below revealed commercial buildings, government offices, hotels, train depots, churches, homes and parks all neatly arranged like an architect's scale model. Fixed spots of light appeared from dwellings and places of business. And moving lights from lanterns on horse-drawn coaches and carriages, as they scurried about carrying their passengers to assorted destinations, appeared from this vantage point like fireflies in a black summer night sky.

The sunset had turned the James River into a shimmering flow of liquid gold. Barely visible, but silhouetted by the slowly disappearing sun, was the panorama of land beyond the James that appeared to go all the way to Petersburg, twenty-five miles to the south.

"Elizabeth, I hope I live long enough and am successful enough to have a home and view such as this. I have never seen anything so grand!"

"Well, my Dad is the one responsible for it. Mother and I gave him some decorating ideas, but he's the one who deserves all the credit."

"Have you always lived here? I would have thought that only aristocrats could live like this."

"Believe me, William, we are quite ordinary, and it was not always this good."

"Would you think me too forward to ask how it all came about?"

"Do you really want to know?"

"Yes Elizabeth, I'm very interested."

"Well, when my father first came to Richmond as a young man from Jamaica, Long Island, New York, he went into business with John Adams, the man who first owned this house. The hardware firm of Adams & Van Lew didn't succeed, and Daddy wound up owing $100,000 dollars as his share of the bankruptcy debts. That kind of start in business might have discouraged a lesser man, but not Daddy."

Elizabeth continued, "Daddy's father came from an Old Dutch family and had wanted his son to follow family tradition by becoming a Latin teacher. But, Daddy had other ideas. He was determined to be an entrepreneur. After a long discussion, his father relented and gave his blessing, realizing that to force his very determined son to pursue a life's work that his heart wasn't into would certainly doom him to failure. When Daddy's first venture into business failed, I'm sure he thought for more than a minute about that conversation with his father and the wisdom of his choice. But Father had faith in his own ability. He was totally devoted to his goals and had made a commitment to himself to work tirelessly to make it happen. We all learned much from Daddy about persistence leading to success.

"After Daddy did some extensive research and soul searching, he opened his own hardware business and took in a partner, Mr. Taylor. It wasn't long before the Van Lew & Taylor business flourished. Daddy's first goal, being an extremely honorable man, was to pay off his $100,000 dollar debt, which he did in record time, thereby establishing a solid reputation with creditors and the banks. However, those were very, very lean years for the Van Lew family!"

"I can well imagine," said the attentive listener.

"When Daddy was in business with Mr. Adams we were small children and had visited this house on many occasions. Daddy saw how much we enjoyed playing and running around the huge yard. He offered to buy it then, but Mr. Adams said he would never sell it while he was alive.

"Several years later, after Mr. Adams died, Daddy bought the house. It was only two stories high and, with the family growing, Daddy decided to enlarge it, and he completely redesigned it inside and out. What you see now is the result of his dreams and hard work."

All the while Elizabeth spoke, William was captivated. He was impressed with her lack of pretension and her openness in sharing very personal family details with him. Her blue eyes that looked directly into his as she spoke and the ready smile of the attractive and honest face captivated him. But, more than that, the flow and sincerity of her words spoke volumes about the influence of her family environment and its value development; the privileged upbringing that did not spoil, and of education and tutoring that was not wasted. Yes, this was indeed a very special person.

Throughout the evening, they chatted continually, before, during and after dinner. Her charm, sincerity, composure, and intellect captivated William. He was unaware that his opinion of her appearance had risen from "attractive" to "beautiful."

As the evening wound to a close and people were paying their respects to the host and hostess, Elizabeth took William aside and invited him to the large party her family was to have the next month with a special guest who would be performing.

William expressed his regrets, which were much deeper than he dared reveal at this time. He told Elizabeth how much he would have enjoyed coming and thanked her for the invitation; however, he would be away in Boston at that time studying medicine.

Expressing her disappointment, but tempering it with her sincerest support of his pursuit of such a noble calling, Elizabeth invited him to call whenever he got a break in his studies and could return to Richmond.

Because Elizabeth had been so candid with him, he revealed in the strictest confidence that this may not be possible. Some unfortunate reverses suffered by his father in an unsuccessful financial investment caused his tuition funds to become badly depleted. He explained that, "It has forced me to seek summer work at the university to sustain myself, preventing me from visiting Richmond for some time. But, I give you my word that I will call at the first opportunity." He thanked her again for the invitation and for one of the most enjoyable nights of his life.

Immensely impressed with William's candor, sweetness, ambition and dedication Elizabeth thought, "This is a very special young man indeed!"

A month had passed, and the much-anticipated dinner party that William had been invited to attend was in progress. The party's guest list included Bishop Moore, Justice Marshall, the Lees, Botts, Stearns, Lewises, Robinsons, Adams, Cabells, Carringtons, and the Stewarts.

The Stewarts were a last-minute addition to the guest list.

This night will be one of the highlights of the social season because tonight, Richmond's own author and poet, Edgar Allan Poe will read from some of his works.

Elizabeth sat observing the author, reflecting on the merit and value of his work, along with the negative criticism it had inspired. Filled with anticipation, she thought, "How I've looked forward to hearing this author's words spoken as he envisioned them during those glorious, inspired periods of creation known to many, but taken advantage of by far too few. The handful of original thinkers who cast aside everyday realities and listen to the words and images within. That same soundless voice that comes to us during the dream state, producing the most unusual and imaginative scenarios, seemingly so far from reality that they are labeled as 'bizarre' and dismissed as farfetched. Those brave artists, composers, architects, and authors, who by the strength of their conviction, risk the humiliation of public rejection, censure and condemnation. And, in doing so, they enrich the world by sharing their inner inspirations through these outward expressions."

Elizabeth's thoughts were interrupted by the sound of her mother's voice, "Elizabeth, I have someone that I'd like you to meet. Elizabeth, this is Boyd Stewart. Boyd, my daughter Elizabeth."

Elizabeth politely responded as always with direct eye contact. She believed that you learn much from looking directly into a person's eyes when communicating with them. She read in Boyd's eyes sincerity, confidence tempered with practicality, and seemed to detect an element of reserve and caution that comes from hurt. Most obviously, she caught a look of pleasant surprise on his face.

"I'm pleased to meet you, Mr. Stewart," she said to the expensively dressed, handsome man standing before her.

"It is a great pleasure to meet you, Miss Van Lew, especially after hearing so much about you from your father" he added admiringly.

"Oh really. How do you come to know my father? Are you from Richmond?"

"No I'm not. Your father was good enough to come to our home and is assisting my father in making some special hardware purchases for our plantation."

The mother's mission accomplished; she politely excused herself to attend to another guest, leaving them alone.

"Where is your plantation?" Elizabeth continued, curious to learn more about him and why her father would talk about her to a relative stranger.

Elizabeth did not know how the Stewarts came to be invited to the dinner. Her mother and father had been talking recently about Elizabeth's arrival at the "marrying age" and the lack of an appropriate suitor. During their discussion, her mother was told that while on a recent business trip down the peninsula to the Stewart plantation, her father met and began to do business with the owner's son, Boyd. In the course of his business transactions, Mr. Van Lew found the young man intelligent, well bred, a shrewd negotiator, and of handsome appearance in face and physique. He added with emphasis that Boyd was not attached nor promised to anyone at the present time.

The mother then asked if he thought the two personalities might be compatible. The Father, having met Boyd and knowing Elizabeth's maturity, education, intelligence, quick wit, candor, and ability to hold her own with anyone, suggested, "Why don't we get them together and let Elizabeth decide for herself."

Mrs. Van Lew promptly posted an invitation to the Stewarts inviting them to the dinner party, which they eagerly accepted.

What neither the father nor the mother knew was that the Stewarts had been trying for years to become a part of the Richmond social scene. In fact, that was precisely the reason they had been inviting assorted successful Richmond entrepreneurs with known social position down to their plantation. Their goal was, under the guise of doing business, to introduce them to their "ace in the hole," their eminently eligible son. The son, unaware of his role as a pawn, has had every unacceptable affair of the heart terminated by his parents who refused to give their blessing saying that the women "were beneath his station, and that they wanted only the best for him."

"And what do you grow on your plantation?" Elizabeth continued.

"Tobacco, mostly for commerce, and the usual farm products for our own table," Boyd replied.

He spoke rather matter of factly about their increasingly successful tobacco enterprise. The truth was the business was declining until he returned from his agricultural college studies and applied the techniques learned permitting him to double, and then triple the plantation's annual crop production.

They continued their conversation exchanging information about themselves, their families, their education and their travels. They made special note of the similarities and differences, of which there were more of the former than the latter. The pleasant exchange ended only because it was time for the guest of honor to begin reciting, and everyone scurried to his or her seats.

Poe was spellbinding, holding the enthralled audience transfixed as he read passages from his varied portfolio. From time to time, Elizabeth and Boyd took subtle looks in each other's direction, as if to learn what impact each portion of

Edgar Allan Poe

the performance was having upon the other to further compare tastes and interests … and they were extraordinarily similar.

At the conclusion of Poe's performance the guests surrounded him, showering him with congratulatory compliments. Elizabeth and Boyd drew together again to discuss their opinions and reactions.

From a distance, both sets of parents observed and thought, "It's a good beginning!"

In the following weeks and months, the Stewarts were included in every social function held at the Van Lew home, and the bond between Elizabeth and Boyd grew stronger and deeper. They relished the talents of the guests at the mansion. They shared the beauty of the written or spoken word. They enjoyed the physical exhilaration of horseback riding, walking and talking in the garden, and the joy of partnered movement and closeness of the dance. They also discussed how sad it was for people to grow old alone.

The culmination of the courtship period arrived one evening when they were alone in the garden. Fearful of another lost opportunity, Boyd had memorized exactly what he wanted to say, and when the moment was perfect, he nervously began.

"Elizabeth, you must know how I feel about you. I have grown close to you in every way and my heart belongs to you alone. I cannot imagine my life without you. I want to spend the rest of my life with you by my side. Will you accept this humble proposal of marriage?"

With scarcely a pause, because she had thought about it and talked it over at length with her parents, she replied, "Yes Boyd, I accept it. I will marry you."

And they embraced and sealed the first step of the engagement with a clumsy but heartfelt kiss. Now they must acquire their parents' formal blessing on the union. The consents and blessings were immediate and enthusiastic.

The Stewarts implored the Van Lews to let them reciprocate their months of hospitality by letting them host the official engagement announcement party. Following acceptance, a lavish ball was planned at which to make the surprise announcement.

There was much excitement and fussing at the Van Lews' in preparation for the Ball. Mr. Van Lew spared no expense. Elizabeth was to have a new outfit for every occasion during the weekend at the plantation. The garments required proper design, purchase of appropriate fabric and many scheduled fittings. Everything was carefully planned and successfully carried out to the smallest detail.

CHAPTER 2

A Timely Revelation

An overcast afternoon sky hovered above the Van Lew family as they were being greeted at the front entrance of the Stewart plantation's manor house. The carriage and the quartet of snow-white matched horses that brought the Van Lews were led away. While their extravagantly filled luggage was being brought to their rooms, the family was given a brief tour of the home and grounds. Exhausted from the long trip, they retired to refresh themselves for dinner.

Dinner was sumptuous and filled with conversation. That was, until Boyd's sister Belle made a comment about the table maid's dropping of a serving of chicken, not realizing that her younger, teen-aged brother had mischievously tripped her.

"What an incompetent nigger! I must apologize for her. She is new and I can assure you that she will pay for the embarrassment she has caused!"

Elizabeth, who witnessed the whole incident replied, "I don't think any punishment is in order for her. It was your brother Bent who tripped her on purpose. I saw the whole thing."

Embarrassed and too proud to back off, Belle baited Elizabeth with, "Well, what would you do under the circumstances?"

Elizabeth replied calmly, "I would correct Bent and have him apologize to the maid for his trouble-making behavior."

"Apologize to a nigger, never!" she snapped.

"Now, now, my dear Belle, Elizabeth is a guest in our home and will soon be a member of our family. Let us show some respect and Stewart hospitality," Mr. Stewart interjected.

Attempting to cool down and swallow her pride, she complied with her father's request and excused her brother's behavior with, "Well, I guess boys will be boys!" She maintained a huffy silence throughout the rest of the meal and never again looked in Elizabeth's direction. After the meal, all retired to their rooms to prepare themselves for the ball and the official engagement announcement ceremony.

There was a soft knock on Elizabeth's door. She opened it to see the table maid. "May I come in?" she asked in a soft, fearful voice.

"Please do." Elizabeth said as she closed the door behind her, sensing the maid's nervousness at being there.

"I just wanted to thank you for telling Miss Belle what really happened and for saving me from a beating."

"A beating?" Elizabeth asked in surprise.

"Yes, and I wanted to do something for you to show my appreciation. You see, I once worked for a wonderful lady who treated me very nice. She would always ask me to fix up her hair ... said I had a real flair for it. Because you were so nice to me, I'd like to fix up your hair real special for the party," she pleaded.

"Well, it is not necessary, but I would be honored to have you fix it special for me!"

Later that night, the house was filled with the sound of music, happy people laughing and talking, the clinking of champagne glasses, and the sounds of many pairs of dancing feet. Elizabeth came down the long hand-carved walnut staircase with her father and mother, and they walked toward the merriment. Elizabeth was absolutely radiant in a stunning, iridescent, black silk gown from Paris. A wide, snow-white lace collar in a v-shape spanned from the tip of each shoulder to her waist. Her hair, fixed "special" by the maid, looked like spun gold as it hung down in ringlets swept back from her face. Her eyes sparkled, and her cheeks were flushed in anticipation of the evening's events. Elizabeth had never looked lovelier!

No sooner did her black satin-slippered feet hit the highly polished wooden floor, than a handsome young man approached and enthusiastically asked for a dance.

Boyd observed the scene from across the room and attempted to position himself to get Elizabeth for the next dance. Having caught the eye of all the young eligibles, they converged and surrounded Elizabeth, blocking Boyd from getting near her, and off she went with another admirer. They all wanted to dance with this attractive newcomer.

Boyd's jealousy turned to anger, and he headed for the refreshment table and downed several glasses of champagne, He made another attempt to approach her for a dance and once again was unsuccessful. Fuming, he vowed, "I'll have the next dance, come hell or high water!"

This time, he headed straight for her, elbowing and shoving men aside as the music was about to begin, but another man started to carry her away. Boyd was not in a mood to argue now. He grabbed her free arm and pulled her away from the dance floor and roughly led her into the library and closed the door behind them. He proceeded to explain to her that, "You are my fiancée, in my house, and will soon be my wife." Emphatically, he continued that, "Being my wife means that you belong to me, and that whenever I want anything you must ..."

A loud, urgent knock interrupts his tirade.

"Who is it?" he shouted angrily!

"It's Calvin, Mr. Boyd!" the plantation's white, burly, slave overseer replied gruffly.

"What do you want?"

"I need to talk to you right away, sir!"

Boyd went to the door and talked to his overseer in low whispers. Further enraged by what he was told, Boyd stormed out of the room, slamming the library door behind him.

Bewildered and somewhat frightened by Boyd's highly unusual behavior, Elizabeth wanted to hear the rest of what Boyd had to say and was curious to learn what would cause him to leave her in the middle of the unresolved situation. She opened the door just in time to see the two of them hurrying out the front door. After waiting a moment, she followed at a safe distance. The night air was cool and damp, and she felt a chill. Her body shivered from the fear of something unknown.

She went down the muddy drive, past the outbuildings, kitchens, and stables to the slave quarters, where a large torch-lit group of Negroes stood in front of dilapidated shanties. The slaves were huddled together dreading what was about to happen, too afraid to speak. In front of them were Boyd, Calvin the overseer, and two other white men holding down a struggling, very pregnant, young black girl by the arms and legs.

Amazed and puzzled, Elizabeth moved quietly behind a huge maple tree and remained unseen, but close enough to hear everything being said.

"Did you catch the other two yet?" Boyd asked impatiently between clenched teeth.

"No, they appear to have gotten away. Sally here, couldn't run fast enough cuz of her condition," the man who held her legs said snidely.

"Well, she'll pay for them too! I'll show you what you get when you try to run away from Boyd Stewart!" he snarled as he pulled off his wide, thick leather belt. The helpless girl's eyes widened as he raised the belt as high as he could to get the full power of the stroke. Then, with all his strength, he lashed the defenseless girl. The crack of the leather on her flesh echoed throughout the area—immediately followed by the girl's scream. The two sounds stabbed the air, piercing Elizabeth's body and penetrating deep into her soul. Boyd raised his arm again and again, whipping the now delirious girl. His face was contorted with anger and revenge as if possessed by some invisible demon, as he ignored the pregnant girl's convulsive screams and pleas.

As a warning to all those present, Boyd promised, "This is what you can expect from me, any of you, young or old, man or woman. This is the way I treat my property when you cross me! And remember, you all belong to me!"

His words rang all too familiarly with the library tirade, and Elizabeth's eyes overflowed with tears of compassion for the girl. Uncontrollable tremors surged through her body.

Finally, the man holding the girl's arms reminded Boyd that, "She's due to have the baby any minute, and any more whupping might kill it and her too!"

Elizabeth had seen more than enough. This was a side of Boyd that she had never known, never imagined. Realizing what a mistake she had almost made, Elizabeth turned and ran for the house. Once inside, she hurried past the people and up the same staircase which, only an hour before, she had so elegantly descended with such high hopes, and entered the safety of her room.

Her mother and father, seeing her distraught appearance and hasty retreat upstairs, quickly followed her to determine the cause of her behavior. In tears, she explained everything that happened, what she saw, and how she felt. Seeing Boyd in an entirely different light now, she said that, "She could not ... would not, under any circumstances, become his property to mistreat. Never!"

After reviewing the entire evening's events and seeing Elizabeth's condition and resolve, the Van Lews were all in agreement that the engagement announcement should be withdrawn, and that they would leave the premises at dawn for Richmond.

It was nearly three in the morning when Boyd returned after inflicting birth-inducing blows on the helpless victim. It had not surprised any of the onlookers that Boyd watched the mulatto baby's birth with a fatherly interest. A birth where the baby had one scream in it's mouth and—another in it's ear.

To avoid observation, Boyd slipped into the library from the unlocked veranda door of the now quiet house and locked it from the inside. After seeing his reflection in the mirror, he decided that he wanted to see no one and would have no one see him in his present condition, especially Elizabeth. He would talk to her in the morning after making up some plausible excuse, "Oh, what the hell; she's practically my wife. She'd better get used to understanding my role and responsibilities in maintaining authority and discipline."

Still angry and half-drunk, clothes covered with mud, sweat, and blood, Boyd reached for the half-filled decanter of bourbon, and with only a few pauses for air, drained its contents. With a frustrated groan, he muttered, "Some heir!" and dropped onto the sofa that would feel his dead weight for the next twelve hours.

When Boyd called at the Van Lew residence the next evening, he was informed by Mr. Van Lew that Elizabeth had been the innocent witness of the inhumane treatment he dispensed upon a helpless pregnant girl. He stated that in no way would he allow his daughter to live in such an environment. And added that it was Elizabeth's wish that he never again call at this address.

Boyd apologized for his behavior stating that he was truly sorry for the embarrassment that they all suffered as a result of it. "I will honor your wishes, and I'm disappointed that it ended this way. Thank you, Mr. Van Lew, for all that you've done for me." They shook hands, said their "Good bye's" and Boyd left none too soon. The tears in his eyes began to flow as the realization of all that he had lost hit him hard, when he heard the door closing in his ears … and in his heart. Once again, he had been denied a loving relationship.

It was an ironic twist of fate that the very day the Van Lews left for James City that young William Parker called at the Van Lew home before returning to school. He had been given leave from his studies to attend the funeral of his mother in Richmond.

The servant answering the door explained to William that the family was away attending Elizabeth's wedding engagement party in James City. He asked William if he could tell the Van Lews who had called and the nature of his business.

William's heart felt as if it had stopped functioning and his hearing along with it. The only sound he could hear was the one echoing in his head, "Elizabeth getting married, Elizabeth getting married!" over and over.

Every leisure moment his mind was not concentrating on his studies, he had thought of Elizabeth. He carried the memory of their first meeting in his head and in his heart. William had fantasized their second meeting; what he would say and how he would say it. Then, he would tell her of the progress he was making toward his professional goal, and how much he enjoyed being with her. He had imagined that after achieving his academic credentials, he would ask her humbly to be his wife, fully knowing that he would not be able to support her in the grand style to which she was now accustomed. He had reasoned that Elizabeth's father wasn't rich when he asked her mother to marry him, and didn't think Elizabeth was the kind of person who would require wealth as a precondition to marriage. "Elizabeth getting married," each repetition cracked the shell of disbelief. There was the painful realization that Elizabeth had made a far greater impression on him than he must have made on her. With nothing more to say and resigned to the hopelessness of his dream, he turned to leave.

"May I tell her who called?" repeated the polite voice of the servant, still waiting for a response.

William turned, and with a heart void of hope, replied softly, "No thank you. It doesn't matter anymore."

The bounce that had been in his step when climbing the stairs to Elizabeth front door was noticeably missing as he descended. As he closed the front gate behind him, William couldn't resist one last look at the beautiful home. On this sad and gloomy weekend, he had lost two people in his life he hoped would share his future. Looking at the mansion now, it seemed to have lost some of its magnificence ... but not much!

William was one of the two admirers who, before the weekend was through, walked away from the house feeling they had seen the last of it and Elizabeth Van Lew. One of them will be mistaken.

CHAPTER 3

The Second Disappointment

The day William had looked forward to for so long finally arrived. Years of dedicated, grueling research, study, and examination; long days of laboring at all forms of work to subsidize the tuition; along with the personal sacrifice of a social life, all for accreditation. Now, he was Doctor William Henry Parker, Jr., and he was coming home to Richmond

As he stepped off the train, filled with such anticipation and expectations of his new life, the first person he saw, not more than twenty feet away … Elizabeth!

She was walking on the arm of a very handsome man and was followed by her mother and one of her sisters. They were boarding the soon-to-depart train directly opposite the one on which the new Doctor Parker had arrived.

Elizabeth looked in his direction and, for a brief moment, appeared to recognize him. But then, she turned her head straight ahead and, with a rather expressionless face, proceeded with considerable difficulty and assistance to climb the steps into the private railcar.

This chance coincidence was a cruel and painful reminder of the missed opportunity sacrificed in the pursuit of credentials.

Elizabeth weakened by sickness and lethargic from medication, thought for a moment that the handsome young man departing the train looked like William! "Could it be? This would be about the time he would have completed his medical studies at the university. Yes, I'm sure it was William! He appeared in need of a good night's sleep—but looks more mature and confident. Periodically, I overheard Doctor Parker tell Daddy about his son's progress. I think Daddy might have had plans for William and me … maybe … I must invite him to call when I return."

With some difficulty, Elizabeth took her seat by the closed window and, once again, spotted William in the crowd. Now she observed a beautiful young lady who had run to William and he to her. They affectionately kissed and twirled about in a hug, as might be expected between two loving people who had long been separated. The affection they had for one another was obvious as they walked arm in arm in animated conversation. The lady gazed adoringly into William's face as he spoke and she appeared to hang onto his every word. Although Elizabeth could not hear their words, their actions seemed to say it all.

The sudden rush of warm healing and excitement that coursed through Elizabeth's body at seeing William vanished upon observing the obvious love shared between William and the young woman. Once again, she witnessed a painful episode; and another potential opportunity for a life of shared love vanished. She closed her eyes in sorrowful resignation. The bright flame of hope in her heart for a shared, loving relationship was only a small flicker now ... but it burned still! Now, Elizabeth looked forward even more to the prescribed lengthy European trip, hoping to recuperate from her lingering physical and emotional state of affairs.

What Elizabeth had been unable to hear the young beautiful lady call when she spotted William on the train platform was, William, William!" as they ran to each other. "Welcome home big brother! Or, do I have to call you Doctor William now?" she playfully teased, full of pride in her older brother, whom she adored and hadn't seen in a long time. Then, she kissed and hugged him and enfolded her arm in his as they walked toward where Doctor William Parker, Sr. was waiting, also bursting with pride.

As they approached him, the beaming elder Parker, thought, "Too bad you couldn't be here on this platform in person with me today Martha to see our two children. And yet, my love, I know you are here in spirit, and you do live on in their goodness and the pleasure they bring to others around them."

Although the Parker home was not at the same level of splendor as the Van Lew Van Lew residence, it was of handsome appearance and much larger than needed for the family of three, and William was overjoyed at being back under its roof. Speaking with his father, he commented, as matter of factly as he could manage, "I thought I saw the Van Lews at the depot when I arrived today."

"Yes," the father answered in rather sober tones, "I recommended that Europe might be a healthy prescription for Elizabeth, considering the advanced medicine and treatment available there, and to get away from the house and all its memories, for a while."

William's mind flashed back to his first memory of the house, and he concurred with, "Yes, I can imagine all the memories, but why would getting away from the house help?"

Doctor William Parker, Jr.

"Oh, of course, you wouldn't have heard about Elizabeth's father, John. Do you recall you met him at their home?"

"Yes, I remember him."

"Well, he passed away recently from dyspepsia, and she took it very hard; they were so close. Elizabeth hadn't been well for some time, and the sudden unexpected loss compounded the illness. Her mother and sister went along to try to lift Elizabeth's spirits.

"So, tell me now, on a more cheerful subject, how are you and Rebecca getting along? She has been working with me for the past six months. Somehow I think her interest in working for me is secondary to her interest in the hope of working eventually with my new junior partner!"

"Well Dad, we have been corresponding for the past several years, but I still just think of her as a very nice young girl with a passion for writing."

"William, William. You've grown a lot and gained a knowledge of medical subjects, but you have a lot to learn about relationships between men and women."

"Dad, Rebecca and I have communicated about many different subjects, and we do seem to have similar tastes, but I never sensed that it was any more than an ordinary friendship. I didn't even know before today that she worked for you."

"Perhaps she didn't feel comfortable writing about it, or maybe she wanted to surprise you. Let me tell you a few things about this girl. Rebecca has learned so much since she came here and has become a valuable and dependable assistant to me in the practice. In fact, it was her idea to use our extra bedrooms as a sort of emergency holding area until patients could withstand the bangs and jarring of the trip to the hospital. She created the facility and has managed it all on her own. She's truly a dedicated and caring person. If I were taken sick, she's one of the people I'd want ministering to me. By the way, when was the last time you saw her?"

"It was at mother's funeral," he recalled.

"Well, my boy, you are in for a surprise when you see her tonight at your welcome home party!"

Surprised? That night William was amazed. Skinny little Rebecca had blossomed into full womanhood, and she was beautiful! He could barely take his eyes from her the entire evening. All the people he had known seemed to have become adults. Everyone added his or her congratulations, and the father basked in the glow of immense pride in his son's accomplishment over adversity.

"Good evening, Doctor William Parker, Jr.," came the cheerful greeting he had looked forward to.

"Good evening, Rebecca," he replied with a smile. "Why didn't you tell me you were working with my Dad?"

"I didn't want you to think I was trying to get too close to you. All your letters were so filled with medical talk and I wanted to be able to speak more intelligently about that with you in the future. What better way to learn about it than from the best? And don't get any ideas that I like you—it's your father I'm after."

"Father, hah," he laughed. "You know he'll never marry again!"

"I know. That is a problem!" she replied in mock despair.

William thought, "I like this girl. She's frank, intelligent, has a good sense of humor, and now we have medicine in common—and I'll be seeing her every day." The fact that she was beautiful came as a pleasant afterthought.

The weeks became months and William and Rebecca fell deeply in love. Both parents gave their blessing, and the couple were married. The Van Lew family was invited but only John Newton Van Lew attended since both sisters and his mother were still in Europe and were not to return for some months.

One day, four months later, Doctor Parker, Sr. asked William, who has shown great medical skill and, like himself, an insatiable thirst for more medical knowledge, to look in on Elizabeth Van Lew. The father had learned that the Van Lews had just returned from Europe, and he wanted William to both check on Elizabeth's condition and to introduce himself as his new partner to provide continuity of the practice as Van Lew family physicians. William was delighted to accept the assignment.

Upon arrival at the Van Lew residence, he presented his card to the servant explaining that he was calling without an appointment and, if not convenient, that he would be happy to return at another time. He explained that he merely wanted to inquire about the health of Miss Elizabeth. The servant politely asked him to wait for a reply.

The response was almost immediate. A much healthier-appearing Elizabeth walked toward him than the sickly one he last saw at the train station.

"William! Or should I call you Doctor Parker now?"

"Elizabeth! How good to see you and 'William' is just fine. Let me first express my sympathy. I heard about your father; he was a remarkable man."

"Thank you William. I miss him so very much."

"How is your health now Elizabeth? Dad told me about your illness and his recommendation of the European trip."

"I am happy to report that the trip was a perfect prescription. My compliments to your father for his excellent physical and emotional diagnosis and proscribed 'medicine'!"

"Dad will be so glad to hear that. He cares a great deal about you and your family."

"And congratulations are in order for you, William—doubly so! Your admirable pursuit and achievement of your goal to become a doctor, and I learned from my brother John of your recent marriage," Elizabeth said politely hiding her tinge of regret.

"Thank you, Elizabeth. I hope someday to be able to walk in the large shoes of my dad as a competent, respected physician and surgeon. I am so fortunate to have such wise and gifted guidance during my early years practicing medicine. And, yes, I married a wonderful girl named Rebecca, who had already been working with my father before I returned home from school."

"William, the day I left for Europe I was so ill and medicated that I wasn't sure, but I thought I saw you arriving at the train station, and the lady who met you must have been your fiancée."

"Yes, that was me, but that was my sister who met me on the platform," he explained.

"Your sister? Oh no! The greeting was so enthusiastic and affectionate that my muddled mind made an incorrect assumption!"

They looked at each other while their minds reviewed the pictures of that day. However, this time the information in Elizabeth's memory was corrected and refiled along with the disappointment at having been deceived by appearances.

Touched by her sincere and honest revelation, William decided to tell his side of the story. "Elizabeth, since you have been so open and honest with me, and that is one of the many qualities I admire in you, I must be honest with you too!"

"William, I hope that will always be the way between us."

"Well, here goes. When my mother died, I was given a brief emergency leave from my studies to attend her funeral. Before returning to school, I came to call on you as you had invited me to do. The servant who answered the door told me that your entire family had gone away to spend the weekend at the home where your engagement to be married was to be announced. I must admit to you here and in private that I was surprised and disappointed, because I had become, well, totally infatuated with you after just that one evening we shared."

Elizabeth listened silently, amazed to discover that he had felt the same attraction to her that she had felt toward him from just that one evening together.

"Dad never mentioned anything about the wedding to me in his letters, so I naturally assumed that you'd gotten married. Then, when I saw the man helping you onto the train, in my mind, that confirmed it for me."

"Oh, William, because of my weakened condition, your father was kind enough to have that man assist me from my home to my seat on the train.

"And I thought he was your husband accompanying you to Europe!"

Once again, there is the re-shuffling of mental images. The "Oh no's!" they inwardly expressed … the opportunity unexplored … the mutual interest too late realized. Only the two pairs of hands that were simultaneously extended and tightly held in mutual affection and understanding expressed their feelings. Though they sat at a respectable distance, under different circumstances, that gesture would have resulted in a long and intimate kiss and embrace. As they looked into each other's eyes, words were unnecessary. They knew their feelings but had to keep the knowledge forever locked in their hearts.

CHAPTER 4

Arrivals & Departure

Only an occasional visitor of prominence, a social event, or secret assistance to the efforts of the "Underground Railroad" made the years of relative calm that followed Elizabeth's return from Europe noteworthy. William and Rebecca had their first child, and the young doctor's reputation and practice had become solidly established in Richmond. Elizabeth occasionally played hostess to a variety of guests as the political rhetoric in the country continued to heat up, polarizing and solidifying men and women on both sides of the volatile issues of slavery and secession.

Some of the guests at the Van Lew's home included staunch abolitionists. Among them, John Minor Botts and Franklin Stearns who never missed the opportunity to speak against the cruelty, injustice, and inhumane evils of human bondage. Their uncompromising egalitarian zeal fell upon more than a few sympathetic ears.

One particularly pleasant, non-political social occasion was an afternoon reception. The guest of honor was Miss Jenny Lind, the "Swedish Nightingale." Elizabeth had invited her not only for her golden voice, but also because she'd heard of the singer's social sensitivities and many philanthropic deeds, which she admired. Elizabeth's own reputation and position on social issues mutually appealed to Miss Lind, and she eagerly accepted Elizabeth's invitation.

The two women had a long private chat and, at its conclusion, Jenny herself volunteered to "sing a song or two" at the ensuing reception at the Van Lew mansion. Her "song or two" included the Norwegian "Echo Song," "I Know That My Redeemer Liveth," Benedict's "Take This Lute," Shubert's "Ich Muss Singen" (The Bird Song), Schumann's "Sonnenschein" (Sunshine), "The Last Rose of Summer," and the song that always brought the house

Jenny Lind

down at each stop of her year-long American tour, John Howard Payne and Henry Bishop's "Home Sweet Home."

The pathos that characterized her unique voice, with its capacity to strike the heartstrings of any listener, was even more intensified by her own longing for a home that she never had.

When those poignantly nostalgic notes and deeply moving words were sung with such emotion and feeling to the mesmerized gathering, there was not one unaffected person in the room. When she finished, there was no immediate applause, just a long hush. Then, people—even the men among them, began to reach for their handkerchiefs. After a long moment, Jenny lowered her own misty eyes. Then came an overpowering, standing ovation that lasted for a full ten minutes. She had totally captivated the hearts and souls of the listeners in the filled-to-capacity grand ballroom!

Needless to say, her single scheduled Richmond performance at the Marshall Theatre that evening was a complete artistic and financial success. It set the record for the highest receipts for a single concert of her American tour, and the music critic for the Richmond Whig said, after his glowing review, that; "We have no apology for the intensity of our admiration."

Another prominent visitor, also from Sweden, was Fredrika Bremer, the novelist. While visiting Richmond in 1851, she wrote about Elizabeth's and her mother's treatment of their slaves; describing them as, "Women of intellect, kindness and refinement of feeling that was evident in their gentle countenances." Elizabeth was described as; "A pleasing, pale blond who expressed so much compassion for the sufferings of the slave that Frederika was immediately attracted to her." And added, "These ladies are so tender hearted, especially toward the Negroes, that I find myself standing upon the moderate and less liberal side, whilst I inwardly enjoy the sight of the warm hearts who only err through an excess of kindness to an oppressed people. Such a sight is very rare in a slave state."

Miss Bremer spent many hours conversing with the Van Lews while she examined, analyzed and photographed the house. She accumulated many details about the Van Lew resi-

Fredrika Bremer

dence that she included in her book, "*Homes in the New World.*" One day while Fredrika was staying at the home; Elizabeth took her to a tobacco factory and, upon observing the hard lot, treatment, misery, hopeless sad faces, and despondency of the slave workers, they both could not refrain from weeping.

Since this humane behavior seemed so unusual in the Southern states, Fredrika asked Elizabeth if she came to acquire her attitude toward the slaves as a result of her teachings from her Pennsylvania governess or during her schooling in Philadelphia

Elizabeth told her that both helped shape her attitude, but the greatest impact came when she was a young woman during one of her family's visits to White Sulphur Springs, the famous resort of the South.

Elizabeth had met the daughter of a wealthy slave trader, a member of a social class that some despised, but tolerated only as a necessary evil. The girl told Elizabeth many stories about her father's slave transactions, relating them in such a cavalier fashion, as if talking about the sale of farm cattle, totally without feeling or compassion.

One story about how her father had sold a young mother and her new baby to different buyers had a powerful effect on Elizabeth. The girl told her "When Daddy handed the mother over to her new owner she saw her only baby being given to another owner from a plantation hundreds of miles from where she would be in bondage. It pained her so much that her heart broke and she fell dead immediately!"

Elizabeth was so moved by that tragic story that it affected her attitude and actions for the rest of her life.

She knew how to take action and did. During that same year, Elizabeth and her mother not only freed all of their slaves but also bought their slaves' relatives and set them free, giving them a small stipend to help them get started. Many of them remained as paid servants, while a few took their families North.

One young black girl, Mary Bowser, caught the attention of Elizabeth. Mary had an extremely quick bright mind, very pleasant disposition, and a touch of independence, qualities not unlike Elizabeth's.

At Elizabeth's urging, Mary's father, Nelson, one of the many former slaves who chose to remain in the Van Lew household as a servant, was persuaded to allow Mary to go to Philadelphia to be educated at a Friends Select School. It was similar to the Quaker-run school that Elizabeth had attended, where many less-gifted students owed their good grades to Elizabeth's sharing of her scholarship by tutoring them after school hours. And many a young man learned not to get into a battle of wits with Elizabeth, for she was far too quick and logical.

Since the entire amount of the trip, lodging and education was to be at Elizabeth's expense, Nelson eagerly gave his blessing for his daughter's unusual opportunity for an education that he himself could not afford to provide. He expressed his gratitude to Elizabeth for her generosity.

Mary's departure was a combination of tears and joy. Her infectious smile, coupled with a youthful energy and brash outspoken comments, brought many a humorous moment to the entire household.

As Mary was leaving, she turned before climbing the steps into the train. With a serious look on her face, she said to Elizabeth, "Miss Liz, I know you're trying to be nice to me sending me to school, but are you sure you're not just trying to get rid of me and get a little peace and quiet?" Then, Mary flashed that precocious smile, and Elizabeth and the rest of the send-off party burst into laughter. Mary's leaving left a void that would not be filled for a long time to come.

CHAPTER 5

The Lonely Reflection

In 1854, the Van Lew mansion witnessed the departure of its last male family resident. The Richmond newspaper's account of the marriage of Elizabeth's only brother read:

"Married on the 24th of January, Mr. John Newton Van Lew of the firm Van Lew and Taylor, to Miss Mary Carter West, both of this city."

Over the course of two decades, the Van Lew household members had steadily declined. In 1833, Elizabeth's six-year old sister Eliza died. The following year, her sister Annie Pauline married Doctor Joseph Klapp of Philadelphia, where she took up residence. That same year, 1843, her father died. In December 1853, her aunt, on her father's side, passed away. And now, with the marriage of John, the occupants of the spacious mansion were reduced to just Elizabeth and her mother.

After the excitement of John's wedding, Elizabeth and her mother were feeling the emptiness as they sat one evening quietly sipping tea by the fireplace. Elizabeth, who had been silent and deep in reflection, broke the silence.

"Is this dreary and meaningless situation to be our lifelong existence? How are we to spend the rest of our lives? I can see our obituary now, 'The two old maids of Church Hill lived and died alone in their house on Grace Street.'"

Somewhat surprised by her daughter's questions, Mrs. Van Lew remained attentively silent.

After another long wordless pause, Elizabeth continued, "At least you raised a family; I have accomplished nothing."

Touched by the words so honestly and painfully spoken, her mother sighed, "Oh, Elizabeth, I never thought it would wind up like this; you and I alone in this house. I thought it would be father and me, with all of you children busy raising your own families. Your father and I were looking forward to attending your wedding. You were the apple of his eye from the day you were born, and you were the one with the most intelligence, culture, and potential."

Mrs. Van Lew looked at her daughter as if she were a hurt little child, while Elizabeth looked off with unseeing eyes but with a mind full of unspoken images.

Another long pause followed. Then Elizabeth launched into a kind of death-bed self-assessment as though dictating to an invisible biographer.

"I never thought I would be an old maid of thirty-six ... but, I guess it's my own fault. From the time I knew right from wrong, it's been my sad privilege to differ in many things from the established principles and opinions of others. That's what has made my life intensely so earnest. It's why I'm so sad right now. I'm sure of it. And, I guess it's also made me intolerant and uncompromising. I have been liberally quick in feeling and ready to resent whatever seemed wrong ... quick and passionate in taking a stand. But Mother, you must agree I'm not bad tempered or vicious. You're probably thinking, like I am, that many a possible relationship was lost while a battle of wits was won."

Elizabeth's mother sat silently, allowing her child to express her feelings to a most sympathetic heart. Then she responded. "Elizabeth, you sound like your life is over. You have so much to live for. You have your health, a nice home, your friends."

"True Mother, but so often I felt out of place here in Richmond, with this accepted practice of buying, selling, beating, and other displays of cruelty upon the unfortunate Negroes. So many warm conversations have turned politely ice-cold when I've spoken against the unfairness of these despicable practices. Mother, I would rather remain unmarried than to attempt to love a man who pays honor to God on the Sabbath, then ignores his words the rest of the week. What hypocrisy! My head has always overruled my feelings in affairs of the heart."

"Elizabeth, it was your father's wish from the day you were born to give you a well-rounded education and the opportunity to develop and use your intelligence. He always marveled at the depth of your knowledge, your quick wit and eloquence in social conversation. Why do you think he invited guests to our house from every station and calling in life? He did it to broaden your education and horizons. It was as if he was preparing you for some future role of national responsibility. He loved and respected you; I'm sure you were well aware of that."

"Yes, and I miss him terribly. I knew that he was proud of my besting men in a match of wits. I think that's why I got such satisfaction from doing it. Then it became a habit. Only two men didn't try to test me and, even then, it didn't work out. I think I held up every man in comparison with father.

"Do you know that I never realized that all our coloreds were slaves because of the decent way you and father treated them. I thought that they were paid servants like they are now."

Elizabeth then recalled early childhood remembrances as she connected pieces of related incidents. "I can remember the origin of our wonderful library. How father always put aside an allowance for you to buy books because you had the time and the desire to read.

"I distinctly recall after we had all gone to bed, because we slept in the room adjoining yours, how you would review for his benefit in such interesting detail what you had read that day.

"I remember father coming in at night from work and waking us and taking us up in our long flannel gowns to sit a while on his knee, or be pressed to his chest, kissed and laid tenderly in our little beds.

"Mother, I have seen so much that is missing in married lives, that I am thankful for the memory of one true marriage. Under God's blessing, we children owe more to you and father than we can ever repay."

Feeling safe to reveal anything at this moment, Elizabeth admitted, "There was one man I could have loved deeply and with whom I could have enjoyed a happy marriage."

With just a hint of a twinkle in her eye, the mother asked if it was someone she knew, to which Elizabeth hesitatingly replied, "Yes."

"It wouldn't happen to be a certain young doctor?" she politely probed further.

Now Elizabeth blushed and, looking into her mother's eyes, realized that she must have known all along, and she decided that a "Yes" answer would be redundant.

"I agree with you. He is so full of integrity and goodness; you would have been wonderful together."

Another period of silent reflective thought was broken by the dependable Westminster chimes of the nearby rosewood grandfather clock.

Then, the mother said, "Elizabeth, I have an idea. What do you say to another trip to the Continent? This time, we are both in good health and could do and see more. I think it would be just the tonic for us both at this time."

"Mother, I think you are right. I'm all for it."

The two women left Richmond in May 1855 on an extended tour of England, France and Germany. They took in all the noteworthy landmarks, museums, palaces, cathedrals, chapels, gardens—and fashionable restaurants.

With both women being such avid readers, they also made it a point to visit the burial places of some of the most noted authors of the accumulated works in their extensive library. They paused at each location to reflect on the author's literary achievements and to pick a flower from the landscape nearby. Upon their return in 1856, they pressed the flowers between the pages of one of the author's books in their library.

The next few years of their relatively quiet and solitary existence was broken only by the birth of a niece or nephew, family holiday get-togethers, and rounds of teas with ladies of their social circle. On October 17, 1858, it was a very solemn and private fortieth birthday party observed by only Elizabeth, her mother, and a handful of faithful servants, as thoughts of marriage and a family of her own slowly faded from Elizabeth's mind.

CHAPTER 6

The Alarm Bell Rings

One of the most significant events that would have an effect on Elizabeth's future, cane in mid-October 1859. The vanguard of abolitionism, John Brown, after his failed attempt to stir the slaves to rebellion in his Pottawatomie massacre in May 1857, struck again. This time at the Federal Arsenal at Harper's Ferry with a handful of Negro and white followers. Brown successfully captured the arsenal but was quickly surrounded by Federal forces.

For two days he resisted, then, seeing the futility of the situation, he surrendered. Brown was tried for conspiracy, treason, and murder, and was hanged.

A number of people who would play significant roles in the events of the lamentable years ahead either took part in, or witnessed the capture and hanging of John Brown. Army Colonel Robert E. Lee was in command of the marines who captured Brown, Lieutenant J.E.B. Stuart led the charging detail on the engine house; and other future Confederate generals John Floyd, Henry A. Wise, Thomas J. (Stonewall) Jackson and one future Federal general, D.H. Strother. In the ranks of the Richmond Militia was an aspiring boy actor, John Wilkes Booth.

John Brown

Just before his execution, John Brown handed his jailer a prophetic message to the world. It said,

"I, John Brown, am now quite certain that the crimes of this guilty land will never be purged away but with blood. I had, as I now think, vainly flattered myself that without very much bloodshed it might be done."

Hundreds of miles away in Massachusetts, on the same day John Brown was hanged, December 7, 1859, Henry Wadsworth Longfellow, at almost the same moment, was writing similar prophetic words,

"This will be a great day in our history; the date of a new revolution—quite as much needed as the old one. Even now as I write they are leading old John Brown to execution in Virginia for attempting to rescue slaves! This is sowing the wind to reap the whirlwind which will come soon."

The nation's newspapers took the opportunity to advance and solidify their positions, inflame the population, arouse deep-rooted emotions, and drive deeper the wedge between those on either side of the slavery-secession issue.

Henry Wadsworth Longfellow

As a native-born Virginian, Elizabeth commented in her diary that turned into an occasional journal, about her fellow Virginians' actions and deeds following John Brown's raid and subsequent hanging. She noted "from that time on our people were in a palpable state of war … I was a silent and sorrowful spectator of the rise and spread of the secession mania." And as the growing, rhetoric-inflamed frenzy and Northern-invasions rumors spread rampant throughout the population, she observed, "The alarm bells would be rung; the tramp of armed men could be heard through the night."

That was also the beginning of her pro-Northern communicating and supporting activities. She used the regular postal channels to inform Federal officials of everything that was happening in the city. She described conditions in detail, gave warnings, and offered advice. Elizabeth commented that the women of Richmond were constantly asking her, regarding the activities of the Virginia Secession Convention, if she thought that the state would go out that day? For if it didn't that they just couldn't stand it any longer! She noted, "Such flag making, such flag presenting—the drums, the fifes and the marching! For my life, I would not have dared to play Yankee Doodle, Hail Columbia, or the Star Spangled Banner, our hallowed national anthems. Instead, it was the bloodstained Marseillaise resounding through the streets. My Country—Oh my Country! God help us, these are sorry days! Loyalty is now called treason. Be true to your section and let your country go to the devil. Every man fears every man and distrust is general. This heavy heart pulses and looks upon slavery as it really is … no pen, no book, no time can do justice to the wrongs it honors."

CHAPTER 7

The Path is Chosen

Lincoln's election on November 6, 1860 fanned the flames of war dangerously close to the flashpoint. Outgoing President James Buchanan, was quite willing to drop this political land mine and republic-threatening problem into the incoming President's lap. When Buchanan told the Congress that the South had no legal right to secede, and the government had no power to prevent it, he opened the door wide for it to happen.

President James Buchanan

Predictably, on December 20, South Carolina started the parade through the doorway, followed in the months ahead by Mississippi, Florida, Alabama, Georgia, Louisiana, and Texas. Later, Virginia, followed by Arkansas, North Carolina, and Tennessee seceded from the Union. Kentucky and Missouri, whose governors were both pro-South, actually never seceded but the Confederate Congress voted both into the Confederacy.

On February 4, 1861, the Montgomery Alabama Convention formed a provisional government for the seceded states, adopting its own Constitution similar to the United States' version and added an amendment recognizing and protecting slavery.

Jefferson Davis and Alexander H. Stephens were named Provisional President and Vice-President of the Confederacy of the seceded states. They were inaugurated formally on February 22nd.

Jefferson Finis Davis

On March 4, Abraham Lincoln and Hannibal Hamlin, the Republican Party victors, were inaugurated President and Vice-President of the legal, national Federal Government of the United States.

Both presidents moderated their inaugural messages, downplaying the necessity or desire for armed conflict as a solution for their differences, but also gave the message that they would not back away from it if it came to that. Both spoke from a sense of deep-rooted lifestyle that their forefathers had developed and fought and died for.

These embraced independence and freedom from disruptive outside influences that wanted to prevent them from living in harmony and prosperity, and doing their duty, concerning what they perceived was best for the people at this most critical moment in history.

Division within the country widened and tensions mounted, crossing geographic, political, religious, occupational, family, economic, and social boundaries. Justification, ideals, principles, tradition, loyalties and resolve were strong on both sides of the issues. In Richmond, there was little or no dissent from the Confederacy's position, except from Elizabeth Van Lew. When Elizabeth first saw the Confederate flag flown over Richmond instead of the forty-three star—spangled banner, she wept, thinking, "Alas for those with loyalty in their hearts." And when torchlight processions were held on the streets of Richmond, she watched through tear-filled eyes and fell to her knees, both in disbelief at the drastic change in temperament and focus of her beloved city and in a personal commitment of her support to the Union. She wrote, "Never did a feeling of more calm determination and high resolve for endurance come over me."

Only her closest social circle of friends understood her feelings and sentiments, because she made no attempt to conceal her Union sympathies and abolitionist tendencies from them. Her very existence was a contradiction and protest against the beliefs of her class and region. She defied old acquaintances, politicians, and military authorities by opposing slavery and war. All but her closest friends thought that she would eventually come around to their way of thinking, but they, like so many others to follow, badly underestimated the intensity of her beliefs, resolve and courage to stand by her convictions—whatever the cost.

Inheriting her voracious appetite for reading from both parents, Elizabeth read with passion, every newspaper's accounts of the political and military activities. She learned that although

President Abraham Lincoln

Fort Sumter, in the harbor of Charleston, South Carolina, was no serious military threat to the Confederacy with about seventy Union soldiers and nine officers; its existence was an irritation to the pride of the political zealots in this hotbed of the secession movement.

Accustomed to getting what they wanted, since President Buchanan had handed over fort after fort to the Confederacy during the final months of his administration, they embarked on yet another attempt to get rid of Union forces and gain a ready-made and armed fortress for their own use. Elizabeth thought, "But now, they must deal with Abraham Lincoln."

She was right. To gain the advantage, the Confederate troops prohibited the sale of food to the Union garrison in an attempt to starve them into submission. Upon learning that the men under command of Major Robert Anderson could hold out no longer, President Lincoln offered several plans and proposals in an attempt to resolve the crisis peacefully. None of them being successful, he allowed an expedition bearing food and supplies to sail for Fort Sumter.

What Elizabeth did not read in the papers was that hot headed South Carolina extremists were impatient with President Davis' caution and were prepared to attack. Davis, not wanting to relinquish power, independence of action or policy making to the seceded states, something he himself was only too familiar with, ordered General P.G.T. Beauregard to demand the surrender of Fort Sumter. Major Anderson refused and, at 4:30AM on April 12, 1861, the firing began. Outside the harbor, the relief expedition Lincoln had sent watched helpless as the Confederates continuously bombarded the undermanned fort for thirty-four straight hours. Near starvation, complete exhaustion, and with little ammunition left, Anderson surrendered.

Fort Sumter

Elizabeth read with a small hint of Southern pride of the Confederate's honorable behavior as it was described in the Pro-Confederacy, Richmond Examiner newspaper. It claimed that the day following the bombardment, with the Confederate's permission, the garrison fired a fifty-gun salute to the American flag. And when the departing men marched past the Confederate troops to the waiting ship, the Rebels bared their heads in tribute to their courage. It was ironic that not one man had lost his life on either side during the bombardment, however, during the salute, a Union private was accidentally killed, becoming the first of the war's unpredictably staggering casualties.

Lincoln promptly called for 75,000 volunteer soldiers to put down the "insurrection" in the South. On May 6, the Confederate Congress countered by formally declaring that a state of war existed and the American Civil War began.

This initial military contact was a celebrated victory for Jeff Davis and the Confederacy, but it was also a quiet victory for Lincoln. His wish was that if hostilities were to begin that the Confederacy should bear the blame for initiating them. He made the right moves, and the Confederacy, itching for the fight, gladly obliged. Not that Lincoln wanted war, because it was the Confederacy that, throughout the agonizing crisis, took the initiative by first cutting off the Fort's food supply, demanding its surrender, and then firing the first shot.

Upon learning the reasons, Elizabeth wrote, "A political solution could have defused this volatile situation." But she knew deep down, that at this point, neither side would have been satisfied with a negotiated compromise.

On April 17, the Virginia State Convention passed a hasty Secession Ordinance to avoid being subject to Lincoln's request for men to fight in the Union Army. On May 21, Richmond was designated Capital of the Confederacy because of its large population, influence, long tradition of leadership, vast natural resources, and its large Tredegar Iron Works.

Elizabeth looked out from her vantagepoint on Church Hill, observing everything. She saw her beloved Richmond take on a new energy, a new life. Not necessarily a better life, she reasoned, but a different one. The railroads, which fanned out in every direction, were being prepared for use as military transportation for the rapid movement of men and materials of war. The manufacturing factories, turning out everything for locomotives and trains, had increased their production to support the war effort.

Now, Richmond was to be given protection from invasion as battery sites were being selected to encircle the city safely in a tight network of security. Their role would be to protect the political leaders from harm or capture, the manufacturing resources from sabotage by outside agents, and to prevent spies from gaining access into or out of the city.

Elizabeth learned that the big State Armory had been reactivated. It hadn't been used for over twelve years since its support of the Mexican War. And that tobacco factories were being converted for military use; and the iron mills, which were the center of iron manufacturing in the South, had tooled up to produce needed war materials.

Almost immediately, the Arsenal and Armory began turning out rifles, cartridges, caps, powder, infantry and cavalry equipment, gun carriages and caissons, artillery harness, ammunition, primers, fuses, and other necessities. Skilled workmen were scarce, and time was needed to develop skills, equipment, and processes. At first, there was little conflict between the military recruiters who needed bodies and the factory recruiters who required qualified workers. The Civil Service screening examination, which stressed mathematics, physics, and chemistry, provided the best people available. Later, the military would dominate, recruiting anyone and everyone, almost without regard for age, knowledge, or occupation.

After overcoming many bureaucratic obstacles, the huge Tredegar Iron Works, on its four acres, finally began to produce much needed material such as cannons, both heavy and field: ammunition, caissons, and other material from its shops, mill, and foundry.

Tredegar Iron Works

On analyzing the assortment of new Confederate flags being displayed by the arriving troops and on several buildings around town, Elizabeth observed, "The azure on our flag is gone. The few stars left are set in blood. The shade-less palmetto, the hissing serpent, examples of unrest and treachery, are fitly chosen as our emblems."

Richmond became the heart of the new country's life and Elizabeth witnessed it all. Nothing of value went unnoticed or unreported. Now, everyone in Richmond must show their loyalty and make their contribution to the success of their new country … the Confederacy.

Friday, May 24, 1861, and Elizabeth's social acquaintances were irritated over her outspoken abolitionist views and lack of participation in their Confederate war-effort-supporting sewing circle. They wanted to give her one last chance to prove her true loyalty and to fall into line. Elizabeth's choice could seal her fate and determine the quality of the rest of her life.

An all-female delegation of Richmond's social elite paid a visit to the Van Lew residence. And, as they have done on many previous occasions, Elizabeth and her mother, Eliza Louise, entertained them with tea and delicacies from their kitchen. There was talk of the hustle and bustle in the city, new babies, flowers, the weather, other social gossip, and some pleasantries. And then, the time for the true purpose of their visit arrived. The ladies, as if on cue, all became silent. Suddenly, the air in the room seemed to turn chilly, and even the fine porcelain teacups sat as silent witnesses while all eyes focused on the unlucky individual chosen to be the spokesperson. At last, she cleared her dry throat to speak, breaking the anxiety-filled stillness.

"Elizabeth, we would like you and your family to help us make shirts for our gallant soldiers!"

Elizabeth rose slowly to her feet and walked to the lace-covered window that overlooked her beloved city. As the women waited in silence, fidgeting in their awkward, nervous impatience, Elizabeth thought to herself, "Where do I really stand? Can I go against my own heart when I know where my true loyalties lie? Can I go along with something that is not morally or spiritually right? And what if I choose to follow my head and my heart? What will the repercussions be for Mother and I? I can choose the easy, safe path, swallowing my pride and denying my beliefs and go along with the crowd. But, by helping them, I will be a willing partner in this shameful enterprise and, God forbid, may even contribute to its ultimate success! If I choose the more dangerous path, one of open opposition, it will bring shame, censure, threats, isolation or worse in these parts upon the entire household. But it might, in some small way, diminish the potential for success of this traitorous government and its ungodly treatment of the unfortunate Negroes. I must consult Mother before I choose!"

Elizabeth turned and faced her mother. One look at that serene and resolute face and she had her answer. All the years of religious education, shared conversations, and the witnessing of so many acts of inhumane injustices were reflected in this gentle parent's countenance. Her expressive eyes and just visible smile acknowledged the admiration and respect for her daughter's integrity. Because they had always been so close, she had already read Elizabeth's mind and knew she wouldn't act on such a critical decision without consulting her. Elizabeth's mother nodded her agreement and consent.

Elizabeth, on seeing that they were of one mind, said to the ladies, "I'm sorry, but we cannot contribute to your cause in this way because we support neither slavery nor secession. Our sympathy is with the North in this unhappy war."

The soft gasps of disbelief and the expressions of shock on the faces of the ladies slowly turned to indignation, then cold contempt. Almost as one, the ladies rose, and a servant brought them their wraps. Without a single word they left. Mother and daughter clung to one another in the vacated room. They must surely have heard the sound of crackling flames emanating from the bridges they were burning behind them!

CHAPTER 8

The Humanitarian Emerges

As expected, snubs, insults, threats, and revilement followed the visit. Old friends turned away when Elizabeth came to town to market. Children and street toughs hooted and hurled insults or mud balls whenever her coach and four white horses passed them by.

One day, during a routine visit to town with her mother, they were stopped on a deserted side street by one of the members from that fateful "recruitment delegation." The woman, wanting to keep their relationship alive out of respect and affection, pleaded with them to consider the social consequences of their stand. But Elizabeth, her mind made up, believing herself to be on the side of right, was unwavering. She explained that, "My mother and I are not just being stubborn, and we're certainly not rejecting your friendship. We are just following our hearts and conscience and don't subscribe to your cause."

Seeing that the Van Lews would not change their minds, the "diplomat" tried another approach. She asked if Elizabeth and her mother would be willing to bring religious books to the soldiers at Camp Lee and to other camps that have sprung up around Richmond in every vacant parcel of land. She added that they should do it if for no other reason than "for their own good." Reluctantly, the two women agreed to "participate" in this small way. Elizabeth and her mother reasoned that by focusing the soldier's attention on "God's words," they might dissuade or diminish the soldiers' fervor for battle and, at the same time, lessen their own hostile treatment by the townspeople. This innocent aid and comfort to the soldiers, for the time being, checked their escalating maltreatment.

General Robert E. Lee

Troops poured in from other states, and the state of Virginia became one large military camp under the Richmond command of General Robert E. Lee.

The population of the city had doubled in only four months. Besides the troops, the additions included political office and military commission seekers. And, as with most large concentrations of men far from home, this was an opportune attraction for gamblers, prostitutes, and many new saloons, all of which were heavily patronized.

For many of the soldiers, this was their first time away from home and parental discipline. The city jails were soon filled with soldiers guilty of drunkenness and disorderly behavior, not unlike the "Wild West" towns to come later in the century.

In June, the western counties of Virginia seceded from Virginia to form the new Union State of West Virginia. On the already significant date of July 4, the U.S. Congress officially approved the war measures that Lincoln had issued earlier without their sanction.

Meanwhile, the ladies of Richmond had kept busy sewing and knitting for the Confederacy, and now they even practiced firing pistols at targets in the event that their assistance might be needed in some future emergency. Elizabeth was also busy. She went out every day gathering important information on the activities in the city and then, in the privacy of her bedroom, sat and wrote long detailed dispatches for her beloved Union with special emphasis on Confederate troop makeup, numbers, training and movement. Only now, she ceased to use the mail and sent them North by special messenger.

May and June had passed into the hot and tumultuous days of July, and dust raised by the marching troops filled the air. Everywhere preparations were being made for the first battle. Elizabeth and her mother watched the soldiers ride off to the sounds of "Dixie" along with applause, roses, and kisses tossed by Richmond admirers.

On July 18, the Confederate and Union forces first met at the Battle of Bull Run at Manassas, Virginia. The Confederate Commander, General Beauregard, aided by the advance military intelligence provided by the South's famous, though short-lived spy, Rose O'Neil Greenhow, was victorious over his fellow West Point classmate, Union General Irvin McDowell.

The battle concluded on July 21, with the taking of over a thousand prisoners, some of who were suffering from serious, painful wounds, and they were headed for Richmond. Beauregard's victory over McDowell rang through the South like the clang of a giant firebell.

The newspapers used many eyewitness accounts to tell about how the "Union troops had been completely shattered and sent running back to Washington like whipped puppies." For a time, it looked like Beauregard and General Johnston would storm and take Washington itself, thus ending the war.

Elizabeth watched with a heavy heart and tear-filled eyes as wagons full of wounded soldiers streamed into Richmond by the hundreds, both Southern men and wretched Northern prisoners. One of her neighbors shook his fist and shouted angrily, "We'll show you, you no account, nigger-loving, Yankee bastards!" Public resentment against the Yankees was so high that no one dared approach or to speak to the Northern prisoners in anything but the most derisive terms. Elizabeth's heart went out to the suffering prisoners, but discretion kept her from showing it, lest she incur the wrath of the hostile bystanders.

There had been no plan to take and hold prisoners, so makeshift prisons which were typically old, dirty, smelly, stifling-hot vacant tobacco and grain factories and warehouses were used.

Only a day or two after the prisoners arrived in Richmond, the Van Lews heard stories about their suffering. Elizabeth, who had anguished for many years about her unfulfilled purpose in life, became immediately energized with the opportunity to provide a useful service. "Now, here is meaningful work to do!"

With a servant carrying a large market basket filled with fruit, Elizabeth headed for the official departments of the Confederate government to ask for permission to visit and perform the duties of hospital nurse for the Federal prisoners.

Her first stop was the office of the Inspector of Prisons, Lieutenant David P. Todd, and President Lincoln's brother-in-law. He chided her in a gruff tone, "You say you want to visit with the Yankees? Miss Van Lew, you are the first and only lady to make such an application."

Then he continued his tirade with, "Let me tell you something, Madam. I have three brothers in the Confederate Army, three sisters married to good Confederate Officers, an uncle who is a Confederate General and, unfortunately for him, one skinny baboon of a brother-in-law who happens to be on the losing side in Washington. Now, if you think you are going to get any sympathy or cooperation from me, you are sadly mistaken. Why, I know people, and I'm among them, that would be glad to 'shoot the lot of them!'"

Lieutenant David P. Todd

Determined in her resolve, Elizabeth trudged from office to office with much the same results. At last, she was told to see Brigadier General John Henry Winder,

Commissary-General of Prisoners in Richmond, the only one authorized to issue a prison pass and that he was a tough person to approach. Elizabeth made several discrete inquiries and was told that Secretary of the Treasury Christopher G. Memminger was "a gentleman who loved flattery," and could be the right one to intercede for her with General Winder.

Once in his office, she told Secretary Memminger of her desire to visit the prisoners. He was horrified and even indignant to learn of the purpose of her visit. He chastised her by telling her that she should be sewing and knitting for the Confederate troops: not visiting prisoners, and that the prisons "are not fit for a lady to visit."

She looked at him, unaffected by his comments, and told him that she once heard him "speak very beautifully on the subject of religion." Her opening salvo hit the mark, and he softened, smiled, and asked, "And you liked my discourse?"

Now she administered the coup de grace, "Very much! You said that love was the fulfillment of the law, and if we wished our cause to succeed, we must begin with charity to the thankless and the unworthy."

Memminger recovered and, with a self-conscious cough, he replied, "Yes, yes, you say you wanted—what was it—a pass?"

"Yes, a note from you to General Winder would help me to acquire it."

Minutes later, she was on her way to General Winder's shanty office on Bank Street with an official letter of introduction. She had already learned that he was stubborn, hot-tempered, profane, and vain. But, at the same time, people respected him for being efficient, honest, and courageous.

General John H. Winder

As she entered his office, The General was conferring with several men. Elizabeth made an indelible mental picture of their faces. The men left the office and Elizabeth was seated directly in front of the general's desk. While the sixty-one-year-old Winder read the letter of introduction, she noticed his snow-white hair was waved in beautiful locks, and it gave her an idea. After sitting for a moment, she said to him, "Your hair looks out of place here; it could adorn the Temple of Janus."

Winder looked up at her with his slate gray eyes; his frown turned to a surprised and almost friendly smile. A few more remarks and Elizabeth had her pass. It permitted her "to visit the prisoners and to send them books, luxuries, delicacies, and what she may please,"

With this first innocent pass, Elizabeth's humanitarian efforts began. Her successful persistence in acquiring the entry pass resulted in gaining valuable knowledge about the workings and personalities of this new Confederate government. Her ability to capitalize on that knowledge will prove invaluable as she embarked on a perilous path and performed one of the most remarkable and unheralded contributions made by any one individual during the entire Civil War.

CHAPTER 9

The First Connections

Delighted and energized by her initial success in dealing with the Confederate Bureaucracy, Elizabeth headed straight for where the prisoners were being held in Ligon's Warehouse and Tobacco Factory on Main Street between 25th and 26th Streets. The servant accompanying her carried a large basket filled with fruit for the wounded men. She presented her pass to Lieutenant Todd, who scowled while reading it, shook his head, and then handed it back to her. After thoroughly checking the basket for any hidden weapons, he took six of the largest and nicest pieces and put them in his desk drawer.

"You there, sit on the floor outside till we get back," he snarled at Elizabeth's servant, "and you'd better not move from there or risk your black ass being shot!"

To Elizabeth, he grumbled, "Now, you don't have to go in if you don't want to."

"If I didn't want to, would I have gone to all this trouble?"

Todd muttered something nasty about "crazy women" and led Elizabeth into the large prisoner holding room. Stopping at the doorway, he gave her a final warning. "The prisoners inside are filthy-dirty, foul-mouthed, and ignorant-minded, worthless animals undeserving of humane treatment. You better not get too close or waste your time trying to be nice to them!"

"Thank you, but I'll be all right," she assured him, anxious to get inside.

Despite the warning, she was unprepared for what she saw when the guard opened the door. With a gasp, she took in her first unforgettable glimpse of the despair, misery, and suffering of the hundreds of prisoners and their wretched conditions.

The huge room was jammed full of men in an assortment of filthy and tattered uniforms. Some were stained with the blood of comrades they had carried from danger on the battlefield or had laid out of harm's way, hoping that the undertakers would get to them before the scavengers did. A number of uniforms were soaked in blood from their wearers' wounds, which were in need of medical attention.

It was hot, and the air was thick with the smell of unclean bodies, festering wounds and rotting flesh, involuntary human waste, and vomit. Cracks in the wooden walls only allowed hot air in to stir the assorted smells into one overpowering stench.

Her ears were filled with the drone of assorted conversations, heated arguments, partially obeyed orders, petty bickering, pitiful whining, shared reminiscences, spiteful chastising and the moans, groans and periodic screams of the badly wounded. Prayers were being spoken aloud by the deliriously sick and dying, calling to loved ones so far away, or pleading for deliverance from their agony to anyone to come and put them out of their misery, oblivious to those close by ministering to them.

There were no beds, no privacy, no washing, bathing, or toilet facilities, except for the overflowing, makeshift chamber pots that were inadequate to hold the body waste from so many bodies.

The men stood, knelt, sat, or lay on anything that offered them even the slightest relief from the hard wooden floor. Their dirty, unshaven faces had a look of disbelief and resentment at their situation. Some were filled with hopelessness and despair. Others were angry with their lot and eager for the opportunity for revenge.

A small group of men were standing off in one corner, speaking softly and observing everything. These were the most senior officers amongst the prisoners. They were constantly assessing their men's physical and mental condition, collecting information on the prison, its location and surroundings, the guards' routines, personalities, and possible weaknesses for the purpose of maintaining some semblance of military decorum and looking for the possibilities, methods, and timing of an escape from captivity.

These were the first men to spot Elizabeth after Lieutenant Todd stepped aside. Todd motioned to them to approach. As they started toward him, the rest of the men noticed the diminutive woman next to him dressed all in black, with the golden curls with just a tinge of gray, and the friendly and compassionate expression on her face. It was such a contrast to the mean, brutish, and contemptuous Todd. The men grew silent in their bewilderment and anticipation of trying to determine who this woman was.

The senior Union officers were brusquely introduced to Elizabeth. The spokesman for the group of field-grade officers introduced the other officers. Her intuition told her that, "Colonel Lee and Major Revere are the friendliest. I must ask the Major if he is any relation to the famous Paul Revere of Massachusetts!"

Elizabeth's genuine mission of mercy was met with some caution and a degree of skepticism. The officers wondered if this was a Rebel trick to gain their confidence and learn about any escape plans they might be making. She handed them the basket and asked if there was anything else she could do for them. Not sure of her true intentions, yet not willing to pass up the offer, they tested her by asking for medicine, food, and books. She replied that she would do what she could, promised to return the following day, and left with Todd.

On her second visit to Ligon's, Todd again inspected all her packages and, when he was again about to siphon off what he wanted for himself, Elizabeth told him that she had "something special for his kindness." She unwrapped and presented to Todd some still warm gingerbread along with some nice cold buttermilk to wash it down. Todd beamed and, for the first time, acted with some civility towards her. Not wanting to leave this special treat unattended, he sent her inside with a guard and the basket of medicine, food, and armful of books.

When the door was opened, and she appeared, the senior officer group came directly to her. One guard was posted on the inside of the door to watch her, while the guard on the outside closed and locked the door behind her.

Elizabeth gave the officers the medicine, food, and books from her own library, and included some recent Richmond newspapers. After receiving their thanks, she asked if there was anything she could do for the sick and dying men. They invited her to check with the men themselves, and she began what would become a daily ritual here at Ligon's, and then later at Libby and Belle Isle Prisons.

One fatally wounded man she spoke to, asked if she could mail his final "good-bye letter" to his family. She waited until the guard was distracted and then took the scrawled note and concealed it in her dress. After she made a few more such stops, she left quietly. She stopped at Todd's office to inquire how he liked the gingerbread. He replied, "Madam, it was of the highest quality!" Elizabeth promised to bring him a like portion the following day if he would be so kind as to have the deathly-ill officer removed to the hospital. For that offer, his stomach overruled his heart, and he gave his word that it would be done. She left and promptly sent the man's letter north.

The next day though still not entirely convinced of her sincerity, the group greeted her more cordially, as her acts of kindness had not escaped observation, and they thanked her warmly. She asked the men for any news that the new prisoners might have brought them.

One of the officers, after some hesitation, asked what was on the mind of every prisoner in the room. "With all due respects Miss ... I ... ah ... we were wondering how it is that a Southern lady is so concerned for the welfare of us Northerners ... I mean, under the circumstances?"

To put their understandable concern to rest and to build their acceptance and trust, she now revealed why she had come to their aid. "Although I was born and raised in Richmond, Virginia, both my parents have northern backgrounds. My father was born and educated in New York, and my mother's roots are in Philadelphia. My father's aunt, Letitia Smith, was a heroine in the Revolutionary

War. She carried secret dispatches to Washington's Army in New York. "My mother was the daughter of Hilary Baker, the Mayor of Philadelphia, who gave his life by remaining at his post ministering to the sick and dying during the Yellow Fever Epidemic of 1798. I was educated in the same Quaker School in Philadelphia that my mother had attended."

Mayor Hilary Baker

"A Quaker school? Does that mean you're a Quaker?" one officer asked.

"No, it means that I had a strong Christian moral education. According to the Quakers, the thought of one human being in bondage to another is against God's Law and is absolutely repugnant to me.

"Partly because of that, but also because I believe in our one and only legal government in Washington and am prepared to do everything I can to see that the Union is preserved in this wretched dispute"

"You're an angel to us, Miss Van Lew."

"My small service to you pales beside your contribution and sacrifices, and so I fulfill it willingly and unashamedly."

Elizabeth's openness in sharing private family details in a voice filled with such conviction and sincerity pierced their shield of doubt. With a better understanding of the motives behind her acts of compassion, they began to develop a trust in her. Now, an officer asked whether she had any news of the war.

"Not as much as I'd like to have, but I'll tell you what I know," she responded.

Based on what the newly arrived prisoners had told the senior officers, everything she said checked out, and the officers realized that she was well aware of what was going on. Elizabeth asked if they had any news from the steady stream of new captives who seemed to be arriving daily. Feeling more trustful, understanding her true allegiance, they provided her with the latest information they had on Confederate troop positions, movements, and strength.

This procedure was continued for several weeks and a solid trust was established. During one visit, they discretely asked if she could send some vital information North. Elizabeth informed them that, since her first visit, she had been sending their information North. They were both astonished and impressed, subsequently increasing the quantity and quality of information they passed on to her.

Two of the prisoners being held in Richmond, from the Bull Run-Manassas battlefield, were civilian spectators who got too close to the action. Congressman Alfred Ely from Rochester, New York, and a fellow townsman who had been Ely's opponent during the previous election, Calvin Huson, Jr. Huson had become seriously ill while incarcerated, and Elizabeth was able to persuade the authorities to let him be moved to her home for medical treatment.

Soon afterwards, nasty comments by the Richmond townspeople were leveled at Elizabeth and her mother for "providing aid and comfort to that 'Black Republican.'" In Richmond, the consensus was that anyone who was a Republican from the North was in favor of the Blacks. Therefore, they labeled them all as "Black Republicans."

Despite every care and consideration, Huson's illness was too far advanced, and he died in a matter of weeks. The Van Lews paid and arranged for his funeral from their home.

Before he died, Huson told Congressman Ely that, "The tender care and attention I received from the Van Lews could not have been exceeded, even by the kindness of a mother and sister."

Another death affected the Van Lew household. On August 19, the Van Lew and Taylor Hardware business lost Mr. T. Taylor, the co-founder of the business with John Van Lew. Now, John Newton, the recently married son, took over full control of running the business.

CHAPTER 10

Gifts & Help

During her daily prison visits, Elizabeth built a close and lasting friendship with both Colonel William Raymond Lee and Major Paul Joseph Revere. The Major confided that it was, indeed, his grandfather who made the ride to notify the populace of the impending advance of the British troops. He felt honored to carry his name and added that his middle name, Joseph, was his father's name.

On Monday, the 11th of November 1862, Lee and Revere informed Elizabeth that General Winder visited them the day before with orders indicating that they would be would be moved to Henrico County Jail to be incarcerated, as hostages, with five other officers. They were condemned to meet the same fate as the pirates, who claimed to be "Confederate privateersmen, and who were being held in a New York City jail under the sentence: "death by hanging!" They told her they also learned that the military authorities had the option of either hanging them or executing them by firing squad. "Some choice," Elizabeth thought.

Colonel William R. Lee   Major Paul J. Revere

The officers' situation was complicated by the fact that they were pawns in a larger game. Jefferson Davis had never received recognition for the Confederacy as a separate and legitimate government by the government in Washington. If President Lincoln changed the status of the wharf-thieves in New York from "convicted pirates," which carried the death sentence, to "Confederate privateersmen," which meant they would be held as prisoners of war, he would be de facto legiti-mizing the Confederacy. This, he was loathe to do. But, by changing his posi-tion on both issues, he would be getting rid of thieves while getting back valued officers because of the opportunity of prisoner exchange. It was an attractive trade and would be a much needed and popular public relations decision in the North.

That Thursday, the 14th, the four field-grade officers were sent along with three captains, who were chosen by lot, to the Henrico Jail. Their seven-by-eleven-foot cell was empty of furniture, but was filled with filth, stench, and vermin. Their nocturnal roommates would the large gray rats that would run over their faces and bodies all night, every night: sometimes even before they fell asleep. The prisoners were not allowed to bathe or wash their clothes, which were the only garments they had.

Their faith and spirit would be challenged in the months ahead as they awoke each day not knowing if it would be their last. Major Revere played a key leader-ship role in maintaining the group's morale.

Meanwhile, Lincoln was still wrestling with the dilemma as the executions were delayed. Politicians and military commanders on both sides of the Mason-Dixon Line debated the issue.

Because of the political sensitivity of the whole issue surrounding the prison-ers, Elizabeth was unable to get permission to visit the prisoners at first. Finally, by bribing the corrupt and poorly paid guards, she was able to get notes to and from the prisoners. By persistence and cajolery, two of her trademarks, she would eventually be able to visit them. She brought food, books, money, letters, news of the war, and their situation.

One cold winter day, the senior colonel prisoner slipped her a secret mes-sage that was to be the forerunner of another of her endless activities. The note explained that there were several men whose experience and special knowledge would be invaluable to the war effort. Their escape to the North was crucial. In order to make good the men's escape, a large amount of money would be needed to pay off a willing Confederate guard. The note asked if Elizabeth knew of any-body who would provide one hundred dollars to pay for the escape.

The incarcerated officers cautiously observed and evaluated the potential vul-nerability of a guard who had some serious gambling debts and whose wife was soon to have a baby. He was discretely approached with a financial solution to his problems. Having little hope of resolving the problem on his own, the desperate guard jumped at the proposal but warned them that he must never be identified or be blamed for his role in the escape.

Elizabeth returned the next day with a note for them. Attached to the message was one hundred dollars taken out of her own personal account, along with a hand-drawn map. The map gave the officers directions to a secluded rendezvous point close to the prison where she would meet and guide them, by the safest route, to her house.

She had also arranged to provide food and secure lodging for them until the furor over their escape subsided, after which she would arrange for their safe passage north. To further reassure them, she revealed that she had been successfully using this strategy as part of the "Underground Railroad," to assist the escape of slaves to the North.

The date selected for the "valuable officer" prison escape arrived, and the plan was successful in every detail.

Soon after their safe arrival at the Van Lew residence, the four men were escorted to a secret hiding place upstairs. One of the men was sick and needed immediate medical attention. Without proper care, he would not be well enough to withstand the rigors of the cold and dangerous journey north.

The escaped officers were made as comfortable as possible. As Elizabeth closed the door and walked away from the secret room, she stopped and looked back at the innocent—looking wall, remembering the day long ago when she was an upset and frustrated little girl.

Elizabeth recalled that her father had been resting in his favorite chair in the library reading the newspaper when she came bursting in and stood beside him pouting.

He put the paper down and asked her, "What's the reason for the long face?"

She explained, "It's no fun playing hide and seek anymore because Johnny knows all the hiding places and always wins. There's just no place in this house that he can't find me Daddy. If only I had one good place to hide so that I could beat him, just once!"

The father glanced down at his little pride and joy thinking, "If that's the biggest hurt you'll ever suffer in your life, you're a lucky girl." He spoke to her in an encouraging tone, "Liz, I've never known anything to ever get the best of you. You always seem to come up with something. So I'm sure you'll find a way to beat Johnny. Remember, you're a Van Lew!"

Her father's words and smiles were always an inspiration to Liz. Reassured, she thanked him with a big hug and ran off to find her brother, determined now to find a way to beat him at his game.

One day, several weeks later, when everyone else was out of the house, the father went to Liz's room and told her he had a very special surprise for her. A secret surprise, that no one else could share. He took her hand in his and led her up to the attic closet room. "Close your eyes tightly, Liz."

Then he opened the door and guided her inside. "You can open your eyes now."

"I don't see the surprise Daddy," she said downheartedly as she scanned the recently finished room, totally vacant of furniture or anything else except her and her father. She looked up and down, left and right, all around and saw nothing!

"That's just it sweetheart."

"Daddy, I don't understand. Where's my surprise?"

"You can't see it, but it's there."

Again her eyes swept the room, as she slowly turned around to see if she had missed something.

Having made his point, he laughed and then explained. "Do you remember telling me that you would like to have someplace to hide where no one could find you when playing hide and seek?"

"Yes Daddy."

"Well, now you have one!"

"But where is it?"

"Let me show you your very own secret room." He walked over to the wall and pressed on a piece of wood molding, and a section of the wall swung open like a door. He opened it wide and invited her to look into the room. She entered the room and was surprised at how much space there was. Then she listened attentively as her father explained how to release the catch from the inside.

"Are you sure I won't get stuck inside and can't get out, Daddy?"

"Of course you won't, sweetheart. Here, let me show you how safe it is," and he closed the door.

"Now you try it while I'm in here with you."

She released the catch as he had done, and the door sprang open. Almost reassured, she said, "Now I want to work it by myself." And the father left the secret room telling her that he would be standing right by the door.

She closed the door on herself. Then, in a barely audible voice from inside the room asked, "Can you tell if I'm in here, Daddy?"

He replied, "No I can't, sweetheart. No one could ever tell if someone was in there."

She then released the spring-loaded catch, came out, and closed the door. Again, she opened the secret door by pressing the locking mechanism, and then re-closed it. She stepped back, admiring the craftsmanship that had her totally fooled. Remembering that her father had done all this just for her, she turned and squealed with girlish delight, "Oh Daddy, it's perfect! I can hardly wait to use it when I play against Johnny. He'll never find me here!"

She ran to him, jumped into his strong arms, wrapped hers around his neck, and told him how much she loved him. She kissed him and proclaimed, "Daddy, this is the best surprise I ever had in my whole life!"

"And," he added, "I will never tell anyone else that it exists. It will be our secret!"

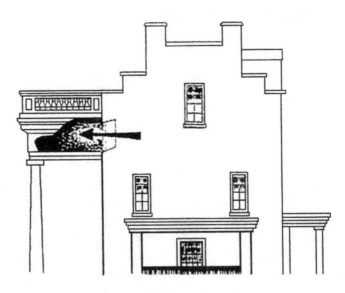

The Secret Room

With the prisoners safely inside the secret room, Elizabeth had a hint of a smile on her lips a glint of a twinkle in her eyes, and a warm glow of appreciation in her heart for the very special man she was so lucky to have had as a father. But, there were immediate needs to attend to. She must go now and see what she could do to get medical attention for the sick officer.

Elizabeth thought immediately of William. "But will he come if he knows who the patient is? Can he be trusted not to reveal to anyone the purpose of his visit? Where do his sympathies lie in this national conflict? Are they with the South? After all, he is a Virginian. What will happen to my family and me if my role in the escape and hiding of the hated prisoners is exposed? Even suspected loyalists are being arrested every day. It certainly means prison for the family and the gallows for me!"

A cold chill and shiver ran through her body at the thought of these dire possibilities. "What should I do? The prisoner might die if he's not treated soon!" She made up her mind quickly after weighing the risks and the advantages and devised a plan to minimize the risks; a technique she will hone to perfection in the hazardous years ahead.

Elizabeth decided to send a servant with a note requesting William to come look in on her mother who had been experiencing a spell of coughing lately. She would use the opportunity as a cover for her real objective — to try and gauge his current political sentiments before requesting his assistance with the prisoner.

Elizabeth herself greeted William when he arrived, and they were both delighted to see each other again. She took his arm and escorted him up to her mother's room. Following a thorough and professional examination, William prescribed the treatment Mrs. Van Lew was to follow precisely. Elizabeth beamed with pride and respect for William saying, "Doctor Parker, we will follow your every instruction to the letter! And now, to show my appreciation, may I interest you in a cup of hot cider on this cold night before you continue on your rounds?"

Since William had no more rounds to make that night he replied, "That would both fortify me and give me an opportunity to enjoy your company." Impressed, Elizabeth thought, "His medical knowledge is graced with a charming bedside manner."

As they sat alone enjoying both the hot cinnamon and clove-spiced ciders, made from apples picked from her own trees, and the compatibility they have always felt with one another, Elizabeth carefully steered the conversation toward her intended goal.

"William, what do you think of this war and our new country's chances for success?"

Having nothing to hide, and always so impressed with Elizabeth's convictions and her willingness to speak them, he answered, "Frankly Elizabeth, I'm against war as a means for settling differences. I don't think we have the resources to wear down or defeat the North. The longer the war goes on, the less are our chances. They outnumber us in almost every important category; namely, manpower, money, machinery, and manufacturing."

Impressed with his answer, she probed further. "And what about all the Northern prisoners we are caring for and feeding in our prisons? Do you think we should send them home, keep paying for their food and medical needs, or should we shoot them, saving the expense?"

He looked at her, a bit puzzled, realizing now that she was setting him up for something, and he didn't like this "cat and mouse" game. However, he barely showed his irritation when asking, "Elizabeth, you seem to have something on your mind What is it that you want to know? I've never held back anything from you, and I've always admired your honesty with me! What is it?"

Ashamed of her cautious and calculating line of questioning of William, she blurted out, "Oh William, I'm sorry that I had to do this to you, but I'm in a difficult situation. I was afraid to speak to you about what I've done, because I wasn't sure whose side you were on in this conflict. I've hesitated as to whether I should take such a large chance on your friendship."

"What have you done that's so terrible?"

"William, would you give medical attention to a northern prisoner?"

"Elizabeth, I minister to prisoners every day in our Chimborazo Hospital and some of the prisons hospitals when I'm needed. It's not my concern to ask a human being needing medical attention what his or her political beliefs or loyalties are. I only want to learn as much as I can about a patient's illness in order to make the person well."

"Then you'll give care to a northern prisoner?" she inquired as she stood abruptly indicating a sense of urgency.

"Yes I will, but it's pretty late to be going to a prison at this hour."

"You won't have to go to a prison."

"Why, where is he?"

"Upstairs," she replied softly.

"Here … in your house?" he asked in disbelief.

"Yes," Elizabeth confessed. "Four officers escaped from Libby Prison tonight, and one of them is very ill."

"But why did they come here?"

"I brought them here."

"Elizabeth, do you realize what danger you're in? Do you know what could happen to you if anyone found out that you willingly assisted a northern prisoner to escape? And what about the danger to your family?"

"Yes, I've considered it all," she said with a resigned acceptance. "I fear what might happen to my family, but my head follows my heart on this path which I have chosen. And when I say 'My Country,' I mean our one and only legitimate country, the United States of America. I am prepared to give my life to defend it against any aggressor!"

William looked at the petite and seemingly fragile woman and thought, "How could any cause lose, with such a determined, dedicated, courageous, and wonderful supporter such as this?" At that moment, he realized that what he had felt for her from the very beginning was, and continued to be, genuine. William vowed to aid and protect her in every way possible. And he said with conviction, "Take me to my patient!"

Elizabeth rushed to him and hugged him, and their secret collaboration was sealed as he wrapped his arms around her in a long-overdue embrace.

William was amazed, impressed, and curious upon seeing the secret room for the first time. He held his questions about its origin for another time. He began to realize that anything Elizabeth did in the future would not surprise him.

After William concluded his medical care of the prisoner, Elizabeth privately discussed her other secret activities with him. She expressed her increased appetite for even more information on the Confederate government and its activities and intentions. William informed her that he was at the Davis home two days ago to attend an "appreciation dinner" held in honor of the surgeons and doctors who were caring for the Confederate sick and wounded.

He laughed in amusement as he related how the whole evening was nearly ruined by the sweet, elderly table maid. The gray-haired servant dropped several of the dinner courses she was carrying to the table. An embarrassed Varina Davis apologized to the guests, explaining that the woman was only a temporary fill-in for the very qualified and experienced girl who had run away to the dreadful North with the boyfriend who had gotten her with child. What appeared to Mrs. Davis and her guests as incompetence, Dr. Parker diagnosed as a severe case of arthritis.

William gave Elizabeth detailed information on who was present and everything that was discussed, but added that he didn't think that it would be of much help to her. He promised to keep his eyes and ears open from now on for anything that might be of value and to get it to her as discretely as possible. Agreeing that their contacts must be minimal and plausible, they planned a safe and timely means of communicating whenever a face-to-face meeting might be too suspicious or dangerous.

If they were unable to meet, William and Elizabeth agreed on a location where messages could be left and picked up by either of them without causing any suspicion. They established a visible signal that would indicate when a message was ready to be picked up. That way, messages could be picked up expeditiously, and their collaboration would be difficult to detect.

Their current business completed, William prepared to leave and urged Elizabeth to use every precaution, not to trust anyone she didn't know, and to take good care of herself, because he thought this struggle could take years to resolve.

"Thank you, William, for all you've done tonight." They kissed each other discretely on the cheek, both regretting the rules of propriety that prevented their lips from touching; knowing that it would be highly improper under the circumstances. "Good night, William." Good night, Elizabeth."

A pensive Elizabeth sat for a moment looking at the two empty cups before taking the stairs up to her room. She soon felt a renewed surge of energy. This was, after all, a very good day! She had visited three prisons; made the prisoners more comfortable and healthy of mind and body. She had safely hidden four valuable Union officers helping them to make good on the first stage of their escape, and also had the sick one attended to quickly and safely so that he would be ready for the perilous trip north. In addition, she had gained an ally in "Dearest William" who would add greatly to her growing network of patriotic informants; and any contact with William was a soothing balm for her unfulfilled heart. The extra bonus was William's comment about the elderly table maid. Without realizing it, he had given Elizabeth a magnificent idea!

She laid her head on her pillow, and it felt so sweet at the end of this exciting, eventful, and typically long, eighteen-hour day. Her body was exhausted, but her mind was racing with possibilities. "I wonder if she would? She would be justified if she declined? And I wouldn't blame her for one minute! But she would be perfect! I could train her ... and I would even be willing to pay her extra. She just might ... and then again, she might not. What have I got to lose by asking? The timing is perfect!" Elizabeth sat up fully energized and quickly wrote a letter that asked for a huge favor without going into detail.

Dear Mary,

How proud I am upon hearing of the completion of your primary education. I long to see you again and to put your education and bright mind to good use. I need you here in Richmond right away and I will pay you very well for your services.

I am enclosing travel money with this note to cover your travel expenses here. If you decide not to come, you may keep the money for yourself. If you decide to accept my offer, you need not reply, just come, as I need you right away.

As always my fondest regards,
Elizabeth

Reviewing the letter she had just written, Elizabeth tried to imagine Mary Bowser's reactions. For ten years, she had sponsored little Mary's education in Philadelphia. Now that it was completed, Mary would probably be looking for employment. The timing was perfect. However, Elizabeth couldn't predict Mary's interest in returning to Richmond, now that it was the seat of the pro-slavery Confederacy. Mary was free, educated, and already situated in the anti-slavery North. Richmond was not the best place right now for a colored person to lead a decent life.

"Well, nothing ventured—nothing gained," she said softly and hid the letter. Her mind work now completed, Elizabeth again laid her head on the pillow. This time, the pillow would not be denied and was allowed to do its job. Elizabeth finally slipped into a deep sleep, the perfect remedy for an overworked body and mind.

CHAPTER 11

A Valuable Return

The Mary that stood waiting in the entrance hall area of the Van Lew residence bore little resemblance to the teary-eyed little girl of ten years ago. That little slave girl who was fortunate enough to have gained the keen eye, the favor, and the affection of one of her owners—Miss Elizabeth Van Lew.

Elizabeth had seen the potential of this bright-minded young girl. She made her one of the first in the household to be given their freedom. Elizabeth also decided that when Mary was of school age, she would arrange and finance her primary education in Philadelphia.

And now, Mary had returned to Richmond; a beautiful young woman, fully matured of body, and enlightened of mind. From the safety of the free North, this former slave returned to the very seat of the Confederacy and its staunch supporters of slavery! The most powerful reason that made her return was her appreciation and gratitude toward Elizabeth. The letter was the perfect opportunity to repay, in some small way, Elizabeth's kindness and generosity. She also wanted to show her benefactress what she had helped her to become.

Mary turned at the sound of rapid footsteps, and there was Elizabeth, now standing frozen in awe at Mary's child-to-woman transformation. After a moment, they ran to each other and hugged with smiles of joy on their lips and tears of gratitude in their eyes, in this open bond of affection between the two women— an affection not unlike that of a mother and daughter.

"Mary, look at you. You're all grown up and so beautiful! I wasn't sure if you would come, but I am so glad that you did. I am very grateful!"

"Miss Liz, I'm the one who is grateful. You have changed my life, and I'll be ever in your debt."

And so, for hours, they sat alone in the library talking of the days and events of the past ten years. After catching up with the years spent apart, they got around to the purpose of Elizabeth's urgent note.

"Mary, what I am about to tell you must be held in the strictest confidence. There is great peril in this city to even discuss what I am about to say to you."

"Miss Liz, after what you have done for me and my family, I'm ready to help you with whatever it is!"

"What I am about to ask you to do is not just for me, but also for your country. The United States must be preserved and the curse of slavery eradicated from it. That is what I believe, and that is why I have chosen my present course of activity.

"This is my plan. I would like to have you work here in this house for a little while as a table maid while I train you for what's ahead. I happen to know that the Jeff Davis household is in need of a quality table maid.

I am having General and Mrs. Winder for dinner soon, and I would like you to impress her with your skills. I will coach you on her likes and dislikes before that night arrives. During the evening, I will, in confidence, let it be known to her that due to our family's diminished means; I am unable to afford your services and would like to see you placed in a quality home.

"Knowing Mrs. Winder and her desire to enhance both her social standing and her husband's military career, I'm sure she will seize the opportunity to recommend you to Mrs. Davis. They will pay you a fair wage and treat you with respect. In addition, I will pay you double their amount.

The Davis Residence

"You will, by arrangement, be a table maid serving the Confederacy's leaders in that small way. By using your eyes, ears, mind, and wits, you will be providing a far greater service to the leaders of our only true legal government in Washington.

"If you choose to do this, you could be in the gravest danger if you get careless or if you get caught doing anything suspicious. If you accept this challenge, I will train you in the safest and most secure manner of accomplishing your assigned tasks. By following my instructions precisely, your actions, behavior, and comings and goings should always be above reproach. From the bottom of my heart, Mary,

I assure you that I would give my life before I would let you risk yours without your complete prior knowledge and consent, and my fullest protection.

"Up to this point, do you have any questions? Do you want to think it over before I go on, or would you like me to end the discussion of this subject here and now?"

"Miss Liz, I've learned a lot in my time away. Believe me, I agree with your position on the Confederacy and I'll do anything to help. Of course I'll be careful and follow your instructions precisely. I have the utmost respect for you and for what you've done for me. And, to prove it, I have already taken the name of 'Elizabeth' for my middle name."

"Oh Mary, that is just the highest compliment anyone has ever paid me! Does that mean you're willing to walk the path with me on this perilous journey?"

"Yes, Miss Liz, Yes!"

Again, their eyes filled and overflowed. This time, they served as binding signatures on an unwritten contract.

"You must be exhausted from your journey, Mary. Why don't we call it a day; tomorrow night, I'll explain everything in detail."

Rising slowly, Mary said, "Yes, I am pretty tired. Thank you again so much for everything and for your trust in me now."

"Good night, Mary Elizabeth Bowser. I am so happy and proud to have you back in our family. For me, this has been the happiest day in so many years. And for that, I thank you, Mary. God bless you!"

"Thank you, and good night, Miss Liz."

Elizabeth's plan to place Mary into the Davis household worked perfectly. Mrs. Winder's strong recommendation to Varina Davis won her the job. Over the weeks, Mary carried out her duties smoothly and, in addition, had boosted the morale of the entire household staff with her sense of humor and infectious smile. Coincidentally, a very short time thereafter, a First Lieutenant's commission was given to William Sydney Winder, son of General and Mrs. Winder, and he was permanently assigned to a safe, non-combat, desk job on his father' staff.

At the same time, life for the prisoners worsened. They were not prepared for the cold weather that had set in. Many who were captured in the summer had no need for overcoats or blankets then. Their rations continued to be gradually decreased, while the cruel treatment was gradually increased. Elizabeth was painfully aware of their heart sick yearning for home and family on this, their first

Christmas in captivity. To avoid the prison censors; she stuffed her coat each day with letters that would help compensate for their absence at their family's traditional holiday gatherings. The families of these soldiers did not look forward to celebrating this Christmas season with the same sense of anticipation and excitement of previous years, knowing that their loved ones were suffering such a miserable existence so far away from home and hearth.

Elizabeth stepped up her marketing for the prisoners to a point where it exceeded what she bought for her own family. She brought as much as she and her servant could carry each day to the prisons. Her generosity also included warm clothing and blankets to help them defend themselves against the cold, and the men then distributed them to their comrades most in need. Besides food and clothing, she also distributed expensive books from her family library, medicine, and even money. All were given without the slightest thought of anything in return. All were dealt out with a lavish, self-forgetting hand. For the prisoners, this kindness meant so much and, in many cases, made the difference between hope and despair.

One prisoner told Elizabeth that her generosity was so appreciated that he wanted to give her something in return. His "gift" was a set of buttons with her initials engraved on them. He said it would be the only Christmas present he would be able to give this year, but it would be to the most deserving person he knew—his Richmond "Mother."

The prisoner never mentioned that he had painstakingly sculpted them out of the only material at hand … left over chicken bones! She accepted this ever so touching gesture but was so surprised and overwhelmed by it that she struggled to hold back her tears. Elizabeth told him in a small voice, trembling with emotion, "I shall treasure these more than my other worldly possessions all the days of my life!" And that she did.

CHAPTER 12

Custards & Prisoners

The year 1862 began just as bleakly as 1861 ended. Several minor military skirmishes were undertaken, but the armies of the North and South yielded to the superior force of bitter cold, snow, and ice of "General January."

In Richmond, C.S.A. Captain George Gibbs replaced Lieutenant Todd as Inspector of Prisons after many complaints about Todd's excessive cruelty. More buildings were being acquired to hold prisoners, as this had not been part of the Confederate leaders' logistical or budgeting war planning. Prisoner exchanges were becoming the subject of much political thought, discussion, and negotiation. For now, the prisoners were at the mercy of their captors and the whims of "Mother Nature," as the prisons were almost totally unheated.

Prison and prison hospital officials were not taking kindly to the courtesies and kindnesses offered so graciously and unselfishly to the enemy by a native Virginian. So it was not completely unexpected that Elizabeth had a blazing feud with Owen B. Hill, the Acting Assistant Surgeon of Confederate Prison Hospitals.

It began on a bitterly cold day in January as Elizabeth was making her daily rounds of the prisons and prison hospitals. The servant accompanying her was carrying many jars of freshly made custard. To her surprise, the guards refused to admit her, a practice the officials will use periodically to try to discourage her from her prison visits. However, they underestimated her determination, and they soon learned that rather than stopping her, it only slowed her down momentarily. Soon, she was able to regain admission through her charm, wit, cajolery, subtle threats, or by making herself a persistent nuisance. But, with this first refusal, she simply left the custard jars to be distributed to the Federal prisoners and returned home.

Later that same day, around noon, a captain from the hospital returned most of the jars to Elizabeth at her home along with a curt note that read:

Miss Van Lew,

Dr. Higginbotham is the Surgeon in Charge of the Prison Hospitals and has given orders that nothing to eat shall go into the hospitals except that furnished by the commissary of the post. Acting as his assistant I cannot violate any order he may give, or I would cheerfully oblige you.

Very respectfully,
Owen B. Hill

Acting Assistant Surgeon
C.S. Prison Hospitals
January 23, 1862

After reading the note, Elizabeth quietly asked the captain, "Did you taste the custard, Captain?"

Caught off guard and slightly embarrassed, the captain felt bound, under the steady gaze of her compelling blue eyes, to answer truthfully and responded, "Yes Ma'am."

"Was it good, Captain?" she continued.

The captain nodded sheepishly and admitted, "Yes it was, Ma'am, and would be good for the prisoners if I could give it to them—but I cannot do so."

Elizabeth thanked the captain for his honesty, and he left.

Within the hour, Elizabeth was at the Richmond Headquarters of the C.S. War Department protesting Dr. Higginbotham's order. Assistant Secretary of War Bledsoe told her that Dr. Higginbotham had no right or authority to issue such an order and he promised to see Secretary of War Judah P. Benjamin and have the order revoked.

To prove the custard was "innocent of all evils," Elizabeth had carried several jars with her to the War Office. She explained in the note left with the jars that "they were for the honorable men, hoping that it might move them to humanity."

The next morning, a note from Bledsoe was delivered to her at home. It read:

"My Dear Miss Van Lew,

The Secretary of War declined to act on your application and referred it
to General Winder. If I can see General Winder, I will try to get him to
grant your request. The custard was very nice and many thanks to you.
I borrowed some cups from an eating house nearby, and brought some
crackers. So it was eaten in fine style.

Truly yours,
A. G. Bledsoe

The next day, Elizabeth went directly to General Winder's office. Through
informants, she had learned that there was no love lost between General Winder
and Dr. Higginbotham.

After showing Winder both Hill's and Bledsoe's notes, Elizabeth gave him several jars of custard along with an ample supply of flattery. He promptly opened
one of the jars, took a spoon from one of his desk drawers, and sampled the custard. Elizabeth had succeeded in appealing to both his prodigious appetite and
his insatiable vanity. Winder proclaimed, "The custard is more than worthy of
human consumption," and not only reinstated Elizabeth's prison passes but wrote
orders for Dr. Edward G. Higginbotham to be placed under arrest for overstep-
ping the authority of his rank!

It was some time before Elizabeth's passes were revoked again, and during
Higginbotham's arrest, it was easy for her to get anything into or out of the prison
hospitals.

Elizabeth continued her visits to the seven Union officers, which included
Colonel Lee and Major Revere, being held hostage in the Henrico County Jail
pending the fate of the "Confederate Privateersmen" being held in a New York
City jail.

Elizabeth brought the officers books, sweets, and anything she could to nour-
ish and sustain their minds and bodies during their deplorable confinement. She
also secretly gave them money to bribe the jailer, "a coarse, ruffianly, drunken
sot," for extra food rations. And, just as importantly, she played secret "postman"
to keep Paul's brother, Doctor Edward H.R. Revere, who was himself being held
prisoner in a former tobacco warehouse, informed of Paul's situation and physical
condition. She relayed to Edward that the hostages were all in reasonably good
spirits, but pale and weak from the close confinement and unhealthy conditions.

The Union leaders' attempts to negotiate a transfer for the seven officers was
rebuffed by the Confederate government with these words:

"Our government will not take into consideration any proposition for exchange of our prisoners taken in our service on the high seas until there is an absolute, unconditional abandonment of the pretext that they are pirates, and until they are released from the position of felons and placed in the same condition as other prisoners of war, and we decline receiving any proposal in relation to the hostages whom we are forced unwillingly to treat as felons as long as our fellow-citizens are so treated by the enemy."

At the end of January, some prisoner exchanges had been arranged for the sick and wounded; one Confederate for one Federal. One of the sick prisoners, Adjutant Charles L. Pierson, from Colonel Lee and Major Revere's regiment, the Massachusetts 20th Volunteers, had been exchanged. Upon his release, Pierson headed straight for Washington to give an eye witness account of the disgraceful conditions of the prisoners. He hoped to influence the politicians and military leaders to deliberate with compassion and act with dispatch for the hostages' exchange.

Meanwhile, the seven officers were kept in their miserable condition not knowing upon rising each day, when they were taken out of their cells, if it was for twenty minutes of fresh air and exercise or for a trip to the gallows. They dispelled their fears through Christian trust, ministering to each other, since General Winder had refused to let a clergyman visit them—a privilege not often refused to prisoners. It was a scene of unfailing courage and faith.

On one rare visit before he was exchanged, Paul's brother Edward, being a doctor, was allowed to come to the jail to look at the prisoners through a small peephole. He could barely see inside or breathe the foul air. He told Elizabeth "I don't know how they survive, escape sickness, or suffer broken minds or powers." Elizabeth noted, from that day on, Edward's face took on a permanent look of one who has seen a terrible sight never to be forgotten.

On the fourth of February, Elizabeth secretly brought news to Edward that the hostages in Henrico County Jail would be freed from their confinement there and returned to be with them in their slightly less cruel surroundings. However, they were told that they were still hostages awaiting the outcome of the decision on the fate of the privateersmen in New York. She related to Edward that the Federal officers were told that they, "were only being temporarily moved while the cell was being cleaned up."

The next morning, the officer-prisoners in Libby heard three cheers from an adjacent warehouse housing Union Army enlisted men-prisoners, many of whom had served with the officers being held hostage. They rushed to the peepholes they had made in the walls, pulled out the material stuffed in them to keep out the cold wind, and saw the approaching officers from Henrico. Many of the enlisted men had served with the hostage officers. Within minutes, the hostages entered the makeshift prison, and their pale and gaunt features lit up with pride and gratitude at the outpouring of affection and sympathy from both the enlisted men and their fellow officers. They gave an account of their living conditions, daily routine, suffering, and privations in the Henrico Jail. The horror of their ordeal shocked the souls of everyone present. The courage and determination of these men etched itself in the minds and hearts of the officers who heard their story and was to stay with them for the rest of their lives.

Thankfully, the hostages never returned to the Henrico County Jail. A few days later, Elizabeth brought them a Richmond newspaper containing excerpts from a New York newspaper stating that "The Rebel Privateersmen, the majority of which were New York wharf-thieves, were turned over to the U.S. Navy Department as 'prisoners of war.'"

Meanwhile, still smarting from their last encounter with Elizabeth Van Lew, and wanting revenge, the Confederate prison authorities made another attempt to stop her from bringing food to Federal prisoners. It happened just after she had paid a visit to a Lieutenant McMurtrie who had just had his leg amputated from a wound that had completely shattered his leg. McMurtrie was devastated because he had always been an active athlete and sportsman.

To cheer him up, Elizabeth had brought an extra special meal, with all fixings, directly to his bed. He was so surprised and pleased that for a few hours on that day, he completely forgot his misfortune.

When she was leaving the hospital, she noticed the Commissary Captain Warner saying something to Captain Turner, the Commanding Officer of Libby Prison. The next day, she received a note from Captain Turner:

February 15, 1862

Lieutenant McMurtrie, being now recently well, I have to request that you discontinue furnishing him his meals. Abundant and palatable food is prepared for the patients in the prison hospital, and I would prefer that they not be supplied by personnel outside as it has a tendency to subvert the consistency of prison rules and discipline.

I am your obedient servant,
Thomas P. Turner

Capt. Commanding

Elizabeth returned to Winder's office with an invitation for the General and his family to dine at the Van Lew home. After he accepted, she related details of the incident and showed him Turner's note. She also quoted to him a conversation she overheard between Captain Warner and Captain Turner about the prisoners' rations, with Warner saying, "I would rather know that I had only one week to live than to live six months on the food the prisoners had. I can't imagine how they stand it!"

"With the custard incident still fresh in his mind, Winder dispatched an order to Captain Turner to "cease and desist his interference with the humanitarian activities of Miss Elizabeth Van Lew." From that moment on, no further attempts were ever made to stop Elizabeth from bringing food to the prisoners.

On Thursday, February 20, it was announced that all the prisoners of war would be forwarded to Fortress Monroe on the following Saturday. Later that day, C. S. General Randolph officially notified the hostages that they would go home with the other prisoners.

On Friday the 21, Elizabeth visited Paul and Colonel Lee for the last time. The meeting was both a happy and a sad one for Elizabeth. She was relieved that they were free from such horrible physical and emotional suffering and happy that they were returning to their families. She was, however, saddened to see them leave Richmond, for she had grown very fond of them.

Elizabeth had learned much and gained great strength from their example during their thirteen weeks of confinement in the Henrico Jail. The ordeal never broke their faith, spirit, or determination to survive, but rather strengthened their resolve and gave them a greater appreciation of what was really important in life.

Colonel Lee told Elizabeth that he was indebted to her, "For substantial comforts that helped ward off the effects of Rebel starvation and cruelty but for the still more exquisite comfort of knowing that even where the Rebel flag waved, the Union had a tried and trusted friend."

They both expressed their deepest appreciation for her bravery in the face of scorn, torment, and threats of her former friends and neighbors. And also for the dangerous risks she took smuggling notes and letters in and out, and her faithful ministering to them throughout their confinement both in the prison and in the jail.

They both said that they knew their families would never forget her conveying news and information to and from them, which kept their hopes alive. Nothing could have made a greater difference during their gravest and darkest hours. They made her promise to visit with them in Boston after the War was over, a promise she looked forward to fulfilling "in better times."

"You are the bravest of us all," they told Elizabeth. "You carry no gun or sword, you are not the physical equal of a war-toughened soldier, you do not fight alongside legions of friendly comrades on horse or foot with artillery for cover. You do not even have to do what you do. And yet, in your work, you display the utmost of courage, wisdom, determination, and bravery equal to any combatant with the same threat of death every day … and an inglorious death tainted with the brand 'traitor.' Soldiers and sailors have days of rest between battles—you take no rest from risk. We bow to your courage, loyalty, and patriotism."

Elizabeth pointed to the "Stars and Bars" that waved above the Confederate Capitol building where the Confederate Congress was in session and replied, "I would gladly see my house lain in ruins if I could once more see the government of the United States restored here. Tell your friends in the North that there are some of us left still who pray day and night that the 'Stars and Stripes' may take the place of that rag of rebellion."

CHAPTER 13

A Hanging Witnessed

In early March, the consequences of Elizabeth's activities became all too clear. Two Federal Secret Service Agents in Richmond, John Scully and Pryce Lewis, both of English birth, were arrested, tried, and put into prison.

Both men had been sent by Allan Pinkerton, founder and Chief of the Military Secret Service of the Federal Army to check on the whereabouts of his trusted missing spy, Timothy Webster. Through her sources, Elizabeth found out that Webster was staying at the Monumental Hotel and got word to the two agents.

When they arrived at Webster's room, they found him very sick and unable to travel. Another member of the Secret Service from Washington, Mrs. Hattie Lawson, who was posing as his sister, was caring for him. Also present was a Confederate officer whom Webster had befriended, but who was unwitting of Webster's true identity.

The officer first asked, then told them that they must go over to the Provost Marshal's Office to get the necessary permits to travel within the Richmond City limits.

Upon their arrival at the Office of General Winder, the newly designated Provost Marshall they were questioned by a recently hired bright detective, W.W. New. New was suspicious of everyone and everything, and he was anxious to make a name for himself. The detective "smelled a rat" when they told him they had their papers checked when crossing the Potomac from Washington. Not wanting to arouse their suspicion, he acted quite friendly and gracious as he issued them the permits. After they left, New had them followed at a safe distance by fellow detectives and sent for Jackson Morton, who recently moved to Richmond from Washington.

Shortly thereafter, New learned that the two men went straight to Webster's room at the Monumental Hotel. When Morton arrived, New hurried him over to the Monumental where they were just in time to see the two men leaving. Morton made a positive identification, stating that the two men were the same two Federal Secret Service Agents who had disgracefully searched his Washington home. Delighted at having had his suspicions confirmed, New arrested the two agents and took them to the city jail.

New now suspected Webster's involvement in the spy ring and returned to question him. Webster claimed he never knew the two men were agents, and that their contacts had been minimal. New only half believed him and later told Winder about a plan he had to catch Webster. Impressed with New's initial success, partly because he had recruited him, the General agreed to support the plan.

The two men were tried as criminals and were sentenced to be hanged. As the day of the execution drew near, John Scully cracked under the threat of death and, for a promise to act as a witness against Webster, revealed Webster's role as head of the spy ring. Both men wound up testifying against Webster to save their necks.

After a three-week trial, Webster was sentenced to hang, and the two men and woman agents were given jail sentences. Fortunately, Elizabeth's name never surfaced because she was careful to use an intermediary whenever she passed information to them.

Lincoln and his Cabinet met and decided to ask Secretary of War Stanton to persuade the Confederacy to change Webster's sentence. They argued that, to date, the Federal Government had not sentenced to death any of the Confederate spies they had caught and warned the Confederate government that if the sentence were carried out, they would retaliate in kind.

Timothy Webster

Despite all the appeals for clemency and the threats from Washington, the Southern leaders wanted to make an example of Webster as a warning to others who were now conducting, or thinking about engaging in subversive activities against the Confederacy. They stood firm on Webster's sentence.

Webster was also an embarassment to Confederate Secretary of War Judah Benjamin, who had hired him to act as a secret agent and courier of important mail and dispatches, little knowing then that all of the messages delivered were read first by Union officials.

The twenty-ninth of April was a cold, raw, gloomy morning on the Old Fair Grounds, now transformed into Camp Lee. With a shawl covering her head and most of her face, Elizabeth was unrecognized in the somber crowd of soldiers and citizens who had gathered to witness the spectacle.

Elizabeth was watching from a totally different perspective than the rest of the onlookers. She admired Webster's composure, although he was obviously in poor health. He stood erect and appeared unashamed, even looking proud of what he had done for his country and clear as to why he did it … even as he was staring death in the face!

Now the hangman placed the black hood over his head, cutting off the last vision of his life, and he felt the noose tighten around his neck. It would soon be over. The crowd turned silent. The deathly stillness was broken by the heavy footsteps of the hangman's boots on the wooden scaffold as he walked the few steps to the trap door release mechanism.

Elizabeth watched the tragic life and death spectacle filled with distress. She was partly angry that she was powerless to prevent them from carrying out the sentence and also saddened that she couldn't protect him from the betrayal of his "comrades."

Every eye was now riveted on the condemned man as he stood erect, waiting for his life to end, looking alone and helpless … and at the same time, courageous, and noble. His heart was pounding so hard and so fast that seconds seemed like hours.

Upon the signal from the presiding officer, the trap door was released, and Webster fell through the opening with a thump to the ground below, as the hangman's knot had come undone.

The attending soldiers were at first stunned and unsure of what to do. Then, they were ordered to pick up the dazed Webster and make him walk the thirteen steps again. This time they tested the noose thoroughly before placing it around his neck.

Elizabeth muttered inaudibly … "Typical Confederate incompetence … surely it's God's sign of the injustice of this beastly deed."

Webster, hooded and noosed, now swayed unsteadily on the trap door for the second time. Again the hangman walked to his position, and a hush swept over the murmuring crowd. From under the hood, Webster cried out, "I suffer a double death!"

Filled with horror and anger, Elizabeth did not utter a sound, but her mind screamed, "Murdering savages!"

This time the knot held, and the lifeless body twitched and then hung limp as the crowd gasped in horror. Webster was the first American spy to be hanged since Nathan Hale.

Elizabeth's knees grew weak from the shock of witnessing, for the first time, the taking of a human life, and from such close range. But the effect of the execution on Elizabeth was the exact opposite from the Confederate government's intention. Their first hanging of a spy of the Rebellion, rather than teaching her a lesson, sent a rejuvenating jolt of determination through her entire being.

Elizabeth reasoned, "If Webster could give his life for what he believed in, so will I if it comes to that … but I must be doubly careful in the future so that my work will not be terminated before reaching its final objectives … ending slavery and reunifying the Republic.

"This cold-hearted injustice against a true patriot must be avenged. Surely God will not let this evil government succeed. I must do everything I can to bring it down."

Detective New had watched the event with much pride. He had his second victory in a row, and he was thinking, "And now I must check on this strange woman who is visiting the Yankees … this Elizabeth Van Lew!"

Detective W.W. New

CHAPTER 14

Hot Water & Information

That very afternoon, Elizabeth was carrying some hot food in a French metal food warmer to the prisoners. The warmer had three pieces, the bottom section which held water hot enough to keep the food in the section above it warm, and a cover to prevent the heat from escaping. Elizabeth had successfully and repeatedly used the bottom section, without the water, as a hiding place for carrying messages in and out of the prisons.

As she was leaving the prison, she noticed a man observing her closely and staring at the warmer. Not wanting to arouse suspicion by turning around, she watched his movement in the reflection from the window of a store across the street and saw him hurriedly enter the prison.

His sinister face looked familiar, and Elizabeth struggled to recollect where she had seen him, as she quickened her pace homeward. Now she remembered. He was one of the detectives in Winder's office the day she went for her prison pass. Her heart pounded as she turned the corner and was out of sight and out of a dangerous situation—carrying a pan full of incriminating messages.

Late that night, Mary reported to Elizabeth that at dinner General Winder was bragging to Mister Davis about how Detective New, under his direction, had so swiftly broken up the Webster spy ring. Davis asked Winder if he thought spying was a problem in Richmond. Winder told him he thought that while it wasn't rampant; they had to keep their guard up, since Webster's example demonstrated that Washington would do everything in its power to learn what was going on in Richmond.

However, Winder elaborated that the steps already taken such as the protective ring of batteries that encircled the city, the pickets that patrolled the perimeter between the batteries, and the mandatory exit and entry permits would control most of the problems of infiltration by the enemy. In addition, the law passed by Congress that ordered all aliens in the Capital to leave, and the thirty civilian detectives he had recruited from Maryland, New York, and Philadelphia would find and clean out any potential espionage or sabotage activity in Richmond. He concluded that he had also directed Detective New to now focus all his attention on subversive activities within the city.

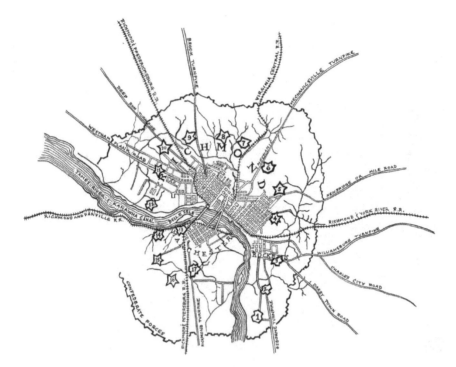

Richmond Defenses

At the same time, Mary was deeply concerned for Elizabeth's safety as well as any possible compromise that might lead to the discovery of her role as informant. She was well aware that there would be no mercy for treason on the part of a Black.

Elizabeth reassured her by telling her, "Mary, I'm grateful for all your information and for your concern—but I want you to know that the surveillance of my activities has already begun." She told Mary about seeing the detective at the prison. "Of course, I'll take extra precautions, and I can assure you that you are in no danger at this time. However, we have to be extremely watchful and circumspect—wise as serpents—and harmless as doves, for truly the lions are seeking to devour us."

The following day, Elizabeth was about to enter the prisoners' room with the food warmer as she had done so often. This time, however, the guards had been ordered by Detective New to "Stop her and search the French contrivance!" The guard blocked her path and told her, "I want to check that contraption."

New, not wanting to arouse Elizabeth's suspicion and possibly preventing her from falling into his trap and to remain anonymous remained out of sight, observing the action from a peephole in the adjoining room. Upon questioning the guards the day before about Elizabeth's activities, New had been told about the suspicious handling of the warmer over the past few months. Crouched at his peephole, impatient to see Elizabeth apprehended, he gloated, "I've got you now … you amateur … you bitch!" He waited anxiously for the guards to find the incriminating evidence before he would burst out and make his third successful arrest.

He stood there, scarcely breathing, but Elizabeth delayed his victory by asking the guard innocently, "Why do you want to see it today; you've never asked me before?"

"Never mind why. Just give me the damned thing!" the irritated guard shouted.

Elizabeth said, "Here it is," and handed it to the guard.

He held it for only an instant, then dropped it screaming with pain, staring at his red palms and then at Elizabeth's shawl-protected hands.

Elizabeth had anticipated this possibility and had filled the bottom section with blistering hot water.

New was stunned. He thought that he was about to make another quick arrest. "Damn her! I know she's up to something. She was lucky this time, but I'll be watching her like a hawk, and the next time, I'll have her—then she'll swing!"

In Richmond, both the weather and the community's emotions were heating up. A steady stream of prisoners were arriving from the Shiloh and Shenandoah Valley battlefields, prisoners for whom Elizabeth shopped for supplementary provisions and medicine. To her, it was just as much a part of her routine as going to St. John's Church on Sunday. However, to the townspeople, it was infuriating and contemptible, and their resentment had turned into ruthless hatred. The Richmond press echoed their feelings in one Monday editorial:

"Two ladies, mother and daughter, living on Church Hill, have lately attracted public notice by their assiduous attentions to the Yankee prisoners … Whilst every true woman in this community has been busy making articles for our troops, or administering to our sick, these two women have been spending their opulent means in aiding and giving comfort to the miscreants who have invaded our sacred soil, bent on rapine and murder … Out upon all pretexts to humanity! … The curse of these two females, in providing them with delicacies, bringing them books, stationery and paper, cannot but be regarded as an evidence of sympathy amounting to an endorsement of the cause and conduct of the Northern vandals."

While another newspaper put it more bluntly:

"RAPPED OVER THE KNUCKS

This is a warning to certain females of Southern residence (not perhaps birth) but of decidedly Northern and Abolition proclivities. If such people do not wish to be exposed and dealt with as alien enemies to their country, they would do well to cut stick with their worthless carcass while they can do so with safety ..."

To which Elizabeth wrote in the newspaper's margin, "These ladies were my mother and myself. God knows it was little enough we could do." She later wrote, "The threats, the scowls, the frowns of an infuriated community—who can write of them? I've had brave men shake their fingers in my face and say terrible things. We've had threats of being driven away, threats of fire, and threats of death."

After the food warmer incident, New had instructed the guards to accompany Elizabeth every step of the way on her visits to the prisoners. They watched her every move for anything suspicious, stayed within earshot, and limited the time of her contacts with each prisoner.

Realizing that this new intense scrutiny demanded another, even more secure method of exchanging information, Elizabeth devised a clever technique. Along with food, clothing, bedding, medicine, and money, she had been bringing books from her library to help the prisoners pass away the empty hours. She would continue daily to bring in new books and take back the ones they had already read. But now, the books themselves would become the carriers of the secret messages.

On this day, Elizabeth revealed the technique and instructed the senior officer in its complete method of usage, right under the guards' noses, without as much as a word being spoken.

She walked amongst the men, handing each of them a freshly cooked hard-boiled egg from her basket. The last egg she handed to the senior officer. He thanked her and went off by himself to his corner to eat it.

From the weight of the egg, he knew that it was hollow and must contain something inside. He turned over the hollow eggshell and saw the tiny hole in the bottom in which a small ball of white paper had been folded and stuffed. When Elizabeth handed him the egg, she had ever so gently scratched the minutely cracked shell against his palm and looked at him with those eyes that spoke more eloquently than most lips.

Safely out of sight of the guards, the senior officer unfurled the paper on which had been written the precise instructions for future communications and intelligence reporting. The plan was so well conceived, and yet so simple, that he smiled in admiration of this remarkable woman.

According to the instructions, the person sending a message could either prick a tiny hole above a letter of a word—only one letter per word, which, when all the letters were put together, would form the words of the message. Or, lacking something to prick the pages, they could use a fingernail to underscore a word. A message could contain a combination of both techniques, words with pinholes, and words underscored, whenever it would expedite the encoding of the message. Scoring diagonally on the bottom left of a page indicated the beginning of the message, and vertically on the bottom right-hand corner of the page indicated the end of the message.

The new system was put into practice that very night. From the numerous windows on all sides of the building, all the officers had been relentless in their surveillance of troop movements into and out of the city. The prisoners even took shifts, so that any information of military value that took place during the night would not be missed. They counted the number of men, horses, equipment, artillery pieces, and wagons. They determined the direction of travel, identified what roads were being used and how supplies were coming into the city—whether by railcar or by water. Observing the water route was easy, because the boats docked just yards away in the adjacent Kanawha Canal of the James River, on the south side of the prison.

They also eavesdropped on the conversations of guards who bragged about a victory here and there or talked about how a lucky someone was going somewhere to "Whip the Yankee dogs."

Another source was the prison hospital, where surgeons and doctors discussed fresh battlefield information while ministering to the sick and wounded. When this was added to first-hand information from the streams of arriving prisoners, it could be of immense assistance to the military strategists. All of this, they passed on to Elizabeth according to her new method. Then, by the light of a candle in the privacy of her bedroom, she painstakingly assembled and rewrote it and passed it along to the military commanders in the Union Army.

The information from the prisoners, coupled with information relayed by Mary, William, and other willing accomplices, added to her own personal observation, increased the accuracy and value of Elizabeth's dispatches a hundredfold. Her ministrations in the prison cells and hospital wards, coupled with the vital information she provided to the military planners in Washington, more than doubled her contributions to the war effort. For the Union, she was a beacon of light in the South.

Her solitary example of loyalty to the Union and outspoken opposition to the wisdom of secession occasionally convinced some people to support her with clandestine information, assorted assistance and errands when required. This pool of loyal and trusted resources would prove invaluable to Elizabeth in the dangerous and eventful period ahead.

CHAPTER 15

Messages, Couriers, & The First Search

As the daylight hours lengthened, Elizabeth was seen everywhere, not missing a single opportunity to glean information to pass on. Because of her newly acquired "watchdogs," she was especially careful to prepare a plausible reason for every trip she took in and around the city; it had to be an innocent cover story that would stand up under close examination or interrogation.

On her visit to the general store, where she normally shopped for the prisoners, she saw a flyer posted near the doorway. It read:

ATTENTION CITIZENS!

Bodies of troops will be marching through the city today, tonight and tomorrow and the citizens are requested to send COOKED PROVISIONS to the store of L. Antlotti at the Central Railroad Depot.

Joseph Mayo
Mayor of the City of Richmond

Elizabeth thought, "Thanks for the advance notice, Mr. Mayor, I'll notify the prisoners to maintain a round-the-clock watch. And then, I'll be happy to take a little food to the Depot so that I can get some first-hand details about the troops and their commanders. When I put it all together in my report, it should help our forces thwart the success of the Confederate's mission."

Sending her reports through the Richmond lines was becoming an increasingly dangerous undertaking. But once again, Elizabeth demonstrated her resourcefulness. She had been paying trusted messengers to carry her reports through the lines. Now, the

Mayor Joseph Mayo

messengers were getting more and more nervous and prone to making mistakes, for Winder's detectives were everywhere. The detectives were so obsessed with ridding the city of any actual or suspected spies, they were becoming an irritant to the population and an especial hindrance to Elizabeth herself.

Winder, who had gone on record with Davis saying, "Spying is not a problem in Richmond," had been busy recruiting civilians to act as agents to cover his premature pronouncement and was now taking a more active role in the effort.

Because the detectives were primarily Northerners whose allegiance rested with the Confederacy, they were viewed in Richmond as aliens and were thoroughly despised for their intrusive and antagonistic behavior vis-a-vis the citizenry. The most despised was the relentless W.W. New, whose suspicions of Elizabeth were slowly turning into a cat-and-mouse game with the grim stakes being possibly a slow death in a disease-ridden dungeon in Castle Thunder Prison or an immediate, early morning appointment with the executioner for Elizabeth.

Most of the information Elizabeth was collecting had to be passed on immediately or it would lose its military advantage. Elizabeth's challenge was to get messengers who could get through the lines whenever necessary, easily, without suspicion—and who could be trusted! She needed loyalty and complete trust. Finally, she hit upon an idea.

Back in the early 1840's, Elizabeth's father had bought a small farm south of the city on the Williamsburg Carriage Road to provide provisions for both their table and as an additional source of income. When Elizabeth and her mother had given all their slaves their freedom after her father died, she allowed the ones who remained to continue to work the farm keeping part of the earnings as income for themselves. Naturally, they had passes to bring their produce in and out of the city on a daily basis.

So, out of necessity, it was logical that Elizabeth should turn to these freed slaves to help her in carrying the messages through the pickets. When asked, and the risks explained, they were more than willing to assist because her cause was their own and because they wanted to repay her many acts of kindness over the years.

Elizabeth began using an assortment of techniques, depending on who would be passing through the lines. When it was the elderly farmhand, Samuel, he would carry the message, maps, and plans in the hollow slits in the soles of his special-made boots. He would wear the boots with the hollow compartment containing the intelligence requests into the city in the morning as he delivered produce to the Van Lew's kitchen. Then, at the end of the day after selling and delivering the rest of the farm products, he would return with his proceeds to the Van Lew kitchen and servants quarters. The boots would be "loaded" with valuable strategic intelligence, and he would quietly leave the city on his way back to the farm.

Sometimes it would be the young Negro seamstress Ruth who carried the messages along with the implements of her trade. She would either stitch them into the hems of dresses, or into the hidden pockets in the bolts of assorted distracting patterned material. After cursory inspections by the patrols and guards, the items were always returned intact. Because the soldiers had been instructed to be on the lookout for weapons, government documents, maps, greenbacks, or contraband—not secret messages.

And when another brave farmhand, Lucy, brought her large country basket of eggs through the lines, one of them near the bottom was but a hollow shell in which a message had been carefully inserted.

After dark, a steam launch from the opposite side of the James River was used to courier the information to the scouts, who would deliver it to the military command posts. Sometimes, the messages would be delivered by horseback to the next relay station, or even on foot, if the other methods were either not available or too dangerous.

Those were some of the methods Elizabeth employed in order to preserve and protect her lines of communication and information flow with the North. Her former slaves, now paid servants, countrymen and women, time after time carried messages which, if discovered, would have caused them to be hanged from the nearest tree. They did so as diligently as they performed their farm chores.

As for Elizabeth, the likelihood of detection one day—any day—seemed inevitable. She wrote, "From the commencement of the War … my life was in constant jeopardy. Yet," she added, "I was an enthusiast who never counted it dear if I could have served the Union—not that I wished to die."

Morning after morning, night after night, her days were full of suspense and threatening danger such as few men or fewer women could even comprehend. She must contend with betrayal, blunders, and the careless disregard for prudence in those with whom she entrusted her life, some of whom she had not previously known, screened, or recruited.

Just at this time of Elizabeth's increased activity, another prisoner escaped from Libby. Now, a highly suspicious and impatient Detective New, determined to bring Elizabeth and any other of her Union sympathizers to bay, immediately formed a pre-dawn search party—and headed directly for the Van Lew mansion.

Upon New's arrival, he posted armed soldiers completely surrounding the entire city block of the Van Lew estate, with orders to shoot to kill anyone attempting to escape the property.

He took the remaining men and quickly climbed the steps to the front entrance. Pounding on the door he shouted in his most authoritative voice, "Open the door, or we'll break it down!"

There was no immediate answer. He waited a few moments and started pounding and shouting again. His second tattoo on the heavy wooden door was interrupted as the door slowly swung open. The men, not knowing what to expect, their hearts pounding, drew their weapons ready to fire. There, holding a candle in one hand and a shawl around her with the other, was Elizabeth. This was the first face-to-face meeting of Elizabeth and her opponent, New.

Elizabeth spoke first, "I don't know who you are or where you come from, but in these parts a simple civilized knock on the door will get a response. Pounding and shouting, especially at this hour of the night, are neither necessary nor appreciated. Furthermore, uninvited gentlemen do not call upon ladies at this time of night."

New was taken by surprise both by confronting Elizabeth in person and by the calling down he received. He quickly regained his composure and his dedication to his mission of catching the hidden prisoner and wrapping up their conspiratorial benefactor.

"I am Detective New, and I have reason to believe that the Union prisoner who escaped from Libby Prison a few hours ago is hiding in this house," he declared, hoping both to intimidate Elizabeth and impress the soldiers.

"And what makes you think he is hiding here?" she inquired with a hint of irritation.

"One good reason. You are so damned cozy with those Yankees at the prison, who else would they turn to in this city besides you?" he snarled.

"And my Christian activities bother you so much that you have prejudged me and attempt to invade my home at this hour as if I were a common criminal?" she snapped back.

New was beginning to lose patience and face in front of the men and felt that to get the upper hand, he must try an oblique attack on her rather than the unsuccessful direct approach. He baited her with, "If the prisoner isn't here, then you won't mind if we search the house. Just to ensure your safety of course."

"If he was in this house, I would know about it," she countered.

"Well, is he?" he demanded.

"I don't think you'd believe me if I said he wasn't, so see for yourself," she said quietly, "but you mustn't wake Mother; she's not well," as she opened the door wider to admit them.

New posted one man at the front door, and then, leading the rest of the men, they moved slowly from floor to floor, room to room, opening every clothes, pantry, and linen closet with guns ready, expecting the enemy prisoner to jump out at them at every turn.

The soldiers, who were predominantly from small farms, were so impressed with the mansion and its furnishings that they might not have seen the prisoner if he were sitting in a darkened corner. But not New. He missed nothing. Starting first in the wine cellar, he looked under tables, behind shelves, around racks, and in wash-up and storage areas. As he and his men worked their way upstairs, he searched behind curtains, under tables, in closets and trunks, under desks and furniture, also looking for any obvious incriminating evidence.

Finally, they wound up in the third floor attic storage room. After completing a thorough search, New looked around, puzzled and irritated, and thought, "The reports that he was seen heading in this direction were from very reliable sources. Everything pointed to this location as the logical hiding place. But where the hell could he be?"

Temporarily stumped, he said grudgingly, "Well, it looks like he's not in this house, but we're going to search every other building on the property!"

"Very well. I'll have one of the servants open them all up for you," Elizabeth obliged, maintaining her air of righteous innocence.

All the men returned downstairs, and before New left he wanted both to instill some fear into Elizabeth and to relieve some of his own frustration. He berated her with, "Miss Van Lew, I don't approve of your activities one bit. I think you are treading on very, very thin ice. I'm warning you, if you're taking part in any treasonous activities, you will be caught and punished without mercy … I promise you that! You are not out of the woods yet by any means. If we find that prisoner here, or see signs that he was here, or learn that you had anything to do with the escape, we'll be back for you, and I will personally take pleasure in watching you come to the same fate as the late Timothy Webster. He thought he could outsmart me too!"

He glared at her for a minute to emphasize his words, then followed the men out, slamming the door behind him. Elizabeth took the lighted candelabrum and sat on the east-facing veranda, watching them as they searched the rest of the property. She wanted them to see that she was monitoring their activities while on her property and to show New her unwillingness to shrink from his attempt at intimidation.

Their fruitless search completed, the men formed two columns, and before New joined the men on their march back to their headquarters, he took one long last look at Elizabeth. They stared unflinching at each other like two boxers who were having the rules of their fight recited to them by the referee, but to whom they pay no attention. They saw only an adversary; an enemy to be defeated … smashed … destroyed!

After the men were blocks away, Elizabeth returned inside the house and proceeded with a single candleholder directly to the attic storage room to make sure the escaped prisoner inside the secret room was comfortable for the night. Then she returned to her own bedroom with a gleam of excitement in her eyes but a look of concern on her face and thought, "This New is trouble … and I think he is as dedicated to his cause as I am to mine! Unfortunately, there can only be one winner in this fight to the finish!"

The next day, Elizabeth gave money to Nelson for distribution amongst some trusted co-conspirators to purchase civilian clothing from different stores around the city for the prisoner.

After waiting a safe period for the furor over the escape to die down, a stroke of luck or divine intervention occurred. A fog rolled in off the James River so dense that houses across the street from one another disappeared from view and completely swallowed up the city.

"Perfect timing, Dear Lord," Elizabeth said to herself, "Tonight, our Union officer will travel north."

Elizabeth breathed a sigh of relief as she bade "God speed" to the officer as he left the protection of her home. Then, she had him carefully and skillfully guided and transported through the city's barricades. It was the first leg of his hazardous journey to repatriation with his command.

The next day, Detective New, impatient that the escaped prisoner had not been found and still suspecting Elizabeth's complicity, decided to follow Elizabeth himself, with the assistance of a junior officer in civilian clothes who was temporarily attached to his department.

As they approached her street, they stopped short. There, with her lace parasol bobbing up and down, was Elizabeth. "What a stroke of luck," he said smugly, "There she is. We'll just see what she's up to today." They gave her time to get out of range to avoid detection, then followed her. As she headed up 20th Street, a pack of ragged young boys heckled her with a made-up street song, obviously inspired by their parents' resentful comments:

"Traitor Bet, Traitor Bet, A Rebel noose will get you yet!"

To avoid them, she had quickened her pace, slowed it down, pleaded with the children, and even scolded them. Nothing stopped their incessant taunting. Finally, in desperation, she used a last resort tactic that she knew they would fully understand. They had maintained a safe distance just out of her reach. Now, Elizabeth charged them menacingly, her eyes blazing, her face flushed with anger, swinging the parasol wildly in swift thrashes, screaming threats of bodily harm.

She had no intention of actually hitting them, just scaring them off, but they didn't know it. So, being satisfied at having achieved their goal of upsetting and angering her with their nastiness, they scattered in all directions, laughing at her vain attempts at retribution.

New and the junior officer smiled inwardly, just a trifle envious of the boys' ability to humiliate her in public, and continued to follow her.

Relieved at having rid herself of the daily annoyance from the street toughs, Elizabeth hummed a tune and continued on her appointed shopping rounds for the prisoners. She was also searching for someone to carry the urgent message she had in her purse which informed Washington about the prisoner she had sheltered and arranged passage for through the Confederate lines the night before.

She entered her regular grocery store and asked Bruce the grocer; "Do you have any sweet butter."

He replied, "My horse has gone lame and won't be able to be ridden till after the weekend. So, I won't be able to buy any before Sunday. Would that be soon enough?"

"By that time, we'll have our own from the farm, but I will take a pound of this rice," Elizabeth replied courteously.

"Of course." He apologized as he scooped out the rice; "I don't like disappointing you or Mrs. Van Lew."

She placed the rice in her basket, paid him, and left. New remained outside but was able to hear the conversation.

Elizabeth continued up Main Street and met a middle-aged woman. They exchanged greetings and a few pleasantries; most of which were inaudible except for the last few words. "Sorry to disappoint you, but not this time."

Puzzled, New started to wonder what it was that she might want that people were unable to oblige her—a neighborhood grocer and a lady on the street. No obvious connection ... yet too much of a coincidence. What could she want? Wait a minute! If she's collecting and passing information to the enemy, she'd need some way to get it to them ... a courier ... someone who could carry her messages safely out of the city. A courier ... of course! That's it!

New signaled to his accomplice who had taken a position across the street. He then pantomimed lighting a pipe and motioned toward a smoke shop. New saw that they could meet there briefly without Elizabeth seeing them, while they could keep her in view.

After he gave the man instructions, New then switched places with him on the opposite side of the street, close enough to witness the execution of his scheme and far enough out of recognition range.

New watched with anticipation as the officer walked alongside Elizabeth and whispered softly, as instructed, "I'm going through the lines tonight!" then continued past her stopping to wait for her as he looked innocently in a store window. He had looked for her reaction, but her sunbonnet hid her face at that moment. However, Elizabeth neither uttered a sound nor changed her step in the slightest. She continued toward the man pretending not to see him. She deliberately bumped into him with her grocery basket and got a good look at his face. "I beg your pardon, Sir," she said with a smile, and continued up the street.

Elizabeth didn't recognize him as one of the couriers she had ever used. Her mind raced. The dilemma raised unanswerable and dangerous questions. "Could this be a new courier sent from Washington? Should I take a chance? This message has got to go out tonight." She thought again, "It could also be a Confederate trap. What should I do? And what about the incriminating message in my purse? I can't destroy it with that man watching my every move."

The man was uncertain if she had heard his offer. If she did, was the bumping an indication that she was accepting or rejecting it? He had to try again to be sure. He approached her again and repeated the offer louder and more distinctly, "I'm going through the lines tonight." His heart pounded as he looked directly into her face.

Elizabeth's heart was also pounding just as loudly as she struggled with the decision. "Is he legitimate? Should I trust a stranger? Should I take a chance just this once? This would be an incredible piece of luck. But, luck comes in both good and bad! I don't feel good about this."

New, sensing Elizabeth's seemingly desperate situation and probable inexperience in coping with such a clever entrapment was ready to move in the minute that she handed him her message. His heart, pounding like a predator at the moment of the kill, joined the other two in a percussion trio.

The man crossed the street and sat on a bench waiting for her to approach him with the message. Elizabeth appeared to be taking the bait as she walked to the curb and lifted her dress delicately from the ground as she headed in the direction of the man on the bench.

"We've got her!" Both New and the man rejoiced inwardly as they anticipated her joining him on the bench. But, in a split second, Elizabeth turned and headed for home, leaving both men surprised and puzzled.

Later that night, with no where else to turn, a small figure with a flower basket under one arm, dressed in buckskin leggings, a worn and wrinkled calico dress, and a large farm worker's sunbonnet slipped out into the formal garden on the south side of the Van Lew mansion. The figure then stopped at one of the many flowerbeds and snipped several roses, tied them in a bundle, and put them in the basket.

Just then, another person moved out of the shadows of a large Acacia tree and headed for the "rose peddler." They joined together and disappeared from the light of the moon, under a large lilac bush bursting with fragrance from the lavender flowers. The rose peddler spoke, "Mary, I was worried about you. Why are you so late?"

"Because there was another box going to Philadelphia," Mary answered. Elizabeth shuddered at the words, commenting, "And I don't know how men can breathe in those things boxed in like that for so long."

Mary explained that the captain of the vessel promised to open one of the boards when the box was safely deposited in the ship's hold, and asked Elizabeth, "And where are you going now in that get up?"

"Off to carry a message. I couldn't find anyone else to take it. At least no one I could be sure of. There was a man who offered to take something through the lines for me today, but I didn't accept his offer."

"Did you know him?" Mary asked.

"No, and I did come close to accepting, but there was something about the situation that seemed a little too coincidental. I had a thought that he might be one of Detective New's men trying to trap me."

"That New is beginning to get on everybody's nerves. He is pushing so hard to make a name for himself with Mr. Davis," Mary revealed, "that even Winder can't stand his pushiness."

"Well, I must be off Mary. I'll see you tomorrow." And off Elizabeth went in a disguise that would be used many times in a variety of situations—all of them desperate and dangerous.

The next day, there was a long column of Confederate soldiers marching toward the train station. Elizabeth pretended to be waiting for them to pass so that she could cross the street, but she was making a mental note of the number and makeup of the units as she waited. Suddenly, she froze. There, leading one of the platoons, was the man who approached her the day before, telling her that he was "going though the lines." A Confederate officer! Now, she experienced a rush of excitement at the realization of how close she came to discovery, prison, and possible death. New's words rang in her head, "If you're taking part in any treasonous activities, you will be caught and punished without mercy … I promise you that … and I will personally take pleasure in watching you come to the same fate as the late Timothy Webster!"

A cold chill ran through Elizabeth's body, and she thought, "Damn him, damn him! How long am I going to have to contend with that man?" Little did she realize that it was only the beginning!

CHAPTER 16

Rooms: One Filled & One Empty

Over 350 Union prisoners newly captured by Longstreet's forces at Williamsburg arrived in Richmond, stuffing the already overcrowded makeshift prisons.

The first prison's overflow were sent to Libby Prison, which opened March 26, 1862, and Belle Isle. Libby Prison was so named because the Luther Libby's Ships Chandlery Equipment Warehouse building was acquired so quickly by the Confederate government that it still had the sign on the building and, thereafter, became known by that name. The prison was be the facility for the incarceration of Union officers, keeping them separate from the enlisted men they commanded.

"Belle Isle," "Castle Thunder," "Castle Lightning," and "Castle Godwin" held other Federal enlisted men as well. The mock prefix "Castle" was used before the more apt names, "Thunder" and "Lightning," to describe the intensity of misery and suffering experienced inside the prisons. Castle Godwin was named after its cruel first commandant, Captain Archibald C. Godwin.

The steady influx tended to give the city's inhabitants a false sense of security that all was going well with the rebellion, despite the dwindling food supplies in Richmond. However, when the people in Richmond learned of the destruction and evacuation of the city of Norfolk, it came like a tornado from a cloudless sky. The authorized destruction of the ironclad "Virginia" was the most unexpected and distressing news. It had been the pride of the South, and its loss was equated in the Richmond newspapers to the loss of fifty thousand fighting men. With Norfolk lost, the naval approach to Richmond was left totally unguarded. First it was the evacuation of Yorktown, then the fall of New Orleans, and now this latest reversal of fortune. The Confederate Congress hastily adjourned, and the officials began dispersing away from their menaced city. Richmond was in a state of alarm, and it triggered a mass exodus of the citizenry.

Elizabeth took note of the numerous boxes being brought out of the different government offices that looked like they contained important documents and records. They all bore the address "Columbia, South Carolina," and indicated a calculated withdrawal from the City of Richmond by the "chicken-hearted" appearing leaders.

The Richmond-protecting fortification at Drewry's Bluff was only half finished and had only four big guns to impede the progress of the dreaded Union iron clad gunboat, the Monitor.

The Union's huge Army of over 100,000 fighting men was heading up the peninsula toward Richmond with General George B. McClellan in command. And, with the flotilla of Union gunboats coming up the James toward the city, the Virginia State Legislature, setting an ominous precedent, passed a resolution declaring its intention to reduce the city to ashes, rather than permitting it to fall into the hands of the enemy.

The citizens left by the hundreds, in all directions, and in all manner of conveyances, although south seemed to be the most popular route to escape the imminent attack. Houses were left deserted, and business was suspended. President Davis sent his children off to Raleigh, North Carolina for temporary safety, while those who chose to remain had their bags packed.

On the 13th of May, the Union gunboats opened fire with their big guns on the Drewry's Bluff fortification. Now the sounds of guns fired in hostile action were heard for the first time in Richmond. Some of the more loyal and wealthy citizens of the Confederacy vowed to defend their beloved city to their death. From a safe distance, Elizabeth listened with mixed emotions about the imminent destruction of her beloved city and almost sided with the townspeople in wanting to preserve it. On the other hand, she wanted to see the treasonous government that invaded and imposed itself upon the city removed—permanently!

As night fell, the big guns grew silent. News came that the shelling from Drewry's Bluff had forced the Union flotilla to retreat down river, realizing that attempting a water-route invasion of Richmond was impractical.

With this current crisis past, the people breathed a sigh of relief and returned to their livelihoods. But there was precious little time to give thanks or rejoice as two great armies that were poised within sight of Richmond.

The 31st was a gloomy rainy day. At about two o'clock in the afternoon, Elizabeth heard the heavy booming of artillery. The mansion windows vibrated near the breaking point, and the strong foundation shook as if in an earthquake. Elizabeth, along with the rest of the citizenry, was badly shaken.

Upon hearing the sounds and seeing the flashes, as brilliant as a fireworks display, Elizabeth was filled with sadness. She watched the sky, only a handful of miles from her lofty vantage point on the roof of the house on top of Church Hill. She imagined the cries of pain and the suffering caused by human beings, bodies battered and shattered, limbs painfully severed, and hearts quivering in a death agony. All because of a mad fury to satisfy political differences. She wept as she thought of the mothers, sisters, and wives collapsing at the news of the loss of their loved ones and vowed, "Cursed war, I must do everything within my power to end this plague on my Country!"

Following daily every detail of the military engagements, Elizabeth read the June 1st newspaper account of the fighting at the Fair Oaks/Seven Pines Battlefields. It reported that General Joseph E. Johnston, who was in command of 60,000 troops, was badly wounded, and that General Robert E. Lee was named Commander of the Army of Northern Virginia.

From her social contacts with General Lee when he was a colonel and a civilian, Elizabeth had learned much about the man. Coupled with Mary's observations of the General while he served as military advisor to President Davis, Elizabeth realized that his appointment was going to bolster both the morale and capabilities of the Confederate forces … and might have a demoralizing effect on her group of "loyalists" in Richmond.

Lee withdrew the Army to more favorable defensive positions closer to Richmond, which he then proceeded to fortify. Next, he hounded the Davis administration for reinforcements so that he could go on the offensive. In the next few weeks, Lee received enough troops from other locations to bring his army, which he named the "Army of Northern Virginia" up to 80,000 men. Meanwhile, McClellan's army had also being reinforced bringing it up to 125,000, still a vastly outnumbering force over Lee's.

During this period of buildup, Elizabeth had continued her humanitarian activities and intelligence gathering, much to the scorn of the community. Her reputation of disloyalty had brought her derision and catcalls such as, "You worthless, backstabbing, Union-sympathizing, nigger lover!" and "You witch! You and your mother both deserve to be burned alive in your fancy house!"

Feeling driven to continue to move about the city and its prisons and hospitals doing all that she could, yet wanting to reduce the increasing danger to herself, her mother, and her home, Elizabeth decided that she must take a different course of action. Besides all of the public condemnation, Detective New's increased surveillance might lead the prison administration to cancel her prison visitation privileges.

After carefully considering several solutions, she still could not decide on the best plan of action. It was only after an evening meeting with Mary that she was able to come up with a partial solution to the problem. Mary told Elizabeth that she overheard Mrs. George Gibbs, the wife of the officer who replaced Todd as Inspector of Prisons, telling another officer's wife about wanting to find a nice home in which to board. In Elizabeth's contacts with Gibbs, she had found him a likeable man though of inferior intellect and low self-esteem. She once heard him say, "I would give my right arm for one word of commendation from Jeff Davis."

The next day while Elizabeth was making her rounds of the prisons, she stopped by Captain Gibbs' office. She reflected on how hard it was to find quality boarders for the large and beautifully furnished vacant rooms in her home. "And with the reputation of my cooks and servants, I am perplexed." While she was sighing, her dilemma, she placed a plate of hot gingerbread on Gibbs' desk.

The aroma and taste of the gingerbread, together with the thought of daily meals prepared in a delicious manner and served in a setting fit for a general, piqued Captain Gibbs' interest. He reflected to himself on the deficiency of Mrs. Gibbs' skills and inclination in regard to culinary pursuits.

Not wanting to appear too anxious, for fear he might drive up the price to an unaffordable rate, Gibbs inquired "And what exactly are you asking, in case I learn of someone who might be interested?"

Elizabeth quoted him a figure that was more than enough to pay for the food for both the Van Lews and the Gibbs yet well within a Captain's means.

He was delighted at the rate but still hesitated to admit a personal interest, so Elizabeth used a timeworn sales technique—"another interested customer"—to make him declare his intentions.

"There is a good chance I will rent it soon though, a Colonel 'something or other' is coming by this weekend to look at the rooms." To leave him a further opening, she added, "I just hate the thought of taking in someone with whom I am totally unfamiliar."

Not wanting to miss this rare opportunity that could soon be lost, Gibbs blurted, "Miss Van Lew, I was afraid to tell you that I was interested in renting rooms in your house because I thought I would not be able to afford it on a Captain's pay. However, I can afford the rate you quoted. If I was to bring my wife by this evening, would you be available to show the rooms to us?"

Anxious to further ensure both Captain and Mrs. Gibbs' commitment to the transaction, Elizabeth offered, "Well, why don't you come and bring Mrs. Gibbs for dinner tonight. After dinner, you can view the accommodations, and that way you'll know what to expect on both accounts."

"That's a wonderful idea. What time do you want us to arrive?" Gibbs excitedly replied.

Elizabeth paused, then offered, "Shall we make it 7:30?"

"We'll be there," and Gibbs asked her address, out of courtesy, knowing full well exactly where she lived.

That evening, an especially sumptuous dinner, followed by a tour of the meticulously prepared rooms led to the renting of the rooms to Captain and Mrs. Gibbs. Elizabeth's strategic "placement" of a Confederate officer in the Van Lew mansion lessened the potential threat of harm or destruction of the home or its inhabitants. Feeling that a Confederate officer within the Van Lew home would restrict any subversive activity within it, Detective New withdrew the round-the-clock surveillance of the house. However, he still maintained surveillance of Elizabeth's movements around the city.

With part of her problem resolved, while earning some needed supplementary income, Elizabeth now embarked on the second part of her plan. As she walked about the city, she began to behave oddly before the eyes of the public. She started to hum songs, then sang them softly, then more loudly. She began to smile into the faces of everyone she met. She laughed at odd times for no apparent reason; gave answers to questions other than those asked; and initiated conversations with people she didn't know about the evils of human bondage and the perils of secession and the war.

Slowly, her reputation was established, and Elizabeth Van Lew became known in Richmond as "Crazy Bet," the harmless old witch. She perfected and played the role so well that long after her death, people continued to use the insulting nickname to describe her, believing that she was, in fact, crazy. What a tribute to her commitment for her mission; a willingness to do whatever it took; no matter what the image or reputation, along with a convincing acting ability.

Wednesday, June 4th. Although there was little word in the press, news spread like wildfire in Richmond that Mrs. Rose Greenhow was in town. Her brief few months of spying for the Confederacy had made her a heroine and a celebrity in the South.

General Winder dispensed with the formality of having Mrs. Greenhow report to him and visited her in her suite at the Ballard House. Later that evening, President Davis also called on Mrs. Greenhow to express his thanks for her dedicated service to the Confederacy. Davis was shocked at her appearance. The once ravishing beauty had drastically changed in only one year. Her sunken eyes, deep facial lines, harassed manner, and rapidly graying hair gave her the appearance of one whose nerves were severely shaken from intense mental stress brought on by continuous exposure to danger—one whose life had hung by the thinnest of threads. He decided that that kind of loyal contribution must not go unrewarded and bowed gallantly as he paid her a high compliment. "But for you Rose, the outcome at the Battle of Manassas might have gone the other way."

Feeling just a bit unappreciated, like many other tired, jaded, and unrecognized former spies, she later commented in her diary regarding his tribute, "I shall ever remember that as the proudest moment of my entire life …"

As with most bureaucracies, several months passed before a check in the amount of $2500 was sent to Mrs. Greenhow by Secretary of State Judah P. Benjamin. This award was taken out of a small fund set aside for secret services "on instructions from the President as an acknowledgement of the valuable and patriotic service rendered by you to our cause."

Mrs. Greenhow accepted the check and immediately deposited it the nearest bank. She drew from the account only when absolutely necessary.

CHAPTER 17

The Mortar & Pestle

The Richmond days were filled with sounds of troops drilling and marching, then departing to the field. The Confederate dead and wounded arrived from the battlefields in a pitiful procession. Some so young that their bodies had felt a bullet or a bayonet long before their cheeks had felt a razor. Faces so full of the promise of youth, with eyes so full of pain and regret—aged by pain and disillusion. The spirited fife and drum music of "Dixie" was replaced by the mournful beat of a funeral march.

The hospitals and prisons swelled with the overflow of captured Federals. For both Northern and Southern troops, the heat of the day and the dust raised by the tramp of marching feet intensified their misery.

As night fell, the drilling troops retired, dust settled, and a refreshing breeze off the James cooled down the city. The air was heavy with the sweet scent of magnolia, fuschia, and jasmine dangling over walls and trellises. The wide streets that rambled over the hills to the James were bordered with a variegated palette of wild flowers. At this time of night, the war seemed almost a bad dream as fine carriages drawn by Kentucky horses still moved along past Elizabeth's home on Grace and Franklin Streets. There were even a few liveried footmen who remained with their households, but slaves no longer sang their hand-clapping songs. Their lives seemed to be more precarious and hopeless as the Confederacy built its army, and the much heralded stories of J.E.B. Stuart's daring raids around McClellan's huge army gave the impression of Federal vulnerability, apathy, and incompetence.

With a lack of military censorship of newspapers and journals, Elizabeth gained much information from their reports and editorials, and from the reprinted stories gathered from out-of-town newspapers. When pieced together with her own personal observations, the bits and pieces Mary was able to gather, along with information from the prisoners and other sources, notably Dr. William Parker, Jr., Elizabeth's reporting to Washington had gained increasing respect and was greatly valued.

Young Dr. Parker became as well known in Richmond as his father. He had built a reputation through skillful surgical work that had saved the limbs of many poor souls who otherwise would have had to face the pain and horror of amputation. Confederate officers and politicians respected and confided in him.

Elizabeth kept in constant touch with William through the use of the secret "post office box" which prevented the compromise of their relationship and communication channel. Since the Parkers were the doctors of record for the Van Lews, it was common practice for prescriptions to be left at the apothecary to be picked up by Elizabeth. She stopped in for the medicine for her mother whenever she saw the signal in the window indicating that a message was waiting for her. The signal that she agreed to, in concert with the pharmacist and Dr. Parker, was to have the druggist turn the pestle, to which only he had access, upside down in the mortar displayed in the window. Then, when Elizabeth came in and purchased her prescription, the pharmacist would hand her, along with her change, a scrap of paper that contained the encoded message from Dr. Parker. The idea for the code came from Elizabeth's past readings of Edgar Allan Poe's "*Gold Bug.*"

Elizabeth's report this day concerned the troop buildup and fortification of the city. To this, she added the news she had read about General Jackson's withdrawal from the Shenandoah Valley and his possible linking up with Lee's forces around Richmond. She reported to Washington, "The smell of a fight is in the air."

She had guessed right, Lee was now ready to move, and on the 25th of June, he started the battle that would rage for "Seven Days." Lee would show the North his military audacity, cunning, genius, and daring that would distinguish him as one of the greatest generals of all time.

CHAPTER 18
A Search, A Trap, & An Exit

Another prisoner escaped, and General Winder was beginning to receive some sharp criticism from the Secretary of War about his "ability to handle the responsibilities of the position." Irritated by the attack on his competency, he summoned Detective New. New reported that "he was working on the problem and was close to resolving it."

Winder exploded, "That's the same damn thing you said after the last two escapes!"

"Well, I'm going to check out a lead at this very moment." he offered, hopeful that he would have something concrete to report at their next meeting.

"Do it then, and you'd better get some results damn soon!" Winder warned.

New's lead is, quite logically, Elizabeth Van Lew. Within the hour, New collected some of the newly hired men from his slowly expanding squad and headed for the Van Lew home. This time, they searched the house with a vengeance. They pulled clothes from closets, removed desk and dresser drawers and dumped the contents on the floor examining them painstakingly, held up ladies' undergarments searching them for hidden pockets, tore up rugs, removed pictures from walls and pried them apart in the search for secret documents, and emptied storage trunks. Whenever they found jewelry or some other item of value that was small enough to be concealed inside a pocket, they secretly "appropriated it." Nothing incriminating was found, and the disappointed New and his men left without so much as a word of apology. The search was thorough, destructive, and extremely humiliating to the Van Lews.

The following day, Elizabeth paid a visit to General Winder to register her complaint. When she arrived, she met Mrs. Winder, who had brought a lunch basket for her husband, in his office. Elizabeth apologized for interrupting and greeted them both courteously. The General asked her the purpose of her visit. Elizabeth responded, "It is in regard to the latest most outrageous search perpetrated upon my household." She proceeded to tell him about the harsh treatment, destruction, insulting searches through her mother's and her own female undergarments, and of the number of missing items of monetary and sentimental value.

"The unprovoked and shameful invasions of privacy upon two unprotected ladies, compounded by the stealing of irreplaceable family heirlooms, are the unchristian acts of hooligans and do not reflect very highly on the ennoblement of this government," she protested.

"Is this the kind of service in which the government wishes to impress my brother John?" she asked.

"My dear Miss Van Lew," Winder responded earnestly, "the search of which you speak was not undertaken by my orders, and regarding your brother John, I assure you I will continue to do all within my power to sustain the medical deferment he now enjoys."

"I told my mother that this latest affront could not be the work of a respectable gentleman as yourself but had the earmarks of an immoral and despicable heathen. My mother is ill over the incident and the loss of the treasured family memorabilia. I just wanted to register my complaint officially and make you aware of the unnecessary indignities and harassment that some of us citizens of Richmond are being made to endure. I also wanted to thank you for all your efforts on my brother's behalf and extend to you and Mrs. Winder an invitation for dinner this Saturday evening to show my appreciation."

In an effort to show his wife that he was not taken in by Elizabeth's words, Winder smugly said to Elizabeth, "You needn't offer me a bribe to preserve your brother's deferment."

"It was not a bribe I was offering. If it was, I would have extended the invitation before your statement of support."

Realizing his gaffe, he stammered, "Well, anyway, we would have been delighted to accept your generous offer, but, in fact, we have dinner plans for that evening. I hope you will be kind enough to repeat the invitation at another time."

Aware that nothing more could be gained by the visit; Elizabeth nodded respectfully to the General and his wife and left the office.

After Elizabeth left, Mrs. Winder commented that she "didn't think Elizabeth was as eccentric as people said she was." She added that she was not even sure that Elizabeth's table maid, whom she herself recommended to Varina Davis, was not "working in cahoots with Elizabeth. I question the loyalty of that girl!" Her last remark was a clear attack on her husband's gullibility in approving her recommendation of Mary.

The General countered her onslaught saying, "Everything is under control. I'm not a fool! It would take more than a little Van Lew woman to outfox me."

He assured her that to prevent any possible military or political intelligence leaks, he had personally taken the precaution of placing a young black servant, Martin Robinson, at the Davis household. His secret role was to watch Mary night and day and to report anything suspicious directly to Winder.

What the General didn't realize was that Elizabeth just happened to stop to remove a small pebble from her shoe outside the door to his office, conveniently left ajar, where she was able to hear clearly every word of their conversation.

Later that same day, Mary had slipped away from the Davis home while on an errand for Mrs. Davis and met secretly with Elizabeth. Mary told her that the boy they hired right after she started working there, Martin Robinson, followed her everywhere.

"Fortunately, he was just sent to the grange to get some feed, and I was able to slip away. He watches me day and night; even goes so far as to peek in the window of my room at night. Today, when I heard him being sent to the grange, I went to look at the maps. He suddenly appeared in the room and asked me what I thought I was doing looking at that stuff. He threatened that, 'If I didn't let him come and lay with me tonight that he would go and tell General Winder what I was up to, and then I would wind up swinging from the nearest tree in the morning! I'm worried, Miss Liz. I don't want to die, and I sure don't want him to even come near me!"

Elizabeth, fully understanding Martin's role and the precariousness of Mary's situation, determined to extricate her from it as quickly and as safely as possible. The feelings Elizabeth had for Mary were more like the love of a mother for a daughter, rather than the bond between comrades engaged in a perilous task.

Mary volunteered, "Maybe if I invite him into my room, and just when he gets inside, I could scream. Then they'll get rid of him for sure!"

"No, Elizabeth said, "They'll only whip him and tell him never to do it again, and then he'll go to Winder. That won't solve the problem—but it does give me an idea of how to get rid of him permanently."

After carefully outlining, detailing, reviewing, and agreeing on all aspects and options of Elizabeth's plan, Mary returned to the Davis home.

Later that night, Mary started to undress for bed. It was a hot and humid night. A beautiful full moon beamed in the clear and starry sky, and the smell of honeysuckle filled the air.

Mary walked slowly to the doorway to catch a passing breeze in order to cool her body before going to sleep. Behind her, the candle on the table next to her bed clearly outlined her perfectly proportioned, lithe, young body. Now the moonlight caught and reflected off her lightly perspiring satiny skin as she stepped out of the doorway and into its light. She raised her arms in a stretch, accentuating her breasts in the moon's bright rays. Her beauty, her graceful movements, and sensuality were capable of arousing most men into complete submissiveness, if she so wished.

Almost as if by magic, yet right on cue, Martin appeared from out of the shadows and lunged at her, pressing his body on hers. He had been watching her from the moment she began undressing, walking slowly outside the room toward his hiding place which was close by in the shadows. Her beauty was such that he couldn't restrain himself.

The heat of his desire was further enflamed by the heat from her body. He was eager and ready to act. He looked at her face. Her eyes were closed; full and lush lips slightly parted. He pressed his own mouth wildly against hers.

His hands traveled the length of her body, squeezing it in anticipation of the property he was soon to possess. His desire was at the boiling point, and he could wait no longer. He reached down to pry her legs apart, but Mary pulled away.

"You're not going any further until you put a ring on my finger … and I mean a good one at that!" she warned him. "I'm going to stay pure as just picked cotton for my first and only man. You see, the first one that gets me has me for life. I am a one-man woman!"

Then she asked the question that her mother told her all men quickly answer in the affirmative when their interests lie "south of the border" … "Do you love me?"

Predictably, he replied, "Sho nuff, I do!"

His physical longings not in the least dulled by her comments and question, he renewed his advances. He pulled her body back tightly to his, and she responded by rubbing her body rhythmically and passionately against his.

"Oooh, dat body! I's gotta hav it!" he moaned to himself. His loins ached with desire and screamed for satisfaction. He kissed her wildly again. Mary was being as provocative as possible while trying not to go past the point of no return. Martin was stronger than she expected, and she tried but couldn't break away from his suffocating embrace. His desire was stronger than she could imagine, and she feared it might already be too late, so she desperately shouted in his ear, "Not until a ring!" in her most determined voice.

Startled momentarily, and afraid of being discovered by someone in the Davis household, he parroted, "Not 'til a ring? Yeah, sur, honey, I's git one tomorrah."

Mary persisted. "I mean it! I want a ring first, and a good one!"

Then, continuing his attempt for immediate satisfaction with Mary, he realized words wouldn't do it, so he got physically rougher, trying to overpower her and managed to pry her legs apart. Mustering all her strength, she pulled away again. With fire in her eyes this time, she warned him, "I mean it Martin Robinson; a ring first, and a good one, or I'll scream!"

Impatient and a little rattled, he blurted, "How yo' tink I kin get a ring if I don got no money? Can we's jes preten' we's marrid up?"

"Sure, and what do I tell Mrs. Davis when I have a belly full of baby? How will I do my chores? They'll throw me to the highest bidding slave trader and sell my baby away from me too! You know how they do!"

He looked half convinced, so she continued with the bait, "Are you sure you love me?"

"Wid al's my heart!" he replied excitedly as his waning desire was rekindled, anticipating that his response would tip the scales back to his advantage.

Softening her tone she responded, "Well then, if you love me and want me so bad, … then I have an idea how you can get the ring and me too!"

"How, tel's me sugah, tel's me!" he begged urgently.

"Well, if you get some silverware from the house, only a few pieces that they would never miss, you could use it to get me a nice ring, and then you could have your way with me every night. Have you ever had a woman who was as ready for her first man? It's going to be like putting a match to fireworks. I know I can't wait for it to happen to me. You're a lucky man to be getting a virgin woman who is so eager and ready to please her man's every wish. And I mean … every wish!"

His hands began to tremble; his knees grew weak and shook; his head was spinning; his body throbbing and aching for satisfaction; his mind filled with a maze of visual images of the two of them in bed, bodies linked and intertwined. Each image of the two of them on that first night more erotic and exciting than the last!

"Oh, yeah, yeah!" he moaned through the lump in his throat, "Buts howz I gets da silvah?"

"That is a problem." She feigned being at a loss to figure out how it could be done and rolled her eyes as if deep in thought.

During the long silence, he began to scheme to himself. "I gotta git on top off dat body. If I git's her a ring, I gets to hav' her. Den, I takes da ring bak, tel' her da massa won' let us'n marry up. By den it be too late. I 'ready hav' her, so I's can hav' my ways wid her anytimes I wants her, an' dat be plenty! Den I sel's da ring an' keps da money, an' Mary too!"

After a reasonable period of silence, Mary, reading his face and mind, suddenly lit up. "I've got it! I've got an idea how you can get the silver. Listen to this. Tomorrow night they're having a dinner with guests, which means a lot of silverware will be out. When the dinner is over, and the ladies have retired from the dining room, and I'm cleaning off the table, you slip down to the wine cellar and set a small fire. Then you come back up and signal me that it's done. Then you go and wait outside. When they notice the smoke, they'll all rush downstairs. Then you come back in and take the silverware I've put in one pile for you. You take it outside and hide it, and then you can come back in and help put out the fire, and they'll never suspect you or miss the silver!"

"An' wat if sumbudy cum back up de stays an' ketch me snitchin' da silva? I's gon' fo' shor!"

"Don't worry. I'll be bringing some pans full of water down the stairs blocking the way until you finish."

She softened her tone again to a seductive whisper, putting her mouth close to his ear, so close that he could feel her hot breath, and purred with a voice filled with promises and possibilities. "Darling Martin, just think about that first time we're together and how easy it will be to get the silver and the ring … and your hands all over this body. That first time could be tomorrow night!"

"I's tinkin', I's tinkin'! he said, and thought to himself, "I kin waits one mor' day to git her, but dat's all, and she gonna pay pleny fo' makin' me wait!"

"Yeah, I do it!

"Good, until tomorrow night my darling, and I promise you it'll be a night you will never forget!"

"Til' tomorra night baby. I's kin hadly wait!" he moaned as he released her, still wanting her but sure that he was going to get everything he wanted the following night! She kissed him quickly on the cheek to show her commitment to the plan and rushed to her room, leaving her ardent pursuer waiting for tomorrow. Tomorrow, tomorrow, and then …

After dinner the following night, which as fate would have it, included General and Mrs. Winder, the ladies retired. Martin, right on cue, slipped down to the wine cellar. He started a small fire in a corner, just big enough to provide time for him to do what he had to do. He quietly returned upstairs unseen, gave Mary the signal, and waited just outside.

Seeing him go outside, Mary slipped downstairs and shouted "Fire!"

All the men rushed downstairs to put the fire out. Mary had already started to put it out, and by the time they all arrived, it was out. Seeing that she succeeded in acting so quickly in extinguishing the fire, they congratulated her and started upstairs, led by General Winder. They arrived upstairs just in time to see Martin running out the door. Startled at being caught in the act, he looked back to see the General's face turn crimson. Realizing that there was no turning back now, he raced out the door dropping an occasional piece of silver. Winder was too old, overweight, and out of shape to catch him and Martin made good his escape. He vanished into the night and out of Mary's life for good.

Hearing that a fire was deliberately set as a diversion to cover the theft of silverware, and thinking that Mary was the thief, Mrs. Winder, whose face had turned ashen, was ready for the humiliating end of her social life and consequent inglorious termination of her husband's military career. She pondered, "Thank God it didn't happen in the dead of night, we would be on trial for conspiracy to murder. Damn that Elizabeth Van Lew!"

The General appeared and bade his wife to prepare herself for the trip home. She proceeded to take leave of the hostess and looked for Varina as eagerly as a condemned man going to the gallows. She suddenly felt a hand on her arm and found herself face-to-face with Varina Davis.

Mrs. Winder's heart was pounding so loudly that she knew that everyone could surely hear it! Her breathing stopped, and her legs started shaking. She felt the perspiration start to build up on her forehead, and her face went pale. Her feeling was not unlike a convicted murderer in a courtroom waiting to hear the judge pronounce the sentence!

"Earnestly," Varina said to Mrs. Winder, "I just want to thank you again for the table maid you sent us. She is the one who discovered the fire. She gave the alarm and then single handedly put it out. If it hadn't been for her speedy response, we might not have caught that horrid boy. He clearly set the blaze to cover his thievery of our silverware. Even though he did get away, I can assure you that he'll dare not show his face in Richmond again."

Mrs. Winder was so taken aback, and the lump in her throat felt so large, that she didn't know if she would be able to speak. She decided to make the attempt. She opened her mouth, and her lips moved but nothing came out. Continuing, Mrs. Davis added, "It is heartbreaking to know that people would stoop so low as to bribe a poor servant to set someone's house on fire to get precious things like silverware—and to support the Yankee effort at that! That is why it is so heartwarming to know that we have such a devoted servant as Mary. We are very fortunate to have her, and we're so grateful to you for your recommendation."

On the way home in their carriage, the Winders both breathed an enormous sigh of relief as they confided to each other how close they felt they had come to the end of their privileged lives in Richmond.

The name Mary Elizabeth Bowser was never mentioned again and they both looked upon Miss Van Lew in a more favorable light. The General vowed to himself to continue to support John Van Lew's deferment and, in the future, to limit Detective New's attacks on the Van Lew family.

CHAPTER 19

A Battle & A Proclamation

Wednesday, June 25, 1862. With the capture of Richmond as a most cherished target of the Union Army, and the protection of it as a major objective of the Confederate forces, both rivals would meet this day to fight for their goal.

Elizabeth confidently imagined McClellan at the head of the largest army ever assembled, sweeping up the Peninsula, liberating the city, and delivering them from the Confederacy's grip. She was filled with excitement as she directed her servants in preparing a fitting room for General McClellan with new matting and attractive new curtains.

The combat began with C.S.A. General A.P. Hill's frontal attacks on Union General Porter's Federal forces near Mechanicsville at Beaver Dam Creek. The thunderous cannonade shook buildings and rattled windows. Elizabeth was overwhelmed with excitement and curiosity. She summoned Nelson, and they rushed up to the roof for a better look, but a heavy screen of smoke, indicative of its magnitude masked the battle scene.

"Nelson, can you tell whose guns those are, ours or theirs?"

"Those be Union guns, Miss Liz. I kin tell cuz they be lower soundin'," Nelson replied authoritatively."

"Oh, if only it was true … I wish I could be certain," Elizabeth thought to herself.

Impulsively, she asked Nelson to saddle up her fastest horse. She then rode toward the home of William Rowley, a staunch loyalist, close friend, and collaborator. Together, they rode toward the battlefield, drawn like moths to a candle flame.

They were stopped by a Confederate picket who was happy to report that they were whipping the Federals, right, left, and in the center and had taken many prisoners. He let them pass after receiving a reward of a few coins for his report.

Then the roar of the cannons grew louder. There, in an opening in the trees behind the Confederate lines, they saw other spectators; Mr. Botts and some of his friends who had a similar desire to witness a Union victory.

Elizabeth thrilled to the rumbling sounds of the battlefield just ahead of her. The rapid succession of the big guns; the sound of heavy hoofs and the creak of the wooden wheels of the supply wagons that brought needed ammunition. The rattling of gear, canteens, and arms; the rush of the horses into and out of the watering pond; cannons on the crop-roads and in the fields; the echoing crack of muskets, carbines, and pistols, and the thick smoke that filled the air with the smell of gunpowder.

Then, there were the commands, shouts, and yells of the spirited onrushing lines of men which served both to encourage their own resolve and to intimidate the enemy, as they charged directly into the merciless blasts of the big Union guns. How quickly the soldiers' resounding voices turned into screams as some part of their anatomy was punctured, broken, or severed.

At nine o'clock, with decreased visibility, the hostilities ceased, and the only sounds were the cries and moans of the wounded and dying as they were being retrieved and attended to. Elizabeth, comparing all that she had witnessed with her past life in society, thought, "No ball could ever be as grand or exciting as watching the action of this evening. I realized the bright rush of life and the hurry of death on the battlefield."

Her ride home was at a slow and somber pace, as if not to show disrespect for the dead. Even though exhausted and emotionally drained, she sat at the small writing desk in her room and incorporated her eye witness account into her daily report. When finished, she placed it next to her pillow in anticipation of yet another surprise search party. If it should occur, she would be able to burn the incriminating evidence in time. She laid her head on the pillow and tried to imagine what it must be like for the men on both sides of the battlefield who were also resting their weary bodies, bracing themselves for the next day, knowing it could be their last. "What must they be thinking?" Finally, sleep overcame her compassionate curiosity.

A gloom, along with the heavy smoke of battle, had settled over Richmond. The stores and government offices were all closed. Men were not to be seen on the streets. The fire alarm bell had sounded almost continuously for days because of the burning woods that threatened the homes and livestock on the city's outskirts.

The city was spared again, and a collective sigh of relief was breathed by most of its inhabitants. However, the price paid in human terms was one quarter of Lee's Army, over 20,000 men; and over 15,000 men of the Northern Army.

For Elizabeth, it would be just the first of many disappointments and dashed hopes for the Confederacy's demise. "McClellan's Room" was not to be opened in welcome to the "American Napoleon."

The sighs of the citizens turned to sobs as the men and boys who paid the full price for their devotion at Mechanicsville, Gaines' Mill, Savage's Station, and Malvern Hill returned home. Day after day, night after night, the creaks, groans, and squeals of the caissons' wheels served as a continuous reminder of just how high a price was paid. Even the summer's powerful floral fragrances could not overcome the air fetid with the presence of the wounded, the dying, and the dead.

Disappointed, but not defeated, Elizabeth tirelessly worked on. In the blazing heat and stifling humidity of the day she bargained in the poorly-stocked markets for food desperately needed by sick men in the oppressive, reeking prisons and fever-ridden hospitals. On any day, one could see her entering the prisons early in the morning and leaving at twilight. At night, dressed in her common farm hand disguise, she silently slipped about the city unnoticed on her secret missions. She met with the small handful of Union loyalists from among the farmers, factory workers, storekeepers, and tradesmen. She listened to them, planned with them, rallied, and instructed them.

Elizabeth's position in society, her impeccable character, and numerous charities gave her a commanding influence in Richmond, and many families of plain people were indebted to her. They rallied, as she did, to the "Stars and stripes," and were able to assist her from time to time by receiving or informing agents sent by Washington. As always, Elizabeth was like a sponge absorbing information from every source. Then, piecing her reports together late at night like a mosaic, to give the readers in Washington a sense of first-hand observation. Now, and for a long time to come, Elizabeth, her family, and her loyal circle represented all that was left of the power of the United States' Government in the City of Richmond.

Following the driving off of McClellan and his huge army, a renewed confidence came to the Confederacy in Richmond. This made the Van Lew family's situation more and more precarious. People pinned threats to her door, warnings by the "white-capped" riders that their home would be burned to the ground along with everyone in it.

Now, Detective New, who had suspended his surveillance activities during the military campaign, was more determined than ever to rid Richmond of this treacherous woman. He thought, "No one should live in such grand style here in this city if they are not truly one of us. They don't belong and, like weeds in a fine garden, they must be eradicated—torn out by the roots and burned!"

New mused, "Having Captain Gibbs in the house must restrict her subversive activities or, at least, make them more difficult. However, Gibbs has not provided one shred of evidence against her, her family, or her servants in any of my interrogations of him since he moved in. I wonder if she's won him over, and he's helping her? I must check it out and, if so, catch them both at once!"

He leaned back in his chair and said enviously to himself, "Boy, would I love to be in Gibbs' boots; to be able to live and eat like that and also be right there to watch her every move. Oh yeah, I'm sure she'd let me board there after the way I treated her the night we searched the place. The witch; she'd probably let me in just so she could poison me! But, if I send someone else …!"

The next day, a young detective knocked on the door of the Van Lew residence and asked Elizabeth if she could take him in as a border. Since she had not advertised for any new boarders, Elizabeth invited him in for tea to learn more about him, his true intentions, and if someone had put him up to it … who!

Although he said all the right things, he was too evasive and unconvincing, so Elizabeth explained that she had no vacancies. The young man finished his tea, thanked her, and left. He reported back to New that his attempt was unsuccessful. Not to be put off by this weak first effort, New ordered the detective to return the following day. "Be forceful, pushy, beg if you have to; but get in there!" New screamed at him.

Once again, Elizabeth graciously invited him in to tea, explaining again why he couldn't board with them. The would-be boarder tried every tactic New suggested, but, Elizabeth's guard being up, she fended off every argument and did not budge from her position. In a contest of will, wits, or words, Elizabeth was a clever and tenacious opponent … and was usually the winner. This adversary was no match for her and, having been so easily defeated, he showed his anger, stormed out, and vowed to return under circumstances less favorable for her.

After New's henchman left, Elizabeth asked Nelson to follow him at a safe distance and to report his destination back to her. Unaware of the surveillance, the detective walked directly up 23rd to Broad Street and the thirteen blocks to New's 10th Street office. He again reported the unsuccessful accomplishment of his assignment. When Nelson returned with this information, Elizabeth's suspicions were confirmed.

Later that evening, Elizabeth saw the same man watching intently from behind the springhouse as she, her mother, and Mrs. Gibbs sipped tea on the rear porch, but Elizabeth gave no sign of her awareness of his presence.

The intense scrutiny and increased hostility by the townspeople caused Elizabeth to magnify her "crazy" antics. The only clothes she would now wear in public had to have been "prematurely aged." She did this by pulling off a button here, ripping loose a ruffle there, and spilling some food on the front of a dress where it might have carelessly fallen while eating. She pulled loose fringes from her parasol, battered her bonnet, let her hair go uncombed, and she hummed or sang songs loudly while walking up and down streets and into the prisons. The song she sang the most was "Kathleen Mulvereen." She gave wide smiles to people she didn't know, or stared point blank into their faces; laughed and talked, with her head cocked to one side as if to some invisible person. Even the street toughs, who continued to harass her, had bought her act because they changed their taunting song from "Traitor Bet" to "Crazy Bet."

To the prison guards, she was "Crazy Bet, the harmless old biddy." Little by little, Elizabeth cultivated and refined the role and reputation. She had already been branded as "strange and eccentric" for her staunch love and labors for the Negro race, but it was a significant step to elevate the reputation to "crazed." While most sane people she knew considered the label the ultimate insult, Elizabeth worked at earning it, because it helped her to be able to accomplish her work with just a bit more safety. She realized that it was harder for people to hate someone they laughed at, and knew she would be seen as less of a threat if she appeared to have lost her mental faculties.

In Richmond, from time to time, Confederate officers and officials, notwithstanding the animosities and suspicions of the city folk, continued to call and were entertained at the Van Lew home. In the after-dinner conversations cleverly directed by Elizabeth, much of importance was learned. In and of itself, it had little strategic value, but when added to what she already knew, its worth was highly significant.

Following the Second Battle of Manassas, Belle Isle was now as badly overcrowded as the tobacco warehouses. Over 2000 new prisoners arrived in early September. Although the Battle of Sharpsburg, near Antietam Creek, was the single bloodiest day of the War with over 23,000 Americans killed, wounded, or missing in action, few prisoners from that battlefield appeared in Richmond. While the outcome of the Battle of Sharpsburg/Antietam triggered great consternation in Richmond, it was propitious in Washington. This stoppage of Lee's foray into the North gave Lincoln the moment he was waiting for to publish his Emancipation Proclamation.

While the Proclamation did not call for the complete abolition of slavery, the impact of its issuance was enormous. European powers hesitated to come into the War on the side of the Confederacy, for to do so would indicate their support for slavery. It gave a ray of hope to the slaves in the South, caused anger and turmoil among the leaders of the Confederacy, and it signaled a clear intention by the government in Washington to end bondage in the United States.

Elizabeth first learned of the Proclamation when she overheard a man reading about it to an aroused crowd on a street corner. She dared not get too close to the angry crowd even though she wanted all of the details. With tears in her eyes and joy in her heart, she proceeded toward the pharmacy to check her private mailbox. Knowing no one was within hearing distance she proclaimed, "Thank you, Dear Lord, for another nail in the coffin of the Confederacy!"

Upon arriving at the pharmacy, Elizabeth noticed the upside-down pestle and hoped it would be some word on the prison hospital conditions. For some time now, she had been pleading with Dr. Parker, Jr. to see if he could tactfully help start a movement from within the medical community to petition the Confederate government to improve the deplorable conditions in prison hospitals. Elizabeth knew that any complaints coming from her would be useless and might even jeopardize her visitation privileges.

Elizabeth picked up both a prescription and the envelope with the encoded message from the pharmacist, carefully stuffed it inside her dress, and left for home.

Acting on Elizabeth's request, Dr. Parker, through his extensive medical contacts, knew of the good reputation of Augustus R. Wright, Chairman of the Army Medical Department. Dr. Parker spoke to Wright during an "accidental" non-official, private meeting. He stated that "The conditions in the prison hospitals are such an obstacle to my work as a healer and a hazard to all our medical personnel assigned to the wards." He then asked Wright if he had personally visited a prison hospital lately. Wright replied, "I've been spending a lot of time at Chimborazo Hospital and at meetings but, no, not lately at a prison hospital. I promise you; I'll look into it William. We don't want to lose any of our good people or our professional reputation," he said as he grasped William's hand in a sincere handshake.

Because of the high esteem for the Parker family's medical tradition in Richmond, Wright took Dr. Parker's comments to heart and shortly thereafter led his committee on an unannounced visit to a Richmond prison hospital. He sent the following report to the Secretary of War, G.W. Randolph, after having Dr. Parker review it in draft form:

"Mr. Secretary:

You will find enclosed a resolution passed this morning at a session of the Committee of the Medical Department. In the discharge of our duties we visited the hospital of the sick and wounded of our enemies now in our custody. All of the wards are in wretched condition. The upper ward was such as to drive the Committee out of it almost instantly. The honor of our Country will not permit us to bring the matter to the attention of Congress, thereby making the matter public.

We attach no blame to the Secretary of War. We know that in his almost overwhelming labors this matter has escaped his attention. We address you in the full confidence that you will have this condition of things altered at once. We think that the hospital for prisoners ought to be on average at least with those of our own soldiers."

Elizabeth, now safely at home and in the privacy of her bedroom, decoded and read the transcript of Wright's report. She put it down on the desk and thought, "God bless William for all that he does. I only hope that someday, someone will pay public tribute to his honorable contributions. This is the second piece of good news today!"

What Elizabeth did not know was that the "very busy" Secretary of War, who had little interest in such minutia, forwarded the report directly to General Winder marked "private and confidential."

Upon reading the report, Winder blurted, "Why those bleeding-hearted, lily-livered sawbones! What the hell do they expect? Do they want us to provide flowers and candy too? Bullshit! This is war, and war is mean and ugly!"

After his initial reaction, he mulled over his response. "I'll wait a few weeks to let him think I'm working on it. Then, I'll write that everything is resolved and that our treatment now matches our enemy's in quality. They'll never go back in there again, so they'll never know that conditions are still exactly what those dogs deserve! Davis didn't put me in charge of prisoners to treat them with love and affection … on the contrary! To hell with the prisoners … and the Committee!", and he buried the report in a bottom drawer of his desk.

Shortly thereafter, Elizabeth learned that there was to be another execution of a spy. The man, Spencer Kellogg Brown, had successfully acquired information on Confederate shipboard weaponry and taken part in sinking a ferryboat secretly used as a Confederate re-supply vessel.

On September 25th, after a year of confinement and many appeals by Union military officials, he was hanged in Richmond to show the Confederacy's resolve and as another public example of the fate of anyone caught engaging in treasonable acts against the Confederacy.

As she had done at the execution of Timothy Webster, Elizabeth unobtrusively observed the hanging and preserved his final words for posterity:

"Did you ever pass through a tunnel under a mountain? My passage, my death is dark, but beyond all is light and bright."

CHAPTER 20

Inflation & Replacement

As the year 1862 wound down, the weather in Richmond had also turned cruel. The nights were bitter cold, the days barely above freezing. Snow, that started falling in early November, continued to blanket the ground. Prisoners who were captured in warm weather did not have adequate clothing to protect themselves from the frigid temperature. Since there was little or no heat provided in the makeshift prisons, men suffered from frostbitten limbs, and a few froze to death.

Belle Isle had become "Hell Isle." The men had little protection from the constant, raw, bone-chilling wind off the James River. Wind, cold, and dampness from the ground they slept on was causing sickness and disease among the weak malnourished prisoners.

For the over six thousand Union prisoners in Richmond, that Christmas was similar to the one experienced by the prisoners who were held captive last year … only worse. Besides the harsh weather, severe treatment and living conditions, food rations were decreased. Despite bumper crops, the company that held the huge contract to supply foods to the government had created artificial shortages by blocking the train depots, preventing farmers from bringing their goods to market in large quantities. Then, they took days to unload the food that they did let through in order to maintain the inflated prices to the community.

With the cost of food ten times what it was prior to the war, there was much hunger and related crime in the city. A turkey cost from four to eleven dollars; hams, ten dollars each; flour, sixteen dollars per barrel. By comparison, a Confederate soldier's pay was only eleven dollars per month. Clothing was expensive when available. Making your own calico dress, which would have cost three dollars before the war, would now cost over thirty dollars, and the government did nothing to check the inflationary spiral.

The tally of the damage and casualties "back home" included parts or all of the many Confederate households wiped out, businesses ruined, properties lost, hearts broken, dreams shattered, lives irreparably devastated; and hope for the immediate future was very bleak.

It had been months since Elizabeth had seen Dr. Parker, so his visit to her sick mother provided a pleasant respite and chance to thank him for all his help. As they sat alone enjoying the hot mulled cider, William recounted some interesting incidents that provided a curious insight into the Confederate psyche.

While examining one of the newly arrived Union prisoners suffering a high fever from exposure during the long trip from Vicksburg, he made a startling discovery. The soldier, named Stephen, was really Suzanne … a young woman! Once detected and encouraged by Dr. Parker's gentle inquiries, she revealed the reason for her impersonation.

She told him of the childhood friendship that continued during and after the school years and grew into love, as she and her husband Donald entered into adulthood. With a far away look in her eyes, she continued to tell of her marriage on May 3, 1861, and shortly thereafter of her husband's burning desire to answer his "country's call."

Suzanne didn't want to interfere with his desire to serve along with his buddies but didn't want to be apart from him either, after seeing him every day for nearly two decades. She also felt that if he was wounded, or worse, she wanted to be there to minister to him. The obvious solution for him to be able to serve and still remain together was for both of them to enlist. They knew there was no physical examination required, so Suzanne cut her hair short like her husband's, put on some of her younger brother's old clothes, and they headed off to a recruiter who did not know them. They were enlisted as brothers Stephen and Donald. After some training, they joined the 3rd Wisconsin Volunteers headed south.

During one of the initial probing assaults on the outskirts of the city of Vicksburg, Donald was mortally wounded in the chest. Not wanting to leave him, she was captured still holding him in her arms only minutes after his last, barely audible, breath whispered, "Goodbye my Angel. I'll wait for you in Heaven."

During the long, miserable, and extremely cold ride in a rail boxcar, Suzanne couldn't stop shivering and fell ill. Actually, she was relieved to be discovered since she no longer had a reason to remain in the Army.

"And what do you suppose happened next?" William asked Elizabeth.

"I don't know. Please tell me," she responded anxiously.

"The guards, corpsmen, nurses and several of the doctors took up a collection and bought her some appropriate women's clothing. Then, when she was sufficiently recovered, gave her enough travel money back to Wisconsin."

"How wonderful!" Elizabeth exclaimed.

"Now, listen to this next story." William told her of an almost identical situation of Emily, a Confederate patient from North Carolina, who was discovered posing as a man by one of his fellow doctors. When her husband Elwyn was killed, she continued to fight valiantly in several encounters with Union forces, killing two of them. She was also three months pregnant.

"Guess what happened to her?"

"Surely they gave her very special treatment," Elizabeth suggested.

"You're right. They sentenced her to prison for three months. And, it probably would have been for longer had she not been three months pregnant."

"Unbelievable," Elizabeth exclaimed.

"My thoughts exactly," William concurred. And so, together they shared several hours exchanging anecdotes as they settled into the roles of close friends bound together by mutual interests and affection.

The parade of unsuccessful Union commanding generals continued as General Burnside was replaced. Upon reading of the appointment, Elizabeth thought, "When is the Union going to get a General like 'Stonewall Jackson?' I bet that 'unconditional surrender' Grant fellow could get the job done like he did at Fort Donelson. Don't know much about this General Hooker. Obviously, Mr. Lincoln knows more about the situation than we are privy to, so we'll just have to hope for the best.

When McClellan was General-in-Chief of the Army of the Potomac, he enlisted Allan Pinkerton, with whom he was friendly, to set up the North's secret intelligence and espionage service. The appointment proved to be a bad move because Pinkerton's reports consistently overestimated the enemy's numbers, causing McClellan to hesitate to attack for fear of defeat on several decisive occasions when he clearly had numerical superiority. McClellan had instructed Pinkerton to estimate high, but he apparently failed to specify a limit. It proved to be a key contributing factor in denying McClellan's success toward his military and political ambitions. When Lincoln fired McClellan, Pinkerton resigned and returned to his famous detective agency.

Colonel George C. Sharpe

Offsetting McClellan's poor selection of Pinkerton as head of the intelligence service, one of General Hooker's best decisions was the naming of Colonel George C. Sharpe of the 120th New York Regiment to create and lead the Bureau of Military Intelligence. Sharpe learned from the mistakes of his predecessor and worked hard to provide the military commanders with reliable intelligence.

CHAPTER 21

Battles, Bread, The Beast, & A Recruit

After a long and cold winter, the spring of 1863 arrived, and Elizabeth was in dire need of some relief. She had been the constant target of scorn, surveillance, and the squeeze of inflation, which the Confederate government had failed to bring under control. In the area of economic hardship, she was not alone. Every person who shopped for foodstuffs in Richmond was aware of the inflated prices and shortages, especially of bread, the staple, and the flour necessary to make it.

Elizabeth decided to give the Confederate government something back in kind. She began a secret word-of-mouth campaign. She told every woman in her loyalist circle to pass the word to everyone they knew around the city, that a protest march was going to take place on April 2nd. Playing on the population's unhappiness about the bread situation, Elizabeth's intention was to force the government to "fish or cut bait" regarding the inflation—and more specifically, the shortage of bread.

Early on that Thursday, April 2 morning, a few women and a scattering of boys began congregating in Capitol Square outside the Treasury Building offices of Davis, Benjamin, and Memminger. As they complained of their hunger, their numbers quickly multiplied to over one thousand.

Getting no satisfaction there, they marched from the Ninth Street end of the Square, past the War Office down steep Main Street toward their target which was the produce stores on Cary Street. Now the group was made up primarily of Dutch, Irish, and free Negro men, women, and children armed with pistols, knives, hammers, hatchets, axes, and other items of protection and possible forcible entry.

From a distance, Elizabeth observed as some of the shop owners who had been gouging the community tried to close their doors, but the women swarmed in, filling their arms, aprons, and baskets full of food. Elizabeth dared not get involved in the activity for fear she might be one of the first to be arrested.

Other shop owners hearing the noise and seeing the angry mob approaching, locked and bolted their doors. Not to be denied, the mob smashed the plate-glass windows and broke down the locked doors to gain entry. They took anything in sight they wanted; boots, cotton, woolen and silk goods, ladies slippers, washtubs, and jewelry. To Elizabeth's dismay, they now shunned stores with foodstuffs and looted anything else of value. What started out as an attempt to protest against the ineffectiveness of the government and the greedy cabal of price gougers, had turned into an ugly opportunity to vandalize and loot, and she was powerless to stop it.

By the time the mob approached the central block of Main Street, Mayor Mayo arrived with the City Battalion and threatened to fire on them if they didn't disperse. Just at that moment, President Davis also arrived and stood up on a cart for the angry crowd to see him better. Moved by this manifestation of their suffering, he made a reasoned, strategic appeal to the mob. He told the crowd that "such acts would only keep all food out of Richmond" and that "the bayonets poised against them should be better used against the common enemy, so that want would be removed from the land."

His appeal took its effect and the crowd, already heavily laden with loot, quietly dispersed. Davis, having such an easy time ending the "Bread Riot," failed to attach much meaning to it. He saw it as only a means of catharsis for the hard-pressed populace and went back to his office to wrestle with other "really important" matters of state.

While unhappy about the course taken by the rioters, Elizabeth was pleased with the results. The event caused the most affected part of the community to rally new courage and, for the first time, to vent their anger publicly against the government's ineffective performance. It caused some brief embarrassment to the government, and it sent a message to some of the price gougers, while achieving a negative blot in the newsprint media against the Confederacy.

With the arrival of good weather, the muddy roads that had impeded the mass movement of armies had dried up, signaling the beginning of active military operations.

Elizabeth was overjoyed when she read the news about the western counties of Virginia banding together, seceding from Virginia, calling them, "West Virginia" and reuniting with the Union. "What poetic justice," she said gleefully, "the place where so many slave traders went for pleasure, flaunting their ill-gotten gains, now spits in their eyes. I love it! It's a fitting first crack in the hard-boiled shell of the Confederacy."

While the victory at Chancellorsville gave the South something to cheer about, there was no cheering in Richmond as

General Thomas J. Jackson

General Thomas Jonathan "Stonewall" Jackson's body was returned. The General had been mistakenly shot by some vigilant North Carolina pickets while he was riding at dusk on a personal reconnaissance of the area surrounding the Chancellorsville battlefield.

The loss of Jackson was a tremendous blow to the Confederacy. From Davis to Lee, to all with whom he served, and to all that knew of him, there was a deep sense of loss. Lee put it best when he first heard of Jackson's wound that took him away from his command, "Jackson has lost his left arm, and I have lost my right arm." His genuine grief was greatly intensified when he learned later of Jackson's death. In reverence to the beloved Jackson, all business activity in the city of Richmond halted on the day of his state funeral.

The procession was nearly a mile long, led by General Pickett, his staff, and two of his regiments with arms reversed; the Fayette Artillery and Warren's company of Cavalry. Followed by members of Jackson's Brigade, his horse with his boots across the saddle, President Davis, Cabinet members, Senior Army and Navy Officers, Mayor Mayo and other City officials, and a long cavalcade of heart-broken friends. The public homage ended with the transportation of the Southern hero to his beloved Lexington, Virginia for burial.

As for the Union—the approach of the long hot days of summer saw the selection of yet another Commander of the Army of the Potomac—General George Gordon Meade. His reputation and success as a tenacious fighter had not escaped Lincoln's notice. His mettle would soon be tested at a small, but significant, Pennsylvania township.

General George G. Meade

The Battle of Gettysburg was widely reported around the country as the bloodiest battle ever fought on American soil. Lee's Army of Northern Virginia suffered losses of 28,000 out of some 77,500 men, while the Army of the Potomac lost more than 25,000 from its total of 93,500 troops.

It would be some time before Elizabeth learned that one of the men wounded on July 1st, the first day of the battle, and who would die from that wound on July 3rd, the last day of the battle, was Colonel Paul Joseph Revere. She would weep the unashamed painful tears one sheds at the loss of a family member. Paul's brother, Doctor Edward Revere, had been killed the year before while ministering to the wounded on the Antietam battlefield.

Meanwhile, Elizabeth continued all her activities, without rest, throughout those hot oppressive summer days and nights. Richmond's Chimborazzo Hospital continued to expand in order to accommodate the thousands of Confederate wounded returning from western and deep-southern campaigns. It was fast becoming the largest hospital in the world. Union prisoner counts rose, fell, and rose again as battle casualties and prisoner exchanges in the thousands continued throughout the summer.

It pained Elizabeth to see the effects of the below-human subsistence level of daily rations given the prisoners in Libby, Belle Isle, and the other Richmond prisons—and to know that they would be further reduced. With the fall of Vicksburg and the occupation of the western part of Mississippi, Tennessee, Alabama, and parts of Georgia, these areas ceased to be providers of the ration supply line for the Confederate troops and their captives. Elizabeth learned from a source that she had recruited in the War Office that even General Lee had pleaded for more rations saying, he "could not be responsible if the soldiers failed for want of food."

Because of the heavy campaigning and casualties, and seeing no end to the fighting, deprivation, danger and suffering, Lee's soldiers began to desert by the hundreds, many appearing in and around Richmond on their way home. This did not go unnoticed or unreported by Elizabeth. She was also given additional valuable resources that she had not planned on.

Because of the manpower needs of the military, men had been zealously recruited from highly skilled manufacturing jobs. The Confederate government, aware of these deficiencies, adopted a new policy. It searched the rolls of the Federal prisoners for the artisans and craftsmen it needed and made them a "gold-plated" offer. If they would take an "oath of neutrality," they would be released from captivity and employed as civilians in the factories, foundries, and armories. Delighted at the opportunity to get paroled, they gladly gave their word not to take up arms against the Confederacy. Now they had a chance to work at their civilian professions again, to wear clean clothes, to sleep in a comfortable bed, to bathe, and to eat regular and decent meals. As a result, they performed their assigned duties with enthusiasm and efficiency.

Since his arrival in Libby, Elizabeth had established a strong relationship with Colonel Abel Streight who had been captured along with his men near Cedar Bluff, Alabama. Through his coordinating efforts with this "release-work" program, Colonel Streight was in a position to help Elizabeth reap enormous intelligence benefits from the workers. He informed Elizabeth of each man's name, profession, and recruitment potential through the book "perforation code" system in the books they exchanged. With his help, she was successful in recruiting enough of the paroled prisoners to gain valuable information about their assignments. They provided production figures, gave information on material shortages, furnished product specifications along with limitations and vulnerabilities, and handed over detailed sketches of new innovations and inventions. Elizabeth also asked them to be on the lookout for opportunities for sabotage without putting themselves in jeopardy, since they were being watched closely every minute of the working day.

Highly significant for Elizabeth and her work was the arrival in September of Major General Benjamin Franklin Butler to command Fortress Monroe located just down the peninsula from Richmond. Butler had been nicknamed "The Beast" mostly from his harsh treatment of civilian men and women while he was in command in New Orleans in 1862.

During his meeting with George Sharpe in the Military Intelligence Bureau, prior to leaving Washington for Fortress Monroe, Butler learned about Elizabeth and her contributions from inside the Confederate capital. Piqued by what Sharpe had told him, he decided to investigate her potential himself. After reading her comprehensive reports, letters, and dispatches, Butler recognized the capability for even greater use of this valuable and proven asset at his disposal.

General Benjamin F. Butler

He resolved to establish contact, increase the volume, and improve the security of all Elizabeth's communications immediately upon taking command at Fortress Monroe.

Fortress Monroe

Shortly thereafter, there appeared at Elizabeth's door, a coarse-looking country-woman of the poorest class who stated she wanted to see Miss Van Lew. When Elizabeth came to the door, the woman stuck a sheet of folded letter-paper into her hand. Elizabeth, ever cautious of a trap, looked around to see if she could detect anyone watching. No one was in sight, so she looked the letter over.

It was addressed on the outside to "Miss Van Lew." On the inside was scrawled a message. It was a request for immediate information as to "the provender and stores in Richmond and where the sick of the hospitals were being taken." It also instructed Elizabeth to send her response as well as all future communications, directly to the correspondent. It was signed "Benjamin F. Butler, Major General, Fortress Monroe, Virginia."

Elizabeth expressed both her shock and horror to the woman for having such an incriminating letter on her person. Indignantly, in response to Elizabeth's concerns, the woman said defiantly,

"I'd like to see anyone try to put their hand in my pocket!"

Elizabeth thought to herself, "As if the papers were the only thing you would have lost had they found it on you!" She gave the woman some money and expressed her gratitude, looking around again and shaking her head as the woman bounded down the steps in a most unladylike fashion.

Butler, however, was no fool. This illiterate and street tough woman was chosen because she would arouse little suspicion and because she had no idea of the purpose, import, or danger of her mission. He also purposely kept the information requested of a lower strategic value; the more sensitive, crucial messages would come into play later. And, he also insisted on an immediate response.

The main purpose of the letter was to identify and establish himself as the focal point of her future communications with Washington, determine the timeliness of her responses to this new "post office box," and, possibly, to demonstrate that his audacity matched hers.

After several successful communications in both directions, Butler sent Elizabeth a letter that he wanted her to have delivered to an officer on General Winder's staff. In the letter, Butler was asking for the officer to "come through the lines and tell everything he knew" for which the officer would be paid a reward. In short, he wanted the officer to desert and betray the Confederacy.

The contents of this highly incriminating letter made it a death warrant for the addressee and the "postman" if it fell into the wrong hands. Elizabeth deliberated carefully over how it could be delivered and by whom. She could not think of anyone she could trust enough or was willing to put into such a dangerous and compromising position. The gains would outweigh the peril, this she knew; so she mustn't think for a moment that it was too risky to accomplish. She had been through too much to even consider not following instructions now.

The letter was meant for Chief of Detectives Philip Cashmeyer. Elizabeth had learned from conversations with some shopkeepers and waitresses in the neighborhood shops and restaurants that he seemed unhappy and disenchanted with his situation and the Confederacy. She discreetly sought the opinion of a well placed and most trusted Confederate War Office confidant on the legitimacy of Cashmeyer's discontent. Convinced of Cashmeyer's approachability, Elizabeth assessed the merits and risks of various methods of contact and decided the time to act was now.

She put the letter in the bosom of her dress and headed for Winder's office, where Cashmeyer worked. Already familiar with the building and most of its occupants, she went directly to Cashmeyer's office and found him busy at his desk. The former Maryland native looked up when she entered, recognizing her immediately. She calmly took the letter from its hiding place, handed it to him, and watched him with some trepidation as he read it.

Her heart was pounding. Located in the next room, was the central network of the dreaded Confederate Secret Police and Detective New. Had she judged Cashmeyer correctly? Would he panic and cause them both to be caught in the act? Was he truly dissatisfied and approachable? Would he be an Arnold to the Rebellion? She had staked her life, once again, on this; the most precarious and bold-faced act to date against the Confederacy. All Cashmeyer had to do was to raise his voice, and it would be all over.

Cashmeyer's face blanched, his lips quivered, his knees shook, and his face turned white with fear. He rose silently, folded and handed the letter back to her, which she returned to its previous hiding place. He gently took her arm escorting her safely outside to a spot where they could talk unobserved or overheard. Softly, he begged her to be prudent. Cashmeyer told her he would come to her home that evening if she would promise never to return to his office or speak to him directly during his working day. She gave her promise and left.

Later that night, as promised, Cashmeyer came to her home. He provided so much valuable information that she realized it would be a mistake to have him "come through" as Butler proposed and to lose such a well-placed resource. So, Elizabeth convinced Cashmeyer to remain in his present position, to do his job above reproach, and to report everything of value to her on a continuing basis. Finally, Elizabeth had someone who could keep an eye on the agents who had been keeping their eyes on her.

CHAPTER 22

Escapes, Vacine & The Secret Room

Shortly thereafter, Elizabeth's pharmacist and collaborator, George Sylvia, mentioned to her that he heard the complaints of some of the prison officers who patronized his apothecary. They needed to find someone they could afford to make new uniforms to replace the worn out ones they were wearing. "On their salaries, and with what money is worth today, they'd have to get them done by convicts." he said wryly.

Ever the opportunist, Elizabeth's face beamed as she got a daring idea, which she promptly communicated to Colonel Streight in Libby. He agreed to the scheme and initiated the action. Streight had to report daily to the Confederate prison officers. Carrying out the plan, he made a comment at his next meeting about the poor condition of their uniforms. He also informed them that if they were interested, there were several prisoners, custom tailors before the war, who would love to break their boredom by putting their skills to use making uniforms for them free of charge.

"All you have to do is supply the material, measurements, room to work in, and the time to do a first rate job," Streight said persuasively.

When the word got around to the other officers, they jumped at the opportunity, and enough material was gathered for scores of uniforms. The tailors worked feverishly, and as each pair of uniforms was completed, they were "road-tested" by the prisoners who donned them, walked through the surgeon's office, and out into the street arm in arm. Now, they walked a short distance away from the prison to a prearranged location. There, Elizabeth, who was waiting in her countrywoman's disguise, met and led them to her home and the secret room. They were then fed, clothed in civilian garb, and prepared for their safe passage North.

This ruse worked for weeks until the material, the officers' patience, and the tailors all became scarce. The duped and embarrassed officers did not report the clever deception to the prison authorities fearing reprimand for their unwitting complicity in the escapes.

New, however, noticed that scores of prisoners were unaccounted for. Never wanting to miss an opportunity to catch Elizabeth with some incriminating evidence, human or otherwise, and even just to harass her, he ordered another search of the home. Once again, nothing was found. As with each time before, Elizabeth immediately protested in an appropriately indignant manner to Winder, who promised to "look into the matter." This was his favorite ruse to get rid of complainers. Winder said nothing to New at this time, but in Winder's mind it was yet another nail in New's coffin.

For some months, Elizabeth had been boarding, free of charge, an undernourished milliner, Miss McGonicle, out of pity for her plight. Suddenly, without any provocation or warning, Miss McGonicle paid a call at the Confederate Secret Police Headquarters to report her suspicions about the Van Lews. Fortunately, she knew nothing definitive and had no solid proof, just suspicions, so the Van Lews were not subpoenaed. However, Elizabeth was deeply hurt by this betrayal of friendship and humanitarianism.

Certain now that "where there's smoke, there's fire," New sent a note to a paying border requesting her appearance to provide testimony against the Van Lews. New added in the note that if the boarder felt the slightest hesitation to testify, she would not have to face either of the Van Lews during her testimony and that her name would not be mentioned in the case. This woman not only refused to testify she declined to say even one word.

New persisted. This time, he started a grand jury investigation against the Van Lews for "trafficking in greenbacks," the official United States' currency. Mrs. Van Lew fell ill upon hearing that warrants had been prepared against her and Elizabeth. She had a deathly fear of being imprisoned in Castle Thunder. The Van Lews had no greenbacks, and no evidence could be presented that they ever took part in the illegal activity. The case was not dropped, only suspended, "to give the detectives time to collect sufficient evidence to complete the case."

New tried again. This time, he subpoenaed the Reverend Phillip C. Price to testify against the Van Lews. Price appeared, was questioned thoroughly, but had not one bad thing to say against them.

Every guest or visitor to the Van Lew home was noted, then brought in for questioning, and asked to testify against them. "Decoy letters" were sent through the post office in order to entrap them, but not one charge of treasonous activity could be proven. Such was life and justice in Richmond under Provost Marshall Winder, because the writ of habeas corpus had been suspended for some time.

Early one cold morning, Doctor Parker came by the house to look in on Mrs. Van Lew. When alone with Elizabeth, he told her of an outbreak of smallpox on Belle Isle for which they did not have adequate vaccine to control. He explained that if not contained, it could wipe out the entire prison population because of the close confinement and weakened condition of the men. Elizabeth thanked him for the early warning of the problem and sent an urgent message to General Butler.

General Butler immediately shipped enough smallpox vaccine to Richmond to vaccinate six thousand persons, along with a note ending with:

"Being uncertain how far I can interfere as a matter of official duty, I beg you to consider this note either official or unofficial as may best serve the purposes of alleviating the distresses of these unfortunate men … if more vaccine is necessary, it will be furnished …"

The December 9th response from Colonel Robert Ould, the Confederate Commissioner of Exchange, was equally cordial:

"Sir: The package of vaccine matter has been received and will be devoted to the purposes indicated in your letter. Permit me, in response to the friendly tone of your letter, to assure you that it is my most anxious desire and will be my constant effort to do everything in my power to alleviate the miseries that spring out of this terrible war."

The Richmond papers reprinted a substantial amount of news from the New York newspaper columns. They reported that General Grant, after many successful campaigns, had been named Commander of the Division of the Mississippi. Elizabeth noted how often Grant's name was mentioned during Federal victories. "Maybe we have a 'Stonewall Jackson', after all, in the Union Army," she mused. She also read and reread reprints of Lincoln's Gettysburg Address. With each reading, she saw more and more of Lincoln's awareness and appreciation of the patriotic sacrifices made in this simple, yet eloquent, consecration message.

In Richmond, food remained scarce and costly as the winter approached. Prices continued to rise while the value of money kept dropping. One Confederate dollar was now worth only five cents in gold. A barrel of flour was now up to $300 per barrel, $60 for a turkey, $35 for a pair of chickens and $15 for a pound of butter. The extensive bartering of goods for goods, and goods for services, showed the lack of faith in the southern currency.

Violence increased dramatically. Gamblers shot it out in the streets in broad daylight, prostitutes plied their wares openly, and drunken soldiers fought amongst themselves in the streets. Robberies were so commonplace in the outskirts of the city that they were not even commented on anymore. One newspaper editorialized: "It appears that every man in the community is swindling everybody else."

Women unraveled and re-knitted old stockings, while window curtains were cut up and served as petticoats, and old clothes were ripped apart and made into serviceable protection from the cold. To write to their soldiers, families and loved ones used old ledger paper, receipts, albums, books, anything; they even tore down wallpaper. For ink, they used the juice of pokeberry and green persimmons, with a few rusty nails thrown in to deepen the color. Since there were no envelopes, letters were folded and sealed with glue made from the gum of peach trees, mixed with starch from ripening corn. Drugs became so scarce that the Surgeon General urged women to grow poppies for the government hospital's medical use.

Families sold everything to survive; family heirlooms and jewelry of irreplaceable sentimental value, furniture, prized silverware, china, glass lamps, and anything else of value. Bottles and odd tumblers served as oil lamps, burning cottonseed or peanut oil mixed with lard. The poor got their light from resinous pine torches. There was no soap for washing clothing, dishes or bodies.

One cold December night, a daughter of Brother John was staying over at the Van Lew home. Ten-year old Eliza Louise, a favorite of Elizabeth and often-called "Little Elizabeth" was awakened by a sudden noise. She sat up in bed in her huge second-floor bedroom. Her little heart pounded as she listened to the howling winter wind outside. Gust after gust caused the bare tree limbs to scrape against the house, while the windows rattled their complaint of lack of putty.

There was a noise from the stairs, and Eliza quietly slipped out of the bed to investigate. Fearful of what might be out there, she silently opened the door a crack. She saw her aunt, with a candleholder in one hand and a plate of food in the other, climbing the stairs to the attic. Her childish curiosity aroused, she decided to follow.

After giving her aunt a head start, Eliza tiptoed soundlessly up the attic stairs. She paused just outside the doorway as Elizabeth set the plate of food on top of the dresser, moved the dresser away from against the wall, and pressed on the wall. She was surprised when a part of the wall sprang open like a door.

From out of the small opened doorway, Eliza saw a thin, haggard looking soldier with a bearded face and long scraggly hair. His thin hand reached out eagerly, but unsteadily, toward the plate of food offered by Elizabeth. When the soldier saw the niece, Eliza put her finger to her lips, and he did not speak or let on he had seen anything. Eliza turned and silently fled down the steps and back to her bedroom unseen by Elizabeth. She listened as Elizabeth also came down the stairs quietly, paused at her door, then returned to her room for the night.

After lying quietly for awhile, Eliza got up and returned to the attic. She struggled with the dresser but managed to move it enough to press on the same spot her aunt had pressed, and the door sprang open. The soldier popped his head out from the black hole in the wall to see who was there. Eliza thanked him for not revealing her presence earlier when her aunt was there. He laughed at her saying, "What a spanking you'd get if I told her you were here." Eliza pleaded, "Oh, please promise me you won't tell her." The soldier agreed and told her, "You'd better close the door, put the dresser back the way you found it, and get back to bed before your aunt comes back and finds you here."

With nervous hands, Eliza started to close the door but, before it closed completely, the soldier winked at her putting his finger to his lips to show her that he would not divulge their secret. Eliza never dared go near the secret room in the attic again, nor told her aunt what she had seen that cold, winter night.

This third Christmas of the War was more about the giving of prayers of deliverance than of gifts. The abounding hope was that the next Christmas would find the sun of peace shining on the hearts now grieving. It was not just the absence of the fat turkey and mince pie, or eggnog and fine wines; those could be accepted. It was the empty chairs at the dinner table that recalled the memory of a loved one's bones being bleached somewhere on a battlefield stained red from the mixed blood of friend and foe. It was not for want of the table delicacies that brought the long, heavy sigh and the tear to the eye of a father, mother or wife this Christmas day.

Christmas did get better for 502 prisoners at Belle Isle. General Butler made a gesture of good will by sending this number of Confederate prisoners, held at Point Lookout, to City Point with a letter to Robert Ould asking for the exchange of a like number of Union prisoners. Ould selected Belle Isle as the prison from which to pick the men. From the sickest, weakest, most malnourished and frost-bitten men, 502 were selected. They were given some vermin-filled, but warm winter clothing, released, and sent on their way back to Washington.

Upon hearing that the exchange had been made, President Davis immediately instructed Mr. Ould "not to hold any further correspondence, without my prior knowledge and approval, with General Benjamin 'Beast' Butler who was in Command at Fortress Monroe."

CHAPTER 23

The Professional Sends A Message

January 1864, and the war was entering its fourth year with still no end in sight. The armies were relatively quiet, and the prisoners in Richmond were suffering horribly from the lack of adequate defense against the extreme cold, snow, and ice, especially on Belle Isle.

Elizabeth received a message from General Butler that she was to meet at the house of her friend, William S. Rowley, on Saturday, January 9th, at seven o'clock. Rowley, a former New Yorker, moved to Richmond in 1859. He had been working with Elizabeth in many capacities, including helping escaped Union prisoners.

When she arrived that night, she was introduced to Captain Harry S. Howard of General Butler's staff. Captain Howard's mission was twofold. First, he was to officially engage Rowley as a $100-a-month paid spy to work directly under the orders of Elizabeth who would get her orders from Butler. His second purpose was to make secure the communications between Butler and Elizabeth, protecting both the message and the sender. The Captain gave Elizabeth a bottle containing a colorless liquid, which looked like water, for writing her secret messages. He explained that once dried, the written "invisible ink" message would not be visible to the eye. However, with the application of milk and heat, the colorless liquid would turn black for easy reading. Howard demonstrated its use and then had Elizabeth try it out while he watched.

He instructed Elizabeth that from that time on, she would address all her correspondence to "Dear Uncle," or "Mr. James," and would sign them with her new pseudonym, "Mr. Babcock." The new mailing address would be:

FLAG OF TRUCE
James Ap. Jones
Norfolk, Virginia

The letters' contents were to consist of innocent news, such as: a recent illness or death of a family member, a new baby, the weather, some romance, or gossip. This "smoke screen" of friendly chatter would be written with enough space between the lines for the real message to be written with the invisible ink. He also told her that she must give each courier a certain token to prove that they were bona fide messengers sent by her. A red rosebud was agreed upon as the token. In winter, of course, it would be pressed and dried.

Lastly, Howard gave Elizabeth a new cipher code to use as further protection for the secret writing. He trained her in its use, explaining that she was to use it to encode and decode every message and then cautioned her to keep it in an extremely safe place to prevent herself from being compromised. "To even possess a cipher is sufficient incriminating evidence to convict a person of spying," he warned her. "That's all New would need to finish me off," she commented, as she folded and concealed it inside the back of her watch.

She then asked if it might not be prudent to send a portion of the message with several couriers. He agreed, "If you can get more than one courier through at a time, that would make the chance of compromise even more remote." Elizabeth told him she would tear the letters into three pieces, giving one piece to each courier. Elizabeth reasoned that in the event the enemy first suspected, stopped, and searched the courier; found and examined the torn piece of the letter; was able to detect the presence of the invisible writing; came up with the correct combination of formula to make it visible; and then, decipher the code, they would still not obtain the full extent of the secret message.

Howard gave both Elizabeth and Rowley an assignment, together with his heartfelt appreciation on behalf of General Butler and the United States' government for their courage and loyalty.

He added a final warning to them both to be extremely alert, cautious, and careful. "Too many spies on both sides have not made it this far and are no longer with us. Please be ever vigilant. This is a life-or-death business. If you live through it, expect no recognition. If you die serving the Union, you may get a very brief moment of fame from our side and significant infamy from the other. Good luck and God speed!"

Elizabeth's Cipher Code

One night in late January, Elizabeth's highly valued contact, Cashmeyer, stopped by the Van Lew home with some disturbing news about the Union prisoners in Richmond. The number of prisoners of war at Belle Isle alone had soared to nearly ten thousand. Because of the cramped conditions, the harsh weather, and the cruel treatment by their captors, they were becoming more bold, belligerent, and getting to be too much to handle. In addition, they were also dying by the score each week from frostbite, malnutrition, or a bullet from the guards' muskets. Escapes were attempted even when there was little chance for success. More often than not, it was an attempt to escape from the living hell they were seeking, not freedom. The raging, freezing waters of the James River claimed the poor souls that were not claimed by the hail of fire from the guards' muskets.

A typical day's ration for the men was a small serving of bean soup, about one pint per man. This consisted of a large kettle of James River water being boiled for a couple of hours to which a few handfuls of wormy, musty beans were added. There were usually two or three bugs in each bean. No seasoning of any kind was added. The soup was so thin that one could see and count the beans clearly on the bottom of the kettle.

The biggest fear of the prison administrators was an uprising and surprise mass prison escape, which would peril the city and the Confederate government officials. They feared that if the Belle Isle prisoners, by sheer force of numbers, got free and armed, they would become an enraged and vengeance-seeking mob.

There was also fear that some of the city's inhabitants would join the prisoners in an uprising. They remembered how quickly the group of women protesting a bread shortage turned into a violent mob just nine months ago; and now, there was a shortage of affordable meat and other commodities. Further, if the people became unruly and the city battalion opened fire on them, the Confederate soldiers might disband and avenge their slaughtered kinfolk. Their solution—send the prisoners away from Richmond, further south to the new facility at Andersonville, Georgia.

Elizabeth called for confirmation from all her sources, and they verified the transfer plans. She met with Dr. Parker and loyal others, both inside and outside of the Confederate government, to learn what might be done to prevent the transfer. Several plans surfaced that Elizabeth helped evaluate and, in concert with her most qualified "military advisors," they selected and refined one plan to send to Washington along with the news of the transfer. Elizabeth's philosophy was, "whenever you present a problem, always have at least one well thought-out solution to resolve it."

Elizabeth carefully worded the cryptic dispatch:

"January 30, 1864

Dear Sir—It is intended to remove to Georgia all the Federal prisoners; butchers and bakers to go at once. They are already notified and selected.

Quaker (a Union man whom I know-B.F.B.) knows this to be true. Are building batteries on the Danville Road. This from Quaker: Beware of new and rash council! Beware! This I send you by direction of all your friends. No attempt should be made with less than 30,000 cavalry, from 10,000 to 15,000 to support them, amounting in all to 40,000 or 45,000 troops. Do not underrate their strength and desperation.

Forces could probably be called into action in from five to ten days; 5,000, mostly artillery. Hoke's and Kemper's brigades gone to North Carolina; Pickett's in or about Petersburg. Three regiments of cavalry disbanded by General Lee for want of horses. Morgan is applying for 1000 choice men for a raid."

Elizabeth never revealed that "Quaker" was actually Thomas McNiven, an abolitionist and a Richmond baker of whom Butler was well aware. His bakery was an active link in the Richmond intelligence-gathering network.

Now, she encoded it using her new, more secure, secret writing technique, penned in between the lines of an innocent letter to her "Dear Uncle," and signed it "Mr. Babcock."

Elizabeth then selected her most trusted courier and briefed him thoroughly on the plan. She told him that General Butler would pay him $1000 dollars Confederate money at the successful completion of the delivery. She then gave him a red rosebud and told him to give it to Butler to prove that he was a bona fide Elizabeth Van Lew messenger. She emphasized the extreme importance of the mission telling him that he must deliver it at all costs-without so much as a moment's delay. Ever since Elizabeth received verification of the prisoner transfer, the experienced courier had been staying in the secret room to ensure his availability for this crucial journey. He was fed a huge meal and given a packet of food to sustain and keep him from having to stop somewhere to eat. She bade him "Godspeed," sent him on his way, and said a prayer for his safe passage.

On the afternoon of February 4th, the courier arrived safely at Fortress Monroe. He was taken immediately to General Butler, to whom he presented the rosebud to establish his authenticity.

At this point, Butler began a cross-examination of the courier. Butler, with his bald head, paunch, bulging, sad eyes, looking remarkably like a life size toad, rolled out question after question while an aide rapidly scribbled the questions and answers. The exhausted, red-eyed, but alert, young man, who obviously was no farm hand, had been well trained and briefed by Elizabeth. The questioning went as follows:

Butler: Well my boy, where did you get this dispatch?

Boy: Miss Van Lew gave it to me. I stayed with Miss Van Lew for a week before I went away. Miss Lizzie said she wanted to send you a letter and I said I would take it. Miss Lizzie said you would take care of me. I left there Saturday night. Miss Lizzie told me what to tell you.

Butler: What did she tell you to say? You need have no fear here.

Boy: She told me to tell you the situation of the army. Mr. Palmer got all the information he could for you. Lee has got about 25,000 men; there are about 15,000 men at Petersburg. The city battalion and two companies—Maryland companies—are at Richmond and about 1,800 or 2,000 at Chaffin's and Dewey's Bluff. Mr. Palmer said two brigades have gone to North Carolina about a week before I left. He found, though, just before I left, that one stopped at Petersburg. The two brigades that went were Stoke's and Kemper's. He thought that what (sic) available force could be got into Richmond in four or five days was 25,000 to 30,000 men. He says to say to you Richmond could be taken easier now than at any other time of the war. He thought it would take about 10,000 cavalry and 30,000 infantry.

Butler: Miss Van Lew says something in her letter about Quaker.

Boy: There is a man who goes by the name of Quaker. This is not his real name but he does not wish anyone to know his real name. He does not wish to be known by any other name.

Butler: What of the prisoners?

Boy: They are sending the prisoners off to Georgia. Mr. Palmer said that he uuderstood Lee was there in Richmond in secret session; but he said that was not reliable. Lee has about 25,000 available men. Miss Van Lew said not to under-value Lee's men. Quaker said his plan to take Richmond would be to make a feint at Petersburg, let Meade engage Lee on the Rappahannock, send 200 or 300 men and land there at the White House on the other side of Richmond so as to attract attention; then have 10,000 cavalry to go up in the evening and rush into Richmond the next morning.

Butler: How did you get past the lines?

Boy: Mr. Holmes got a man to guide me. He paid him $2,000 in Confederate money. He brought me to the Chickahominy and left me there. He fooled me. I came across the river. I got a boat. I don't think there are any men on the Chickahominy, or only a few cavalry. There are none nearer than Lee's army. At Chaffin's farm there is about a regiment. He told me to tell you that Dewey's Bluff is their strongest point; he said you must come around Richmond on the other side. Morgan is applying for a thousand men. The papers say he is going to make a raid into Kentucky. I don't believe that, though, for the papers would say so.

Butler: Anything else, boy?

Boy: Miss Van Lew said to stop the women passing from Baltimore to Richmond. She said they do a great deal of harm. She also said there was a Mrs. Graves who carried mail through to Portsmouth. She hoped you would catch her.

Butler now had corroboration of the letter's contents and, based on his own information regarding the Confederate forces, drafted an urgent letter to Secretary of War Stanton:

HEADQUARTERS EIGHTEENTH ARMY CORPS, FORTRESS MONROE, February 5, 1864.

Honorable E. M. Stanton,
Secretary of War

Sir-I send enclosed for your perusal the information I have acquired of the enemy's forces and disposition about Richmond. The letter commencing "Dear Sir," on the first page, is a cipher letter to me from a lady in Richmond with whom I am in correspondence. The bearer of this letter brought me a private token showing that he was to be trusted.... You will see that the prisoners are to be sent away to Georgia. Now or never is the time to strike.... I have marked this "Private and immediate," so that it shall at once come into your hands.

Respectfully your obedient servant,
Benj. F. Butler,
Maj.-Gen. Commanding.

Butler's dispatch, once decoded in the Military Intelligence Office of the War Department in Washington, was taken by a major straight to the Secretary of War's Office. Secretary Stanton was not in his office, but President Lincoln was, awaiting his temperamental adviser. The major was not surprised to find the President there, as he was often found either in Stanton's office or the telegraph room waiting for a code clerk to finish decoding a message that might bring some good news from the front.

The major handed the message to the President. Lincoln took out his spectacles while signaling him to wait for a reply or elaboration. After reading both the Butler and Van Lew letters, he asked, "Can you tell me anything about this lady?"

Anticipating the very same question from Stanton, the major handed Lincoln a thick file of Van Lew correspondence. "From the day John Brown was captured at Harper's Ferry, this woman has bombarded us with warnings about Virginia's preparations for war," the major began.

"Indeed," Lincoln muttered while reviewing the file, "these are not crank letters. They are the work of someone with a loyal heart, good mind, and a keen eye."

"Exactly! It sounds like hindsight now, Mr. President, but if you remember before the War, we thought Virginia was more Union than Secessionist. Miss Van Lew kept writing us that the rabid, vocal minority would stampede the more docile majority. If we had listened to her then, we might not be chasing Lee and his army up and down the Old Dominion," the major commented.

"Sometimes, I'm not sure who the 'chaser' is," Lincoln sighed. The President read aloud certain phrases that caught his attention, "All the ladies are busy making clothing for the soldiers ... 'kill as many Yankee savages as you can for me ... bring back the head of Mr. Lincoln, or at least a piece of it.' 'These are the favors the families ask of their departing loved ones.' 'Dr. Revere said his brother Major Paul Revere and Colonel Lee are ...'" Lincoln paused in disbelief. "And these came through the mail?"

"For quite a long time," the major admitted.

"Did we correspond back?" he probed further.

"Not until after the First Manassas, when one of Major Allen's detectives looked her up in Richmond. He was convinced of Miss Van Lew's sincerity, and arrangements were worked out to improve the focus and security of future correspondence. She managed somehow to wrangle a prison pass from hard-nosed old General Winder and, when she started getting information daily from the freshly-captured prisoners, the value of the information she sent became significantly more valuable."

The major continued as President Lincoln listened with interest. "The most amazing thing is the daring she displays. We sent a request to her, through Butler, to set up a meeting between one of our agents and an officer in the Confederate War Department whom she had been observing. Miss Van Lew told us that she thought that he 'was almost persuaded to come over to our side.'"

A little surprised, Lincoln asked, "Isn't that a rather delicate job for an amateur?"

"Sir," the major confided, "for quite some time, this woman is all that is left of Federal authority in Richmond."

"And how did she manage to get word of the proposed meeting to the officer?" Lincoln inquired.

"She hid it in the bosom of her dress, went straight to his desk in the War Department, and handed it to him. When he read the request, I'm told that he nearly fainted. In the next rooms were secret service detectives and armed guards. However, Miss Van Lew just stood there calmly until the officer quietly asked her to please come with him outside the office so that they could talk safely."

"And who told you this fable?" Lincoln laughed.

"The officer himself. He told us that he was so fearful of discovery that he would have done anything to prevent her from persuading him out loud. In addition, she convinced him not to come over as we requested, but to remain at his post. He has been providing us with invaluable information ever since. In fact, because of his excellent access, I'm positive that he provided a good part of the information contained in the plan in your hand."

"Incredible!" Lincoln smiled, "And do we pay her well for such important and dangerous undertakings?"

"Not a penny," the major revealed, "In fact, we really owe her for all the money she has expended from her own pocket and for the invaluable service she has rendered and continues to render."

"Then, why does she do it?" Lincoln inquired a bit puzzled, "A Southern woman aiding and abetting the North."

"Well, as I understand it, her parents were both from the North, and she was educated in Quaker schools in Philadelphia. So, I think she has strong abolitionist convictions mixed in with her loyalty to the Union," the major explained.

"Hmmm, an abolitionist spy born in the South. That is someone to whom I would listen," Lincoln confided just as Stanton entered the office.

"That will be all for now Major, and thank you. You have been very helpful," Lincoln said appreciatively.

Once alone, Lincoln and Stanton reviewed the letters and discussed the plan's advantages, disadvantages, and feasibility. Anxious to end the War, especially in an election year, the thought of a decisive attack on Richmond and the end of bloodshed was irresistible.

The two biggest initial problems they saw were the rapid deployment of troops in such unpredictable and inclement weather and preventing leaks about the operation from getting to the enemy.

Back in Richmond, the Confederacy's unflagging commitment to ferreting out and making examples of people caught engaging in spying activities was emphatically demonstrated once again. This time, it was 36 year-old, Tennessee native, Spencer Deaton, who was accused of spying for the North. He was hanged February 20, 1864 in the yard of Castle Thunder Prison.

CHAPTER 24

Escape From Libby Prison

Lincoln's meeting with his top military advisers, Generals Meade, Pleasonton, Humphries, Kilpatrick, and Secretary Stanton, and others was spirited. Although the decision to conduct the raid at this time was not unanimous, a consensus was reached, and the plan finalized.

The number of men allocated for the mission would be only four to five thousand; a tenth of the specified amount considered necessary for success in the plan sent by Elizabeth's courier to Butler. There would also be a battery of artillery sent, but no wagon trains, which would slow down the operation. The raid would consist of three commands with different objectives. General George Custer would lead one group making a diversionary raid in the vicinity of Albemarle County, Virginia. A second group of 500 hand-picked men led by the youthful, but courageous, Colonel Ulric Dahlgren, would swing south, coming in through Richmond's back door and effect the release of the prisoners. The largest force, led by General Judson Kilpatrick, would make the frontal attack on the city to smash through the city's defenses.

Dahlgren was the son of Rear Admiral John A. Dahlgren, who was on duty with the Union Navy and who had previously invented the Dahlgren gun now in use by both sides. The plan included the liberation of the ten thousand Federal prisoners on Belle Island who, when brought into the city, would free the additional five thousand being held in the city's makeshift prisons. They would then all be repatriated with Butler's forces at Fortress Monroe.

Lincoln set three main objectives for the raid: the destruction of war installations and supplies, the widespread distribution of his amnesty proclamation amongst the civilian population and lastly, and most important to Lincoln, the release of the prisoners in the misery-filled Belle Isle prison on the James River.

For the next few weeks, Washington buzzed with rumors about the mysterious comings and goings of the generals and their meetings with Lincoln and Stanton. When General Kilpatrick, nicknamed "Kill-Cavalry" for a few perilous missions that had cost the lives of cavalrymen under his command, was seen going to the White House, it confirmed to those trained observers that a raid was planned.

The Willard Hotel at Fourteenth Street in Washington was the favorite watering hole for officers, members of the government at every level, congressmen, senators, and businessmen seeking government contracts. Discussion and debates filled with strategic military implications flowed as freely as the liquor. With such a wealth of free information readily available, the hotel's bar was also a magnet for newspaper reporters and Southern spies. Many a bartender and waiter were supplementing their income as paid informers, passing on every scrap of information of military use during their clandestine contacts with Rebel agents.

For the past few weeks, there had been so much heated discussion over the merits and pitfalls of the raid that the Confederate government in Richmond knew almost every general's position and most of the possible options concerning the upcoming raid. The only thing they didn't know was the precise timing of it. That was why they began to strengthen the city's defenses and to conscript every available man and boy, regardless of their draft status.

Meanwhile, the prisoners in Libby had been busy with their own form of "liberation." For some weeks, they had been working on a plan of which Elizabeth had been a contributing accomplice.

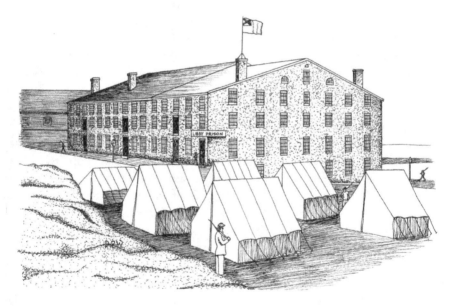

LIBBY PRISON

The two initiators of the plan at Libby, Colonel Rose and Lieutenant Foster later took into their confidence Colonel Streight and Major McDonald. Rose and Foster had made several attempts to find a way out of their captivity. Finding a weakness in the masonry holding the stones behind the cook room fireplace, they removed the stones, crawled into the narrow passageway and, with the help of an improvised rope ladder, made their way down to the cellar, known as "Rat Hell."

Finding their way in the dark, they calculated how far up the wall they needed to go to safely dig a tunnel out of the east side of the building, which would lead them past the sentries, to the nearby nearly-vacant lot of the Virginia Towing Company.

Night after night, they had returned to their digging using a jackknife, a tin sugar scoop, a chisel, and their fingernails. They did this without so much as a sound, which would have aroused the sentries on duty outside on Cary Street or those inside the heavily guarded cook room, the main above ground area of the escape route.

The officers used an old wooden spittoon as their major tool. The person doing the digging took the implement into the hole with him. The spittoon had two long strings tied to it; one held by the digger, the other by the man waiting at the entrance to the tunnel. When the spittoon was full, the digger pulled on the string that was held by the man at the entrance. The receiver of the signal would pull the spittoon full of dirt out of the hole and dump it under the straw that also covered all the rats' nests. Once the dirt was dumped, a pull on the digger's string silently signaled the digger to pull the empty spittoon back into the hole for refilling.

As with tunnels of any length, air became a problem for the diggers. The person waiting for the spittoon would fan the opening with an old hat to force air into the hole helping the digger to breathe better while at work. Once or twice, a man fainted from lack of oxygen and had to be pulled out of the hole.

As the work became more arduous, more men were recruited to help with the digging. They now had three teams of five men, each team digging every third night. Upon returning after each night of digging, the men pulled up and hid the rope ladder, replaced each stone in exactly the same position. They then covered the crevices so skillfully with soot that no trace of any disturbance was visible to any of the 1100 officers who used the fireplace for cooking each day in Libby.

The escape cabal was taking no chances, because there were strong indications that at least one of the officers was leaking information about prison escape plans in exchange for extra rations. The officers were close to pinning down the identity of the traitor, or traitors, who had been recruited by Detective New.

Once, due to impatience, the operation was nearly discovered. One of the diggers, thinking he had dug far enough away from the prison wall, dug a hole vertically until it reached the surface. The digger slowly inched his head up through the tiny opening to verify his location. Only fifteen feet away was an armed guard! Luckily, he was facing the other way at that moment, and the digger quickly popped his head back into the hole. His impatience had put the entire plan in jeopardy, almost negating all of the men's work on the tunnel. Yet, he was still curious about the tunnel's progress. So, when he heard the guard's boots on the cobblestones walking away, he took off his old hat and pushed it through the hole and then began packing dirt very tightly back into the vertical hole. At first light the next day, the hat's location, safely observed from the second floor window vantage point, provided the diggers with precise information on where the tunnel's construction ended and how far it had to go.

Finally, just at dawn one week later, the tunnel was finished. It came up into a shed just on the other side of a fence that was out of sight of the sentinels. Exhausted and fearful of discovery, the diggers covered the hole over with a large, empty, wooden box and returned back into the prison. They informed the other two teams of their accomplishment, then entered a message, in the usual manner, in a book to Elizabeth informing her that they were to escape the next day, February 9th. She had already supplied them with directions to her house where she would meet them, put up as many as she could, and have the rest housed in other loyalists' homes until the furor and search activity subsided.

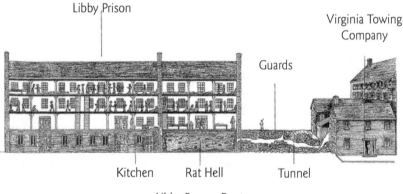

Libby Escape Route

As fate would have it, the very night before the tunnel was completed, word came to Elizabeth that her brother John had been ordered to report for duty with the Army to help shore up the city's defense forces. To avoid conscription, he slipped away to the home of some old friends on the outskirts of the city.

In disguise, Elizabeth went to the house of the very kind, brave and poor family where John was secreted. Elizabeth spent the night discussing possible solutions to the situation. In the morning, Nelson came with a basket full of supplies to help the family feed their unexpected "boarder." He reminded John of the penalties for a deserter when found, and for all those harboring and aiding the deserter, which now included Elizabeth. Fearing a firing squad for John and prison for the compassionate family who were sheltering him, she thought, "desperate times require desperate measures," and immediately headed home to change her clothes.

Quickly changing into one of her "prematurely aged," tattered dresses; she headed straight for General Winder's home. Upon her arrival, Mrs. Winder greeted her suspiciously, but respectfully, remembering the favor she had gained with Varina Davis thanks to Elizabeth. A surprised Winder looked up from his breakfast and asked Elizabeth the meaning of her visit to his home at that hour.

Elizabeth began by telling them that she deeply appreciated all their past favors and pleaded that they keep in the strictest confidence what she was about to tell them. Bursting with curiosity, the General blurted out impatiently, "Well, what is it, Miss Van Lew; tell us what's wrong!"

Elizabeth took a deep breath for effect, then said slowly, "My brother John has deserted. He has run off and hidden from the men sent to conscript him into the Army."

The General, so greatly relieved that it was not a confession of some crime against the state that would prove New right, also breathed a deep sigh … one of relief. Desertion in Richmond at this time was as common as a head cold. "He shouldn't have done that; he should have come to me first."

"Well, after the deferment you got John previously, he probably thought you were overruled this time," Elizabeth rationalized softly.

"You say he's hiding; you know where?" he asked.

"Yes, indeed. Do you want me to tell you?" she inquired, wanting to appear totally cooperative.

"No, there's no need of that," he said as he pondered the predicament.

Elizabeth volunteered her well thought-out solution, "I wouldn't want to impose on you on our behalf, but I've been thinking perhaps John should serve. If he could be assigned to some position where he could use his extensive bookkeeping skills and not be on a battlefield …"

"A bookkeeper!" Winder blurted as he rose from the table, "We have been looking for a Regimental Bookkeeper on my staff. Tell your brother to report to me tomorrow. I'll have him assigned to Company C, Eighteenth Virginia Infantry stationed here in Richmond, and he'll start to work right away."

"And where would he be quartered?" Elizabeth asked.

"At home, if you wish. Technically, he should be housed in the Regimental barracks, but I wouldn't require it."

Surprisingly, Elizabeth said, "He may prefer the barracks, just as long as he can come home for a visit now and again so mother wouldn't worry."

"Well then, we'll leave it up to John," Winder said as he sat back down and continued to eat his breakfast.

"I am ever grateful to you both for your understanding and your help, I'm just about at my wit's end about all that's going on. Everything seems to be coming down around my head. It's almost more than I can bear." She took out a worn handkerchief and put it to her cheek, "Having to put up with all the degrading and destructive searches resulting in the loss of irreplaceable family things of deep sentimental value. Then, there's mother's illness, the struggle to make ends meet, and now John's situation. You don't know what a relief this is to me to have your friendship. I don't how to repay you," she said wiping her eyes, her hands shaking.

"No repayment is necessary," the General chided gently, "and now if you'll excuse me, I must be off to work. I have a very full day ahead."

After Elizabeth left, the General confided to his wife that "We are pressing every available man and boy into the city's Defense Battalion to prepare for an upcoming raid. John's deferment doesn't matter a hoot at this time, but I didn't want to let on to her about it and get her more distraught than she already is. The poor woman is heading for a nervous breakdown."

Elizabeth immediately headed back home to change clothes again so that she could return to the home where John was in hiding to tell him about Winder's offer, before any zealous searchers found him. At this time, she was still unaware that the planned escape from Libby had been scheduled for that night.

As soon as it was dark, the prisoners in Libby, anxious to be free, began to make their escape in relays of five men at a time, spaced thirty minutes apart. Not until the last group was leaving did the news spread through the sleeping prison, and there followed a wild, but silent, stampede by the rest of the prisoners to leave.

The noise made by a guard rattling the bolts on one of the Cary Street doors, as part of his routine perimeter checks, started a panic in which several men were trampled unconscious, but there was still not enough noise to alert the guard, and he proceeded on his rounds.

Afraid to speak, the men groped in the dark of Rat Hell for the opening to the tunnel. It was higher than most expected and only 103 men were able to get out before the loud, pre-dawn prison staff activity began. In all, the number included eleven colonels, seven majors, thirty-two captains and fifty-three lieutenants.

The original escape planners and tunnel diggers headed straight for Elizabeth's home, as pre-arranged, along with a large number of other escapees who observed and followed the initial groups.

The remaining men in Rat Hell, unwilling to risk being caught either in the cellar or on the streets, returned upstairs to the mass sleeping room. To preserve the integrity of the escape route for future use, they pulled the ladder up with them into the crawl space and just as carefully as the original group had done, covered their tracks by replacing the stones and covering the crevices with soot.

Knowing that the large number of missing prisoners would be discovered at the morning count, and to further protect the tunnel from discovery, they hung a makeshift platform out from a back third story window which faced the Kanawa Canal, giving the impression that this was the escape method.

This decoy baffled Winder for two days until the tunnel was discovered. He and New's men had questioned every guard, prisoner, and person who lived or worked within the vicinity of Libby about the platform. It was only when a Virginia Towing Company worker had accidentally knocked aside the box covering the opening that the tunnel was discovered. Even then, Winder couldn't believe that the men were so desperate or resourceful that they could have tunneled their way out undetected. He forced a reluctant black youth to fearfully crawl down the hole into what, he knew not. Only when he screamed after he fell into Rat Hell and the rats set upon him, did the guards find him. The ensuing thorough search soon revealed the opening that led to the cook room fireplace.

There were some heated discussions with two Federal officer prisoners who were warned that they would be sent to Castle Thunder Prison if they did not learn about and warn prison officials of any future plans for a prison escape. Besides having the security around the prison increased, Winder gave orders to have Libby and the entire surrounding neighborhood mined so that it could be blown up in the event of another escape or disorder. However, he failed to warn the prisoners about the order, and their lack of awareness kept it from serving as a deterrent to further escape planning.

Some of the prisoners who made it out, lacking knowledge of the original escape plan, did not fare so well without Elizabeth's assistance. Two of the men stole a boat and attempted to navigate the swift and frigid James River rapids. The boat capsized, and they drowned. Some got as far as the circle of batteries around the city and were recaptured. Mercifully, others were found a day or two later, half-frozen and starving by squads of searchers. These men were returned to Libby for severe punishment for attempting to escape. Of the 103 men who escaped, minus the two who drowned, 50 were caught and returned to their miserable existence in Libby.

CHAPTER 25

The Modified Raid Plan Revealed

As expected, the Van Lew home was subjected to yet another search and, as before, the search was fruitless. However, the search was not as detailed as in previous visits because, upon Elizabeth's pleading, Captain Gibbs, her Confederate boarder had accompanied the searchers and nothing further was stolen. It was also the speediest investigation. This might have been due to Gibbs' awareness of the aroma of the hot meal that had coincidentally been placed on the dinner table at the right moment.

After dinner, Elizabeth was warming her hands at the library fireplace and checked her in-house, secret "mailbox" which was part of the ornamental iron fireplace grate. Two pilasters, one on each side of the grate, were capped by a small sculptured figure of a couchant lion. From wear or by design, the lion on the left could be raised like the cover of a music box. The shallow cavity beneath the lion held the numerous messages and notes that were picked up or inserted by Elizabeth, Mary, or Nelson.

Elizabeth could come into the room alone, select or replace a book, and warm her hands. While in front of the fireplace she could remove the previously prepared dispatch ready for delivery from inside her sleeve, lift the lid, slip it inside the cavity and then leave undetected. Later, when Nelson came in to dust the fireplace, he could remove the dispatch and leave for the night. No one would be the wiser that they had any contact with each other. With Captain and Mrs. Gibbs coming in and going out of the house so often, the secret mailbox was used almost daily.

On the evening of the same day of the search, there was a note in the box for Elizabeth to meet that evening with Mrs. Abbie Greer, one of her trusted loyalists. Having set pre-arranged times and suitable locations for meetings, Elizabeth set out alone.

After meeting Mrs. Greer, they both set out for Mrs. L.A. Rice's humble home on the outskirts of the city. The four officers, who had been hidden there, all stood when she entered and gave her a warm welcome. Only Colonel Streight appeared in good condition. Knowing they were eager to be on their way, she gave the officers journey instructions.

With the important business out of the way, they enjoyed some friendly talking and laughing together, which was the first time she had seen any of them in such good spirits in all the time she had known them. "They appeared much more at peace now having the horrible prison ordeal behind them," she thought to herself, "I guess unless you have been through it for yourself, it's impossible to know what it does to you." And, as an afterthought, "It's the first time I have laughed in a long time too!"

Elizabeth bade them "Goodbye" and the most fervent "God help you" from her heart toward every one of them.

The next day, there was an on-site visit to Belle Isle by members of the Confederate Congress, including Jefferson Davis, Judah Benjamin and Howell Cobb to assess the magnitude of the overcrowding problem at the prison. They also discussed the upcoming raid by Union General Kilpatrick and what might happen if these ten thousand prisoners were released upon the city. Unbeknown to them, their entire conversation was overheard by a solitary prisoner who was working behind the building on a burial detail.

When the prisoner returned inside the compound, he told what he had heard to a fellow prisoner, who told another prisoner, who told another, and within fifteen minutes, every prisoner gave out a shout that continued for a half-hour. The departing congressional contingent, still on the bridge leading from the island, heard the shouting that caused a cold chill to run up their spines.

During that entire night, the Belle Isle Prison officials hung hospital signal lights over the island in order to help direct the city's defense batteries' fire upon the prison in the event of an uprising. Considering the degree of density of the prisoners and lack of any form of protection, it was inevitable that the vast majority of the ten thousand prisoners would be blown to pieces during the very first volley.

February 14th, and the first six hundred prisoners from Belle Isle were sent away to Georgia. Additional groups, of similar size, were being scheduled to follow them south. Although the men would still be in captivity, the thought of leaving the unrelenting cold weather on the island prison lifted their spirits. They wondered if they would be better off to tough it out on the island until Kilpatrick's Raid, but thought, "What if he doesn't come, would we be sorry that we missed the chance to go to a warmer clime?" The fact that it kept their minds active and gave them something to think, talk, and argue about, other than the lack of food, was a welcome benefit.

On the evening of February 27, Elizabeth received an urgent note from Mrs. Rice asking her to come to her house at once. When Elizabeth arrived, she was greeted by one of the prisoners who had escaped through Rose's Tunnel, Captain Paul Silman. It was such a pleasure to see him. He looked so different … so handsome. In fact, she was quite astonished! She marveled to herself, "It's amazing what decent food, rest, personal hygiene, and new clothes can do for a person."

"How nice to see you again, I hardly recognized you. You look so … well … compared to when I saw you last."

"Thank you, Miss Van Lew. My comrades and I owe you and all your friends a large debt of gratitude for our safe passage North," he said with a voice filled with emotion, "we learned that almost half of the men didn't make it."

"Yes, I saw most of them in the Libby Prison ward. They didn't fare well at all, poor souls," she commiserated, "but tell me, why are you back?"

"I came to give you first-hand details of the plan to raid Richmond, to provide my assistance with any duties you may require here in the city, and to tell you that the plan is to commence tomorrow! In fact, I just left General Kilpatrick's camp yesterday morning so that I could be here in time to notify you."

"You do know," Elizabeth interrupted, "that all Richmond is aware of the upcoming raid, including the prisoners on Belle Isle!"

"I don't think Washington is cognizant of the extent of the knowledge you speak of. How could they have found out?"

Elizabeth postulated, "I've heard, from my conversations with people who have come from Washington, that the Willard Hotel is the best source of strategic military news. So many officers and politicians go there and talk as if it were a safe haven. If I wanted to gather Federal military intelligence, that would be the place.

"I would put a few good listeners on the hotel staff which would provide a perfect cover for their true activities. They could observe 'who's who,' who's in town to see the President, how long they stay in town, find out whose tongue loosens up the most from liquor and then serve them the largest drinks. Then they could listen to every scrap of useful debate, news or gossip, collect any scribbled notes or battle plans sketched on paper, tablecloths, or napkins, etc. You get the idea."

"Unbelievable! You really know your stuff. I'm glad you're on our side," he said, quite impressed with her professionalism. "So, I guess that's how they learned about it. I must remember to warn my fellow officers about the dangers of the Willard Hotel."

The Willard Hotel

"Now, Captain, tell me about the raid details," she said feeling the heat of his admiring gaze.

The Captain was amazed at how much Elizabeth already knew, unaware that she had sent the original raid plan to Washington ... at which time, she had asked for ten times the amount of men. He explained the roles of Generals Kilpatrick and Custer and Colonel Dahlgren. When he talked about Dahlgren's route, Elizabeth interrupted "How is Dahlgren to follow the route with so many forks and branches in the road, and how will he know the best place to cross the James?"

"Dahlgren was given a guide to get him to Richmond, and he picked up another one who said he knew the areas leading into the city. The second one was a young black man, who said he knew all the fords between Richmond and Goochland Court House," he answered.

"And where did they find this second guide?" she inquired.

"We didn't, he just showed up and asked us if we could use a guide. He said that he was a freeman who worked the crops but was now out of work and needed the money."

"And you didn't think that it was a little too coincidental?" Elizabeth probed.

"Jud, I mean General Kilpatrick, questioned this fellow at length, and said that he seemed to know his stuff, so he got the job."

"You said that this stroke-of-luck guide was young; how young?"

"I'd say about twenty or so," he guessed.

"Do you happen to know his name?" Elizabeth continued.

"I don't remember now, sorry."

"Was it by any chance 'Martin?'" she asked fearfully.

"Yeah, that's it, Martin … Martin Roberts, or something like that," he smiled.

"Could it have been 'Martin Robinson,'" she asked now as if her suspicions and worst fears were about to be confirmed.

"Yes, Yes, that's his name! How did you know?" he responded excitedly.

"Then it is him! He's a traitor!" Elizabeth shrieked, "He must have been sent to deliberately scotch the raid! I told you they knew it was coming and who was to lead it. All Martin had to do was to wait until Kilpatrick's Cavalry appeared and then volunteer … so simple. It's a trap, and we fell for it hook, line, and sinker." Elizabeth derided.

"We must call off the raid now before he betrays us and ruins the opportunity. You must ride back to Stevensburg and call it off."

"Are you serious," he replied in astonishment, "at the eleventh hour, with four and a half thousand men primed to act, with military careers and political ambitions and huge egos involved? Everyone wanted to go on this mission of mercy to liberate our brothers in uniform and to smash the Confederacy. To call it off would demoralize the men, embarrass the leaders in an election year, and take away the opportunity for instant fame and glory for all the generals with political ambitions. Not a chance!" For additional emphasis, he added, "And whom would I tell them ordered the raid called off?"

"You mean because I am a woman?" she challenged testily.

"No, I didn't mean it that way. I meant it would have to come from some high-ranking military officer," he said apologetically.

"I'm sorry, but we don't happen to have any running free in Richmond right now. It's just you and me who know about the very real threat to the mission's success."

"Is there another way to save the mission?" he asked trying to change her thinking about wanting to stop the raid.

Elizabeth reviewed all the plan's details and started to think out loud. "One of the most important objectives and elements needed to pull it off is the liberation of the Belle Isle prisoners. Without their support, Kilpatrick will have a tough time fighting his way past the fortifications on the Brook Turnpike. With the prisoner's support, they will have the Home Guard in a vice grip from behind."

"I wouldn't hold the Belle Isle prisoners totally responsible. We do have thousands of additional men in the city, and I know the men in Libby can be counted on to put up a good fight."

"But the prisoners on Belle Isle are the lion's share Captain, and the only way to set them free is to cross the James upstream and approach the island from the south side. There are no bridges and only a couple of fords upstream safe enough to use when the water in the James is this high."

He nodded his head in agreement as she proceeded. "So, you can see how important it is to have the right guides. Martin will either take them on a wild goose chase, lead them into a trap, or send them into the jaws of a cold and hungry river at an unsafe location; and in the turmoil, make his escape."

"The die is cast," he conceded with finality.

"Not if you ride out and intercept Dahlgren and tell him to beware of Martin's treachery!" Elizabeth pleaded.

"What will I say to Dahlgren? A woman in Richmond says the guide you have is a traitor; beware. And what would you expect him to do … shoot Martin and proceed without a guide?"

"He'd be better off. Dahlgren could ask any Negro he met on the road, once he identified himself and gave the purpose of the mission, and they would gladly help." she reasoned.

"All right. It's worth a try," he relented. "Miss Van Lew, you are a darn persuasive lady. I bet you could talk a man into doing just about anything."

Elizabeth blushed a deep red, smiled, and thought, "Why does this man affect me so? I haven't blushed in years." And now that he had agreed to make the trip, she softened, adding, "Please call me Elizabeth, or Liz, if you like."

"I will, if you drop the 'Captain' and call me 'Paul,'" he reciprocated as he got up to leave. Elizabeth also got up and handed him his hat saying. "I can't emphasize enough how important it is for you to catch up with Dahlgren. You could save the mission and, at worse, the lives of Dahlgren and his men."

Elizabeth extended her hand and Paul took it. With his other hand, he compressed hers tenderly. "I make this trip out of my deepest respect for you and your judgement."

"And for your country." she added, "May God watch over you. Please be careful. When you return, I'll expect a full report from you over a well-earned dinner in my home in your honor."

"Now, that's an incentive I'll look forward to collecting. Good night, Elizabeth."

"Good night, Paul." And the smiling Captain headed out into the cold, dark night.

Once the Captain left, Mrs. Rice re-appeared, and after a brief business discussion, they shared some pleasant social conversation. More than once, the name of the handsome Captain came up as the topic of conversation.

Elizabeth departed, humming a romantic tune all the way home. Not the eccentric humming of "Crazy Bet," but the sweet, soft humming of Elizabeth Van Lew, the woman. The nearly extinguished flame in her heart had been rekindled. Then, the final stanzas of another song, a familiar hymn flowed into her mind:

> Above the maddening cry for blood,
> above the wild war-drumming,
> let freedom's voice be heard, with good
> the evil overcoming.
>> Give prayer and purse
>> to stay the curse,
>> whose wrong we share,
>> whose shame we bear,
> whose end shall gladden Heaven!
>
> In vain the bells of war shall ring
> of triumphs and revenges,
> while still is spared the evil thing
> that severs and estranges.
>
>> But blest the ear
>> that yet shall hear
>> the jubilant bell
>> that rings the knell
>> of slavery forever.
>
> Then let the selfish lip be dumb,
> and hushed the breath of sighing;
> before the joy of peace must come
> the pains of purifying.
>> God give us grace,
>> each in his place
>> to bear his lot,
>> and murmuring not,
> endure, and wait, and labor!

CHAPTER 26

The Richmond Raid

February 28th began with a heavy blanket of fog along most of the entire eastern seaboard. It burned off slowly while the men were making their final preparations for breaking camp. At 2 PM, Custer, in his velvet uniform with its embroidered gold stars, led his Michigan Brigade out towards Madison Courthouse and Charlottesville on their diversionary raid on Stuart's troops.

General George A. Custer

At dusk, a second 500-man group mounted up and formed a long column. They had been hand picked from detachments of the 1st Maine, 1st Vermont, 5th Michigan, and 1st and 2nd New York Volunteer Cavalry. Now, young Colonel Dahlgren, wanting to impress, rode up the entire column, exchanging brisk salutes with officers he didn't know and who didn't know him. He took his position at the head of the column and, imitating Custer, raised his saber, nudged his horse with his left foot, and gave the order, "For-wa-ar-rr-d Yo-o-o!"

Colonel Ulric Dahlgren

Once underway, the clatter of utensils and the chatter of men drowned out the sounds of the hoof beats. Dahlgren gave orders for the silencing of the noise of the rattling cookware and the loud talking and singing of the men. Although it was only quarter-past six, and they were not to arrive at Ely's Ford on the Rapidan River until eleven, he was nervous about the lack of discipline and respect for the element of surprise. Dahlgren realized that scouting parties or roving pickets could be anywhere in the woods that bordered the road and would be well hidden by the darkness before the moon rose.

An hour later, Kilpatrick led the third division on the same route south over the Rapidan.

Dahlgren sent a small group of men ahead to Ely's Ford where they silently surrounded and, without a shot, captured the small group of pickets camped near the Kilpatrick's entire troops to cross the carefully selected, thinly guarded spot on the Rapidan uneventfully.

However, only a mile past the ford, crouching in the brush close to the road were Scott and Topping, two of Confederate General Wade Hampton's "Gray Ghost" scouts. These members of the "Iron Scouts" who roamed for days behind enemy lines picking up all sorts of information silently observed from the safety of cover. They watched, counted, and listened to the loose boasting of one of the men as they rode only a few feet away, "Yeah, and after we sack Richmond, I'm gonna get me one of those pretty Southern Belles and do some celebratin'!" As luck would have it, for the scouts, along came three of Dahlgren's men who by stopping to relieve themselves, created a large

General Judson Kilpatrick

gap between themselves and the rest of their group. The scouts ambushed the men, dragged their lifeless bodies into the brush, commandeered their horses, and headed straight for Fredericksburg to warn General Hampton.

When Kilpatrick's men passed one section of road, Martin, trying to further establish his credibility with a suspicious Captain said he knew exactly where they were.

"And where are we?" the Captain checked.

Martin said confidently, "Chans'lo'vil!"

"And how do you know we're at Chancellorsville?" the Captain probed skeptically.

"Da smell" he answered, "ifs it be da' rit tim,' yoos sees da bones of da mens an' da hosses. Da fros tro's 'em up fum da groun' cuz de don puts'em down deep."

"My God," the Captain said shaking his head as he detected the odor coming from the battlefield and trusting Martin a little bit more now.

Early the next morning, Dahlgren's column rode through Spotsylvania Courthouse where a few early risers barely showed them any notice. The young Colonel commented to himself, "I guess they'll know we're on our way now!"

Several miles later, they swung right, toward Frederick's Hall Station, one of the Virginia Central Railroad's stops. Meanwhile, Kilpatrick's main force split off at Mount Pleasant and headed directly south toward Chilesburg, roughly the half way point on their route to Richmond.

As Dahlgren's cavalry approached within a few miles of the Frederick's Hall Station, they saw the smoke of a three-car train from Richmond heading their way. There was great enthusiasm to attack the train and raid the station. "Nothing doing," Dahlgren snapped. "The station is the artillery depot for the II Corps, and they probably have five thousand men guarding the guns. Besides, we can't risk discovery just to capture a Rebel train. Our objective is Richmond."

What they didn't know was that inside the train a high ranking Confederate officer, on his way back to his headquarters at Orange Court House, was mulling over the intelligence he had received while conferring with President Davis. It seemed that President Lincoln was about to name a new Commanding General of the Army of the Potomac. The appointee was a stubborn "West Pointer" named Grant who had an awesome reputation for persistence earned in western campaigns. The officer didn't know how much hammering the ragged and gaunt Confederate forces could take from this vast army headed by an officer of Grant's caliber.

"Major," he said, "make a note to all officers who were contemporaries of Grant, who went to school or served with him, especially Longstreet, to make private reports to me about his character, personality, strengths, weaknesses, habits, and the like. You know what I mean?"

"Yes sir, General Lee, I'll get right on it!"

Dahlgren's column swung wide to avoid the station by taking secondary roads that turned eastward toward Bumpass Turnout, a smaller way station of the same Virginia Central Railroad. They then turned south again heading for Goochland Courthouse and their first sighting of the frigid James River.

As Dahlgren's five hundred-man force receded in the distance, Confederate General A.L. Long, the commander of the Frederick's Hall artillery depot grinned and breathed a sigh of relief.

General Ulysses S. Grant

Dahlgren would have been chagrinned if he had known that there were only 120 sharpshooters stationed at the Frederick's Hall depot to guard the 120 artillery pieces of the II Corps; and, had he attacked the train, he would have captured the Confederacy's preeminent general.

General Long decided to ask for a couple of infantry regiments to be rushed to the station to help protect the valued equipment and munitions, more adequately, in case the column returned.

Just west of the Bumpass Turnout Station, Dahlgren's force dismounted, tore up the rails, and stacked the wooden ties into several piles. They ignited the stacks into giant bonfires and threw the rails over them, heating and warping them beyond usefulness.

To the east, paralleling Dahlgren, Kilpatrick's men reached the Virginia Central's Beaver Dam Station. Kilpatrick's men captured the telegraph man before he could tap out his warning to Richmond. Then, they completely demolished and burned the station and its fuel supplies, ripped up the main and spur tracks, and then tore down over a half mile of telegraph poles in both directions.

Sergeant George Shadbourne, another one of Hampton's scouts, observed their movements and passed it on to Hampton, who passed it on to his superior, General J.E.B. Stuart. Just as Kilpatrick's men finished their destruction at the station, a winter storm began to rage.

Clothed in ponchos, with heads bowed to protect themselves from the wind and stinging sleet, both commanders cursed the fact that they were unable to fire rockets into the darkened skies, which was their prearranged means of communications between the two commands.

"Damn" Kilpatrick cursed, "I don't know if Dahlgren's men got through, were jumped, turned back, or what!"

"Knowing how determined Dahlgren was to be on this raid, I'll just bet he's still on his way. He does not seem to be the sort that would turn around," General Davies of the First Brigade commented in response.

"Well, I'll tell you one damn thing. He damn well better be in Richmond at ten o'clock tomorrow morning!" Kilpatrick declared.

"He'll be there, Jud, but shouldn't we pick it up a little to make sure we'll be there on time?" Davies queried.

"Not in this storm we can't," Kilpatrick admitted. As the contingent moved past Ashland Station, they began to be slowed down by occasional bushwackers and makeshift barricades manned by snipers who fired, then disappeared into the pines and brush.

In spite of the periodic delays, the men rode quietly and miserably, trying like seasoned troopers to catch some sleep in the saddle whenever possible. They were dog tired, wet, and cold. The periodic attacks from the scattered militia and civilians who posed opposition were not as punishing as the driving, slashing, stings of the rain on their hands and faces.

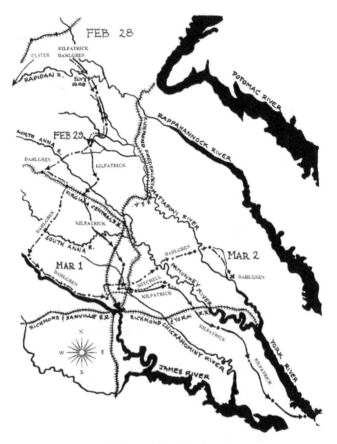

Richmond Raid Routes

Shortly after dawn on March 1, Dahlgren's men reached the Kanawa Canal of the James River, which was a twenty-one mile ride from Richmond. Dahlgren sent Captain Mitchell with about one hundred men, mostly from the 2nd New York, along the north side of the canal to destroy locks, canal boats, mills, granaries, and factories that lined the busy waterway. The group was to rejoin Dahlgren in the city after leaving a flaming trail behind them.

Now, Dahlgren had to depend on Martin to get him to the best spot to ford the James with the remaining four hundred riders. Where's the spot for us to cross?" Dahlgren asked Martin.

"Is rit ahaid suh … thar it be!" he shouted as he pointed to the spot.

Dahlgren looked at the not very promising location. The water was reddish brown with silt from the heavy rains. The heavy and deep current was swiftly driving all kinds of debris past the crossing point. Anxious to be rid of the men and be on his way, Martin urged the men into his trap, "Sheez riz up sum, so's youz prob'ly get wet sum."

Willing to risk his neck for the rest of the men, one of the sergeants started across with an, "I'll test it out for you Colonel!" He got no more than fifteen yards before his horse lost contact with the ground and attempted valiantly to swim against the raging current. The sergeant was swept off the horse and carried downstream flailing wildly in the frigid water. Troopers galloped downstream to head him off. They threw him a rope and managed to pull the soaked and shivering sergeant ashore.

"So this is the ideal spot," Dahlgren snarled at Martin. "This is where the men can almost walk across without getting wet?"

"It sho nuf is, I's pos'tiv. Not my faul' ifs da watah riz up!" Martin said defiantly.

"That water's got to be at least ten feet deep, and, judging from the past high water marks on the trees and the banks, we never would have made it across here even if it hadn't rained! Martin, you're a goddamn liar!" Dahlgren snapped, getting more frustrated and angry at being taken in by this treachery, knowing that the entire raid depended on Martin getting his men safely across the canal.

In an effort to bluff Martin into either telling him the true best spot to cross or to admit his guilt, Dahlgren ordered the corporal to bring the rope he had used to pull the Sergeant from a sure death in the river.

"Youz aint gonna hangs me, I knows it. I'z dun my job rit fo' you," Martin said a little less defiantly.

"You mean you did your job on us," Dahlgren corrected, irritated by the traitor's attitude. "Hang him!" he added with authority.

Martin, seeing the Colonel meant to carry out his threat, started to run for the safety of the woods which he knew would prevent the horses from following and allow him to escape. Three riders chased and pounced on the fleeing man just as he got to the wood's edge. They held Martin's struggling body as the rope was fashioned into a hangman's noose, placed around his neck, and thrown over a nearby tree limb.

He screamed, "Don' hangs me, pleez, I sorra wat I dun! I need' da money bad. Dey beats me if'n I don' do wat de tells me! Der's no place dat yo' kin cross dat riv'r!"

"Proceed Corporal," Dahlgren said with cool contempt. Several officers protested the hanging, promising to make a full report of the incident when they returned from the raid; other officers agreed with the Colonel's action.

Furious that they would not be able to cross the River and feeling caught in the web of his officer's disagreement, Dahlgren sought to rally support for his "swift justice" decision. He turned to the officers, "Gentlemen, do you realize what this man's treachery means to the achievement of our mission? His act of deception has condemned ten thousand of our brothers in uniform to remain in a living hell on Belle Isle.

"Many of them that we could have saved this day will die ... about a hundred a week! This entire mission's success might just have been wiped out because of this one individual's betrayal! When you weigh the cost in human lives of this traitorous crime against the punishment, you'll see it's entirely fitting. Remember what they did to our man Webster!"

There was a long moment of silence as the officers weighed his words. Feeling he had made his point, Dahlgren broke the silence and gave the fatal command, "Hang him! Hang the bastard now!" This time there was no opposition, and the men hoisted the struggling Martin in the air. He struggled and gasped for air for a few minutes as the men looked on in horror at their first hanging. Then, the body went limp.

Just then, a rider was brought in by two of the point men." Colonel, this man says he has an urgent message for you."

The rider asked, "Are you Colonel Dahlgren?"

"Yes, who are you, and what is your message?" Dahlgren replied.

"Colonel, I'm Captain Paul Silman, 1st Division Cavalry Corps, Army of the Potomac on special assignment from the Bureau of Military Intelligence in Washington. I just came from a meeting with our top agent in Richmond to tell you that your Negro guide, Martin Robinson, has been paid by the Rebels to prevent you from successfully crossing the river and to cost you as many men's lives as he can. He is a traitor!"

"You mean he was a traitor," Dahlgren corrected, pointing to the lifeless body hanging from the tree.

The officers who had protested the hanging and heard the Captain's pronouncement were now silent and felt somewhat relieved. Dahlgren asked the Captain, "And what is the situation between here and Richmond?" As Paul was about to answer, they heard the sound of big guns.

"It's Kilpatrick ... give'em hell. We'll be there soon to pitch in!" someone hollered.

"Wait," said Dahlgren, as he listened more carefully, "we only brought six guns, and there were more than twenty firing!"

The Captain interrupted, "That's another thing I want to tell you. The Rebels know you're coming, and General Custis Lee's Richmond City Battalion has prepared a 'welcoming committee' for you. They know most of the details of the raid, so the chances of freeing the prisoners on Belle Isle are nil. Libby is also too risky, because the protective fortifications on Brook Turnpike are now heavily manned by regulars, thus freeing much of the Home Guard to block off the western and southern approaches to the city.

"Even to wait for the protection of darkness to make an attack would be a mistake. They have men posted all over the city, and one man, hiding in the dark behind the cover of a solid wooden fence, is worth ten on horses in the open street," Paul advised.

After mulling over the Captain's information, Dahlgren decided to ride toward Richmond, join up with Mitchell's men, and test the strength and resolve of the old men, boys, clerks, and bookkeepers. The young Colonel felt that he didn't come all this way without getting some satisfaction; at least, he would not leave without trying. He also dispatched five men to tell Kilpatrick that they would not be able to attack Richmond until dusk. Dahlgren never saw the men again, nor did Kilpatrick, as they were captured after going only one mile on their assignment.

Five miles outside the city, Dahlgren's men encountered a volley of fire discharged from a clump of bushes. This same sequence was repeated about every half mile until Dahlgren's men ran into the most punishing concentrated fire about two and a half miles from the city.

Dahlgren ordered a cessation of hostilities and a strategic retreat northward, realizing that the prisoner rescue opportunity of the mission had been lost. If only they could still damage or destroy the Tredegar Iron Works, the grain mills, and the Armory, their efforts would not have been totally in vain. But, he realized that to do so, he would be making his men easy prey for the enemy. For this reason, he ordered the abort order in the form of a retreat.

Captain Mitchell, whom Dahlgren had sent ahead with one hundred men to cause as much destruction as possible on the northern side of the canal, came to the same conclusion earlier. Mitchell led his group north, away from the city, toward Hungary Station, which was the agreed upon rallying point in the event things went wrong. Mitchell's contingent eventually linked up with Kilpatrick's bivouacking troops near the hamlet of Mechanicsville.

The ill-fated raid ran into more bad luck … once again, it was the weather. A storm of mixed snow and stinging sleet lashed out without mercy at the weary men and horses. Nothing destroys the spirit of men more than to be totally, and continually, at the mercy of that over which they have no control.

Kilpatrick, who had arrived and taken a position on time facing the protective five-mile breastworks on Brook Turnpike, waited for Dahlgren's rocket signal. It never came. Still not certain of Dahlgren's position, he ordered General Henry Davies, Jr. to "go in and flush them out." The area in front of the breastworks was wide open for hundreds of muddy yards on both sides of the road as it approached the man-made barricade. The mud slowed the horses' charge to an unsteady trot and, with no shelter from enemy fire, the situation looked bleak.

A few men parried on the left, while a small group tested the right. Accurate musket fire and a few artillery rounds halted the initial attempts. As the number of men attacking increased, so did the response from behind the breastworks. It was a hopeless sacrifice of the men. The enemy fire appeared not like that of inexperienced clerks and bookkeepers, but of seasoned veterans manning the twenty artillery pieces and hundreds of muskets. All attempts to mount an attack were easily repelled and fresh Rebel reinforcements appeared to be arriving continually.

Now, Kilpatrick had a decision to make. Should he hold onto his dream of the conquest of Richmond, which included the capture of Jeff Davis and his henchmen, of ending the war, and returning home to "hero" status; and then to the Presidency itself? But, at what cost in bloodshed? The reality was that he had very poor battlefield position and conditions, the Rebels had clear superiority in numbers of Secesh troops and firepower, his men and their mounts were bone weary from their grueling trip … the dream painfully faded from his view.

It was now beginning to get dark, and the General was close to his decision. He thought, "After all, we did accomplish a lot on this raid. We've destroyed an important rail link, put a good scare into the Rebs' capital, and have suffered relatively few casualties. To continue would only mean added bloodshed for his forces. Dammit, I was where I was supposed to be. Where the hell was Dahlgren?"

His mind made up Kilpatrick sent orders to his commanders to swing north falling back on the main column to begin the short ride to the far side of the Chickahominy River to rest for the night.

CHAPTER 27

Arrest & Questioning

As Captain Silman was traveling with Dahlgren and his men, he worried about Elizabeth. Upon Dahlgren's rocket signal, she was supposed to assist the plantation workers and other loyalists, inside and outside the Confederate government, with the attack on Libby. In the event that Paul failed to reach Dahlgren in time to prevent Martin from negating that part of the raid Elizabeth's had an alternative plan. It was to have Nelson, along with Palmer the grocer, set off an explosion at the State Armory that would signal the plan inside the city to action. As part of the plan, the officers in Libby were to be told that upon hearing the explosion, to be ready to direct the activities of the thousands of released prisoners.

However, the notification of the officers in Libby had a major obstacle. Winder had issued a new temporary order forbidding entrance to any of the prisons during the current "emergency period." Somehow, someone had to get word to the trusted men in Libby about their responsibilities upon hearing the signal. There was no one Elizabeth dared send who knew which of the prisoners could be trusted and which were informants; so, once again, she decided to take the risk herself. Since it was Sunday, Elizabeth decided to take her bible with her to the prison and say, as a cover story, that she wanted to "read to the men from the Good Book on the Sabbath." Upon her arrival, she was promptly arrested and taken to Detective New's counter-intelligence office.

For some time, it had been the deadly dance between "the spider and the fly." Now, the fly was firmly snared in the spider's web! At last, New could interrogate the prey he had stalked for so long. He suspected that with the imminence of the raid and the planned liberation of the prisoners that she would somehow be involved. He believed that her amateurish participation might create a blunder as the time for the raid grew near.

New wasted no time. He told her he wanted every detail she knew about the raid, its timing, the names of all the parties involved, and a full confession from her about all her traitorous activities, past and present.

He questioned, probed, baited, badgered, cajoled, accused, shouted, and threatened ... with no results. He could not get her to admit to any impropriety, to make a slip, or change her story. After three hours, New was frustrated, exhausted, angry, and impatient at his fruitless attempts to get the results he wanted.

Elizabeth had answered that she could not expect a non-Christian like him to understand the value of spiritual nourishment. She knew that if New pressed her case, she would find more understanding and sympathetic ears by pleading the purpose of her visit to the devoted churchgoer, Jeff Davis.

"Who sent you to Libby today? I want the name of the man, or men, who tells you what to do, where to go, and what they're up to … was it Botts?"

"I have told you that I was sent by God," she said softly.

New persisted by asking her if she knew "this person" or "that person;" if they were the ones that sent her, and what was their message?

Elizabeth now changed to her next defense—a good offense. She suddenly lashed out at him in a convincing show of temper. She accused New of being a "parasitic leech, petty blackmailer, and a Southern imposter who preyed on the unsuspecting, innocent, law abiding, tax paying, legitimate citizens of the city."

Elizabeth continued, "And, General Winder has promised to sweep the city clean of your sort. All I have to do is report your uncalled-for attacks upon myself this day, and you will be unemployed, if not a guest of Castle Thunder!"

New almost laughed at her feigned audacity until he realized that she had learned more from him than he of her.

Elizabeth pressed further, "If I am held here much longer, my mother will be inquiring to General Winder of my whereabouts. The General will track me down, and when I am found, I will bring the wrath of every official in the Confederate government down on your worthless head."

Not to be intimidated or sidetracked, New counterattacked. "I'll just wait until they find you before I worry about that … and it may be a long wait. That is entirely up to you. If you answer my questions now, it will be over quickly. If you refuse, I'll put you behind bars upstairs until you are ready."

Beginning to be concerned about her ability to fulfill her assorted roles in the raid, she tried another approach to gain her release, "My mother's health is very delicate. If she has an attack over this insulting arrest, I shall hold you responsible and accuse you of murder. Do you hear me … I said murder! There's no other way about it."

"Why don't you save the dramatics for someone who appreciates theatre? I don't."

"Oh, so you don't think my mother is ill?"

"If you care about her so much, why don't you answer my questions? Then you can go home and hold the 'old biddy's' hands," New added, showing his frustration.

"You are a disrespectful lout, and I have answered all your questions. It's just that you have some paranoid delusions probably left over from your childhood, that keep you from accepting them," she fired back.

New's irritation was getting the best of him, and he wanted to take time to mull over everything that had transpired to see if she had given him any openings to explore. He led her upstairs, leaving her with a huge, mean-looking, ox of a female guard to watch over her. As he was leaving, he warned Elizabeth, "You will remain here until you are ready to answer my questions to my satisfaction or until it's over."

"What's over?" Elizabeth asked, feigning puzzlement.

"What you went to Libby about; the escape, the raid. You know damn well what I'm talking about," he bellowed. He watched her face for the slightest indication of a surprised reaction at either his or her knowledge of the raid, but she revealed nothing. He barked to himself, "Dammit! She's as guilty as sin and as slippery as an eel, this woman. But, I'm not finished yet!"

To buy more time, and to cover himself in case things didn't work out the way he wanted, New scribbled and sent a hurried note to Captain Gibbs requesting him to report to his office immediately. Upon Gibbs' arrival, New explained that he had Miss Van Lew in custody and instructed Gibbs not to inform the Van Lew family as to her whereabouts. The captain reminded New that he was a military officer and didn't take orders from civilians and, in fact, he "was duty bound to report the entire conversation to General Winder."

New said that he had proof that Elizabeth, her mother and Mary Bowser were all spies in order to influence Gibbs to cooperate with his needed stall for time. Gibbs, astonished, and taken in by New's bogus "proof" allegations, returned to the Van Lew home prepared to follow instructions—and to pass on his fear to his wife.

As Elizabeth lay on her prison bed, she reviewed the situation. "If everyone knows about the raid's plans, they will fortify the Brook Turnpike earthworks and be on the alert, undoubtedly, doubling or tripling the number of guards at the prisons. It's even more imperative that Paul Silman gets through to Dahlgren. He has to; he must!" And, with Paul's face so clear in her mind and exhausted from the interrogation, she fell asleep, dreaming of the two of them—alone—together, and far away from the war.

When Captain Gibbs arrived back at the Van Lew home, he related to the mother while at dinner, that Miss Van Lew had stopped by his office. And, as she was leaving the prison, had asked him to tell her family that she would not be home until quite late ... if at all. She said she would be staying with a friend who was quite ill, and that they shouldn't worry about her absence. Mrs. Gibbs believed the captain, but not Mrs. Van Lew, Mary, or Nelson. They had seen the number of men surrounding the house and knew something was wrong, but they had no choice but to wait and see what happened next.

Elizabeth was awakened on the morning of the 29th of February by the voice of Captain and Mrs. Gibbs speaking with Detective New. "I searched her room as you requested, but I didn't find anything of significance," the Captain said in a most cooperative manner.

"I wish I had been warned earlier, but I did add a few names to your list," Mrs. Gibbs chimed in.

"Good work," New praised. "We'll put our best surveillance men on them until we get the proof we're after. By the time Winder finds out, we'll have all the proof we need to hang the witch and her warlocks," New relished.

"Do you plan to try Miss Van Lew first?" Gibbs inquired of New.

"No, not until we get the entire network. We'll let one lead us to the next, and so on. For now, the entire household, except for you two, are under 'house arrest.'"

Elizabeth heard their footsteps fade away. Then a fresh, louder set was heard on the stairs leading to her bedside where they stopped. She kept her eyes closed and controlled the evenness of her breathing to give the impression she was still asleep.

New pulled up a chair and began to speak in a softer, more empathetic tone. "I know you have been listening, Miss Van Lew. I just wanted to tell you I've come to give you a reasonable offer. You can think it over and give me your response when you are ready.

"I know why you have been reluctant to provide me with the names of your superiors. You don't want to hurt others; that's your Christian training. You've probably carried a message or two, maybe sheltered a prisoner, and found yourself caught up in the web. You didn't know how to get yourself out of it gracefully. Isn't that pretty much what happened? All you need do is give me the names of the men who got you involved in this mess, and I'll give you and your mother safe passage to Butler."

Elizabeth almost reacted to the suggestion but controlled the urge to sneer. New continued, "If there is to be a prison escape from Libby, you had better tell me now. You will be saving a lot of lives. For your information, Libby is mined. Libby and everyone in, or near it, will be blown to pieces if anyone tries another escape. In addition, Belle Isle now has many cannons aimed at it, all the time, in the event they try to attempt an escape."

He waited and, as he watched, a barely perceptible bead of perspiration formed on her upper lip at the news of Libby being mined. A reaction! New was ecstatic but stifled his urge to react because he felt she was about ready to crack. He decided to let her stew for awhile. He figured that after she had time to mull things over, she would see the futility of her silence and tell him everything he wanted to know. "Think it over, I'll be back in one-half hour."

When New returned, Elizabeth appeared delirious. She screamed at the top of her lungs, thrashed about so much that he called for the female guard to hold her down. Her flesh seemed fiery hot, and she was gasping for air. New could make no sense out of her words. Not wanting to be held responsible for any illness to her, he summoned a hospital doctor to calm her down. When the doctor arrived, Elizabeth fought off his hands so frantically that he was unable to examine her. He recommended that New call her family doctor, which would know her medical history, to give her the appropriate medicine to calm her, before there were grave consequences.

New glared at Elizabeth, sensing her slipping through his fingers once again just when he was so close to having the evidence needed to prove her guilt. But, he was not willing to have her die here and now. That would be cheating him of the chance to expose and sentence her publicly ... and reaping the reward of revenge on Elizabeth and Winder! Her death now would give Winder just the amount of ammunition he had been looking for to punish his "maverick subordinate."

New grappled with the positives and negatives of calling for her doctor, and thought to himself, "Maybe, just maybe, her doctor is part of the conspiracy! Wouldn't that be nice! If the doctor comes here, no doubt she'll give him a message to take to their leader. I'll have him followed and when he delivers the message, I'll be able to nab the whole ring ... Yes! I'll get you one way or the other 'Miss Van Shrew!'" he vowed to himself in confident ridicule.

Elizabeth awoke with the feel of a cool cloth on her forehead and, as she opened her eyes, she saw the concerned and friendly face of Dr. William Parker, Jr. who smiled and asked her how she felt. Elizabeth saw New standing behind William and although she wanted to respond, she dared not. Sensing the predicament in her eyes, William proceeded to examine her by thumping with two fingers on the ribs below her heart. He then moved his head and body close to listen to her heart, blocking New's view of her face. Without moving a muscle on her face, Elizabeth whispered so faintly in William's ear that she was not sure if he heard her. William straightened up and told New that he must administer a sedative to calm Miss Van Lew's irregular heart beat.

"Do it then, Doctor." New obliged.

"I must have water." he told New. The detective sensing that this was the moment that Elizabeth needed to give her accomplice the secret message, walked to the door and called for the female guard to bring some water. In those few precious seconds, Elizabeth whispered the rest of her message. William administered the sedative and advised her, "Not to get excited, but to rest," in a voice loud enough for New to hear. Weakened from lack of food and the effects of the sedative, she closed her eyes and slowly slipped into a deep sleep.

New asked, "Doctor Parker, exactly what's wrong with her?"

"She's had a weak heart for some time. Due to overexertion and lack of nourishment for the past few weeks that condition has worsened. How long has she been here?"

"Since yesterday."

Parker continued, "And what has she eaten?"

"Nothing," New said defiantly, "She didn't ask for anything!"

Doctor Parker stared at New with disbelief and a bit of anger as New smirked.

"You are aware that her father died at a young age from such a condition, so it looks as if it must run in the family," the doctor said gravely.

"But, there is really no immediate danger, is there?" New quizzed.

"Yes there is. I hope you have good reason to hold her here. She could go at any moment."

New regretted asking the question. He thought, "What else would an accomplice say?"

"What if I were to send her home and confine her to her house?" New suggested.

William said to reassure New, "Her illness will confine her to her home for weeks," and then he added the coup de grace, "if she recovers at all."

New mulled this one over in his mind, and concluded to himself, "Alright then, I'll send her home. Even if she gives messages to her servants to deliver, none of them can leave the house. They're all prisoners there now. And you, Doctor Parker, will lead me to the rest of your dirty little band of Yankee-loving traitors!"

When safely in his carriage, Doctor Parker hastily scrawled a note and rolled it into a tiny ball as he headed for home. Along the way, William passed his favorite newsboy, young Charles Phillips, and quickly tossed the tiny paper ball toward him. Phillips recognized the doctor's carriage as it approached and had a folded newspaper ready to hand to him.

The alert newsboy had also noticed another carriage following the doctor with two strange men in it. Now he knew why Doctor Parker's carriage did not stop for his paper, and why the doctor put his finger to his lips. Phillips had seen the tiny paper ball thrown into the street toward his feet. He waited until both carriages were out of sight, then stooped to pick it up and nonchalantly put it into his pocket. Making sure he was not being observed, young Charles went into a nearby alley, opened up the paper ball, and read its contents. Within one hour, everyone was warned not to leave their homes this day and night and that Libby Prison was mined.

Tuesday morning, the first day of March 1864, found New reviewing the reports of his surveillance teams. No one left the Van Lew estate with the exception of Captain Gibbs who went to his place of duty. The doctor went to homes of people who had legitimate illnesses and perfect political health, and then he spent the rest of the evening at home with his family. Mary Bowser had tried to leave the Van Lew property to serve at a small dinner party at the Davis home, which they were hosting. She was refused exit and her story verified.

"Damn!" New exploded, "Despite every precaution and a suffocating blanket of surveillance … nothing! The guilty parties must have been warned, but how?"

Just then, his thoughts were interrupted by the sound of Kilpatrick's guns. "Damn, the raid has begun. I'd better go to Libby to tell Gibbs about the mines." After being informed about the explosives, Gibbs decided to tell the prisoners about them, since it would serve as a powerful deterrent to any revolt attempt by them during the fighting … and he was afraid he might be in the building when they went off. He immediately rushed to notify the senior Federal officer prisoners about the mines. The guards snickered to each other as he passed, "That's the fastest I ever saw the Captain move."

What Gibbs didn't know, was that the prisoners had been meeting and discussing plans for a revolt at the very moment they heard the guns. Upon hearing about the mines, however, they dejectedly abandoned the idea, deciding to wait until Kilpatrick's arrival and liberation.

Meanwhile, General Winder was anxiously and angrily searching through his desk for the list of auxiliary guards, cursing New for scattering all of his men around the city on some damn foolish surveillance activity. "He's probably on the damned Yankee payroll, the miserable dog!" Frustrated at not finding the lists, he stormed out fuming and continued his litany of profane opinions of New, swearing vengeance.

Just after dark that same day, Mary took a tray of hot soup up to Elizabeth's room. When she opened the door, she was stunned. There was Elizabeth, out of bed in her countrywoman's clothing rummaging around for a matching, warm outer garment to protect her from the storm. "Listen," she said to Mary, "Firing in the west. It's Dahlgren coming to release the prisoners on Belle Isle. I must warn him about the guns that will annihilate them all."

Mary put the tray down, closed the door, and pleaded with Elizabeth, "Get those clothes off before someone comes and sees you in them."

"Mary, I must go and warn them of the cannons!" Elizabeth insisted, trying to pass by Mary on the way to the door.

"Are you out of your head, Miss Liz? You're still sick and weak and the house is surrounded." Elizabeth struggled with Mary who was younger, taller, heavier, and healthier.

"Don't tell me I can't go. I can, and I will."

"And what if you're caught and what of your mother and the rest of us? It's Castle Thunder and the kind of torture that would force even an innocent man to confess. Do you want that for your mother? If the questioning, the horrible conditions, or the prisoners don't kill her, the rope certainly would!" Mary said sternly.

"There's always that risk for us. We've always known what the penalty would be if we were caught," Elizabeth said calmly.

"You're right. I'm not speaking about you or myself right now. I'm speaking about my daddy and your mother. Although your mother has not done all that we have, her sentence would be the same. Would you want that on your conscience?"

"No, and I don't want the lives of the raiders and the prisoners on Belle Isle on my conscience either." Although she hadn't mentioned his name, Elizabeth was also thinking of Captain Paul Silman. She knew that he would have joined up with Dahlgren's cavalry by now and would be with the men who were attempting to liberate Belle Isle. That meant he would be subject to the same fate as everyone else on Belle Isle. "Oh, Dear God!" she gasped.

Just then, the door slowly swung open. Both Elizabeth's and Mary's hearts began to pound. Was it Captain Gibbs, due home at this time, which would see Elizabeth in her disguise and report her to Detective New? Elizabeth would have a rough time explaining the getup, and Mary would also be arrested on the spot as an accomplice.

No, it was Elizabeth's frail looking mother. Mrs. Van Lew had been awakened by their discussion and came to check on her daughter's condition. She, too, was startled to see Elizabeth out of bed, and she quickly closed the door behind her. Mary's words about the possibility of the imprisonment, or worse, for her mother were still echoing in Elizabeth's head. The thought of being the cause of such a fate to her wonderful mother pained Elizabeth deeply. She rushed to her mother and embraced her, long and tenderly, trying not to let her mother see the tears.

"Elizabeth, you mustn't go out in this weather in your weakened condition," the mother admonished.

"That's what I've been trying to tell her; especially with the house being watched from all sides," Mary added.

"It's all part of God's purpose, child. None of anyone's suffering is lost; not ours, not the prisoners, the soldiers, the slaves …"

Just then, the front door slammed shut, and the sound of military boots was heard coming up the stairs toward Elizabeth's room. It was Captain Gibbs coming up to check on Elizabeth so that he could report back to New. There was a frantic scramble to remove the countrywoman clothing, but there was not enough time. Instead, they put Elizabeth's long nightdress over the other clothing and tucked her into bed. The captain knocked on the door and, when invited in, entered. Elizabeth managed a weak smile for him as Mrs. Van Lew and Mary acted out their "bedside vigil" roles.

"I'm delighted to see you awake and recovering, Miss Elizabeth. General Winder is very concerned about your welfare and plans to stop by tomorrow. He's anxious to hear the complete details of what happened," the captain stated gallantly. Mrs. Van Lew thanked him for conveying the general's wishes and asked him if he would be kind enough to offer his arm while escorting her to her room. She added, "Elizabeth needs the rest and nourishment now more than company."

As Mary spooned soup to her frail and old-looking friend and collaborator, the weak and spent Elizabeth asked, "Do you think the raid will succeed, Mary?"

"I don't know, Miss Liz. If it had come as a surprise, and with enough men … yes! It sure was worth a try … and could save a lot of suffering and bloodshed on both sides. Like your mother said, 'It's in God's hands.' You should try to get some sleep now. Remember that there are a lot of people who are depending on you. It won't do for you to be ill." Mary said encouragingly.

"Yes, you're right, Mary, and I thank you for those comforting words. I must think of what to tell Winder tomorrow. I would like to take advantage of the opportunity to play Winder against New to get some relief from New's meddling.

CHAPTER 28

Winder & New: The Showdown

Around noontime, General and Mrs. Winder called at the Van Lew residence. The general was infuriated to find his way blocked by some of his own men. The day before, Captain Gibbs had confessed to him of New's plot and Winder immediately countermanded New's orders. The men were instructed to return to their posts at once to receive their new assignments. Here it was a day later, and the men were still posted at the Van Lew home. Winder's order was totally ignored! "Damn that New. Who the hell does he think he is, and who the hell is giving him his orders, backing him up, and making him think he's going to get away with this insubordination! Well, I came here to get some ammunition to use against the bastard and, by God, I'll use it!"

Mary answered the General's knock. She immediately proceeded to apologize to Mrs. Winder for being unable to serve at the Davis' reception and begged Mrs. Winder to relay her apology to Mrs. Davis since she was still a prisoner and unable to do it herself. The general replied, "That is no longer so. I have dismissed the guards from their duties here, and they will not be back."

Just then, Elizabeth came slowly and unsteadily down the stairs. She was the epitome of poor health; deathly pale, with dark hollows under her eyes, hair that looked as if it had been abused by the tossing and turning of a fitful night's sleep. Her shoulders were slouched and her facial expression was that of one who has been pushed to the brink of sanity.

Mary took Elizabeth's arm and escorted everyone into the parlor. The general apologized for disturbing Elizabeth before her ordeal was through, but explained that he wanted to resolve the matter as expeditiously as possible. He declared that New was solely responsible for her incarceration and interrogation and, in his opinion, was "an enemy of the country and our cause. I need your help in ridding us of the likes of him."

"When you were being held incommunicado, did New say anything about me; threats, accusations, proposals?"

"He spoke of you, but it was nothing but trash. Knowing you personally, I knew he was lying."

"What exactly did he say?" Winder pressed, eager for the ammunition he could use against New.

"It was not worth remembering. I put it out of my mind."

"You must try to recall it, Ma'am. Remember that we all depend on each other in this matter. If you help me, I can help you so that we can both rid ourselves of this nuisance."

"I don't think I understand what you mean."

"New accuses you of treason because of your humanitarian ministrations to the enemy prisoners. He says you are a Yankee spy. He charges you with being involved in every prison escape from Libby, every piece of treachery, sabotage, civil unrest, bribery of guards, and leaks of military information. He accuses you, and he blames me for protecting you. Take my word for it, I am all that stands between you and the severest punishment."

Feigning trying to remember, she cocked her head to one side and said hesitatingly. "He wanted me to ... told me I had better ..."

"Yes, yes, what did he want you to do?" Winder asked impatiently.

Suddenly, the door swung wide and there stood an angry-looking New. The men returning from guard duty on the house had told New of Winder's visit and countermanding of his orders. Furious and concerned about what Elizabeth might say, he thought it wise to be present at Winder's interrogation. Now, he confronted the two people in the world that he most detested.

Elizabeth shrieked, "Why are you here? What are you going to do to me now?"

"I'm only here to find out what you've said about me." New snapped.

"I've said nothing about you; nothing. Please don't torture me again!" Elizabeth pleaded pitifully. Mrs. Winder gasped, while the General's eyes turned icy with contempt.

"I never tortured you!" New shouted defensively, adding "Not that you don't deserve it!"

Elizabeth rose unsteadily to her feet. Her voice filled with fear and anger; her face livid with rage. "Not torture? You bound me to a bed, left me at the mercy of your guard, gave me no food for days, accused me of atrocities and threatened me with death! Why? Was it to explain away your inadequacies, or to mask your own involvement in the activities."

"You bitch! How dare you accuse me? Nice try, but no one here is buying your lies and accusations," New sputtered, trying in vain to convince those present of his innocence and Elizabeth's histrionics. Winder was well aware of New's methods, as he had heard accounts of his "questioning" of other detained innocent citizens.

New moved toward Elizabeth threateningly, but Mary jumped between them. "Leave her alone. Can't you see how ill you've already made her? Do you want to finish the job by beating her to death here and now?"

"Get out of my way 'darky' before I take the lash to you!" New threatened, raising his hand to strike Mary.

Elizabeth screamed, "No, No! If you must whip someone, let it be me …"

Just as New was about to strike Mary, Elizabeth's eyes rolled in her head, and she fainted to the floor.

The Winders both stared in disbelief at the turn of events. New glared at Mary who had bent over and was cradling the unconscious Elizabeth; his arm still poised to strike.

Abruptly, Mrs. Winder told Mary to have Nelson send for the doctor at once. The general regained his composure and ordered New to report to his office immediately and to wait there for him. New, anticipating the confrontation to come stared unblinkingly at the General. Torn between wanting to have it out right there and, at the same time, wanting to better prepare his rebuttal, decided to wait for the meeting in Winder's office. The disgruntled detective left, slamming the door behind him.

The Winders also left, but not before being assured that Elizabeth had been placed safely back in bed to await the doctor and expressing their sincere regrets for the unfortunate results their visit had brought.

New, while on his way to Winder's office, felt that he had better report to his secret benefactor, Judah P. Benjamin, before having it out with Winder. He went first to the office, then to the residence of the Secretary of State, but was unable to see him. New was beginning to feel "stonewalled."

Winder, at the same time, was concerned that New's unknown protector might have the President's ear, so he quickly headed for the Davis residence to present his account to the man who had selected him for his position. Mrs. Winder, who had accompanied her husband, explained to Varina Davis the reason for Mary's inability to appear at the dinner and then gave her a woman's point of view of the present situation.

CHAPTER 29

Exits, Capture, & Contraband

At five-thirty, the evening of March 2nd, Kilpatrick ordered his troops to make camp at Tunstall Station about twenty miles east of Richmond on the Richmond & York River Railroad's route to West Point.

Meanwhile, Dahlgren's soaked and miserable men, constantly besieged by sniper fire, wretched weather, and horrible road conditions, were fifteen miles away from the main force. They had crossed the Mattaponi River at Aylett's and headed for St. Stephens. With no hospitable place to make camp and the certainty that they would be sitting ducks in daylight, Dahlgren decided to keep moving. Many of the men and officers were taking turns sleeping in their saddles during the ride.

The column of men under Mitchell's command, who had gotten separated from Dahlgren's, was now part of Kilpatrick's forces. This main body of the raiding party, temporarily camped for the evening, was down to thirty-three hundred men.

Suddenly, the woods near the campsite came alive with the sound of musket fire from Hampton's Cavalry who had been ordered to dismount and attack on foot. The men rushed around in disarray, looking like moths circling around the giant bonfires built to warm them. In the firelight, they were easy targets, and many fell on the spot. A makeshift line of defense, ordered by Kilpatrick, provided cover so that regiment after regiment could escape into the night on the way to Williamsburg. Their hasty retreat cost them scores of good horses, food, equipment, and the dead and seriously wounded men they left behind. When the campsite had been completely evacuated, General Hampton himself rode in to witness his cavalry of less than three hundred men who were savoring their victory and gathering the spoils. They had routed a Federal contingent that outnumbered them by better than ten to one. He grinned and echoed his men. "Yes indeed, we whupped them good!"

At midnight, near the Mantapike Hill Crossroad, Dahlgren and his men ran into an ambush by Company H of the 9th Virginia Cavalry of the Army of Northern Virginia, led by Lieutenant James Pollard. Pollard had gotten word of Dahlgren's movements and had set up in the woods to wait for him.

After surviving countless ambushes, sniper attacks, miserable debilitating weather conditions, a betrayal, and treacherous road conditions, this would be the final crippling blow to Dahlgren's command. The four hundred men he had left the Richmond area with were now down to just eighty men. As he had done on every occasion, whether it was a charge or a retreat, Dahlgren was at the front leading his men. Thinking it just another attack of the "shoot and run" home guardsmen hiding in the pines, Dahlgren drew his Navy Colt .44 pistol and ordered the snipers to "Surrender!"

The response was a swift and terrible volley of flame and smoke from at least fifty weapons; all aimed at the lead riders with the best-looking horses. Dahlgren's horse whirled around at the flash and, almost instantaneously, the young leader was thrown from his saddle from the force of five balls ripping into his back.

He was dead before he landed face down in the mud. Many others were killed, wounded, or had their horses shot out from under them. Panic ensued as the men ran into and over each other on the dark and narrow road while attempting to pull back.

Captain Silman, who had been riding with the third group near the rear, had to constantly prod the men. "Come on men; close it up, don't straggle behind! The woods are full of Rebs; close it up!" Finally, he advanced toward the group that was under fire. Quickly assessing the situation, he realized the futility of attempting to go forward, and he headed for the fence between the road and a small clearing surrounded by trees. Removing the fence rails, Paul called to the men to assemble in the partially protected clearing.

The Major, who had now become the ranking officer, told the men that the situation was so serious that they were free to choose from several options for themselves. They could attempt to fight it out with the Rebs. But he was quick to point out that it was a poor choice, because they had only a few dozen rounds left between them.

The second choice was to try to pick their way through the countryside to the safety of Butler's command, about six hours away on horseback. The major told them that if they were to select this option, attempting it on horseback would make them easy targets for snipers. He said that he would assist the men with the second, and least hazardous option, by attempting to trick the Rebels into thinking that they were making a stand there by tethering all the horses together. The men could then leave on foot, in groups of four or five, spaced minutes apart.

He didn't mention the last option, which was to remain there waiting to be taken prisoner and join their fellow men in one of the horrible prisons they were sent to liberate and destroy. Unfortunately, this was the option the many sick and seriously wounded were forced to accept.

Paul took a group of four enlisted men and started out for Williamsburg. They crawled for about a half-mile till they were clear of the ambush area, then they stood and walked stealthily through the underbrush.

The weary and anxious men covered about a mile, when they heard the sound of someone running on the road toward them. They dashed into the bushes as the runner approached. As he passed in front of them, they heard him shouting, "I made it sweetheart; I'll be home to see you and our new baby!" The man from Dahlgren's emaciated force was so delirious with fever that he thought he was on the entrance road to Fortress Monroe. So relieved to have made it, and anxious to get inside the fort, he came out of the underbrush and began to run up the road.

Suddenly, several shots rang out. One hit the runner in the neck, silencing his shouts of joy, and he fell dead instantly. One of the other errant bullets struck Paul in the shoulder. Being fired at such close range, the velocity of the bullet sent it clean through his body. He was thrown back, bleeding profusely; in great pain, and unconscious. A small group of Hampton's Cavalry rode up to examine the dead runner. The dead "new father" was one of Dahlgren's seriously wounded men who were initially prepared to stay behind and be captured. But, after weighing his chances of survival in Belle Isle, decided to risk it all, in order to see his wife and their new son.

Just as the Rebels were leaving, Paul screamed, "No, Elizabeth, don't go!" Hearing his scream, the cavalrymen returned and immediately set upon the men, taking them all prisoners.

Meanwhile, the scavengers were claiming their spoils of war from the dead bodies on the Mantapike Turnpike, clothing, boots, money, watches, tobacco, weapons; anything of service or value. From Dahlgren, they took his billfold full of greenbacks, his expensive leather holster and revolver, his uniform, and the fine wooden leg that would bring a good price. When they couldn't get the ring off the middle finger of his left hand, they cut off the finger to acquire the valuable diamond ring. In addition, they also seized his dispatch case that held a notebook, ink, pens, papers, maps, and blank 3rd Cavalry stationery. The valuables were kept and the dispatch case was forwarded immediately to Richmond. A shallow, muddy grave was dug, and Dahlgren's body was unceremoniously dumped in and covered over.

Back in Richmond, New entered Winder's office prepared for the general's diatribe. They glared at each other for a moment, then Winder began, "You have been a thorn in my side for far too long. So, what do you do to a thorn? Very simple, you remove it. You're fired!"

New had been thinking of this moment for far too long to go down without a fight. This was his opportunity to tell Winder exactly what he thought of him.

He countered with, "And what about the glory you stole from me when I nabbed Webster and his spy ring? Was I a thorn then?"

"That was then! What the hell have you done lately? You've misappropriated manpower making me look bad with Davis during a crisis. You've harassed innocent citizens of the city, and I got blamed for that. You've wasted the Grand Jury's time hearing cases based on trumped-up charges for which you have only hearsay and rumors, rather than substantiated evidence. You've ignored my orders. In short, you are the most disreputable and unmanageable subordinate I ever had to put up with!" Winder bellowed.

Matching Winder's escalating intensity and volume, New snarled smugly, "Well, of course, most of your subordinates are members of your own family. And, what the hell have you done lately? You sit there, day after day, on your pompous, fat ass while any self-respecting military officer would be out in the field fighting the enemy!"

Winder, momentarily stung by the nepotism and cowardice charges, quickly recovered. "Oh, really. Let me tell you something, you worthless skunk! I am responsible for more casualties to the enemy's ranks than any of our field commanders!"

Holding up a file, Winder continued his tirade, "Here are statistics of the number of Northern men already dead and, with the miserable food and living conditions, thousands more will die in just the next year from sickness, malnutrition, and exposure! Which general out there is causing those kinds of casualties on the enemy on a continually escalating basis?"

Only slightly beaten down by Winder's effective counter argument in defense of his military contributions to the cause, New attacked again, "You know, and I know, that the Van Lew home is the center of all the espionage activity in the city. What the hell is she doing for you that makes you defend and protect her?"

"You son of a bitch! Are you accusing me of something? Come on, let me hear your latest paranoid cock and bull story!"

"Weren't you the one who signed her original prison pass? Weren't you the one who had Dr. Higginbotham imprisoned when he crossed her? Weren't you the one who was always telling me to lay off her? Haven't you been a dinner guest in her home? Who knows what lewd things the two of you do there alone in that big house with all those bedrooms!"

"You bastard; don't you dare insinuate that there was anything going on between us. Every time I dined at the Van Lew home, I went with my wife, and frequently there were other government officials or officers and their wives present. Both Mrs. and Miss Van Lew are citizens of long standing in this community.

They have strong Christian characters, high intellect, and a very generous nature. Their reputations are above reproach.

"You have insulted them, defiled their home, stolen family heirlooms and other irreplaceable valuables, harassed and almost murdered one or both of them. Only time will tell. If Miss Van Lew doesn't make it, the shock may kill her mother too."

"Come on! You're a blind old fool if you were taken in by her amateur theatrics!"

"I know Miss Van Lew a hell of a lot better than you do, and I say she is goddamn sick!"

"You're right in saying you know her better than I do. That's been the problem all along," New said, continuing his sarcastic, fabricated goad at Winder's carnal impropriety.

"You son of a bitch! I'll kill you!" exploded Winder who, whatever he had been accused of, had never been unfaithful to his wife. He came up off his chair and around the desk. New backed away just as the door opened, and Cashmeyer told him that Secretary Benjamin wanted to see him at once in his office.

Winder glared at New; his face crimson with rage, his meaty fists balled to strike. "I'll finish with you later!" he vowed while putting on his hat.

Anticipating the result of Winder's meeting, New said snidely, "Maybe you will, and maybe you won't," and beat the General to the door.

Secretary Benjamin greeted Winder with unusual cordiality, a rare occurrence since he had never displayed any signs of friendship before in any of their dealings. Benjamin hated Winder's coarseness, and Winder hated Benjamin's arrogance.

"General, let me come right to the point. We are sending more and more of our prisoners south and need direct, on-the-spot supervision of those activities. You already have two sons handling various aspects of the prisons, and you work well with them. Therefore, President Davis has instructed me to retain you as the Commanding Officer of all the Confederacy's prisons and to move you and Mrs. Winder south with all courtesies and dispatch."

"But what about my Provost Marshall's duties?" Winder inquired.

Judah P. Benjamin

"Those will be handled by a replacement officer," Benjamin said without emotion.

"Do I have any say or choice in the matter?" Winder asked.

"Yes. If you don't accept the post, you will be assigned to serve in Lee's Army in the field of battle." Benjamin said provocatively.

Winder thought, "I'd rather walk into the crater of a volcano than to serve in Lee's Army. I'd have about the same chance for survival!" Winder asked dolefully, "When do you want me to head south?"

"At once. And, one thing more, General. As of this moment, all the detectives are to take their orders from me until your replacement is announced. Is that clear?"

"Very!" Winder said in an equally brusque tone. Winder now knew the source of New's protection—Secretary Benjamin! He thought to himself, "Benjamin's never liked me, and now he had a legitimate excuse to get me out of Richmond. All along he was the one who prodded New to make me look bad. And now, I am the one to be shipped out!"

"That will be all, General. Have a pleasant trip." Benjamin said gleefully, dismissing Winder.

As the portly General walked out, resigned to his fate, he was baffled by New's ability to resurrect himself after this latest screw up. How did he do it? I thought Davis backed me up on firing him?"

What Winder did not know was that New finally got to see Benjamin in his office earlier in the day trying to avoid being fired. Benjamin was uninterested in saving him this time, and it did look like New was finished in Richmond. While New was with Benjamin, an officer brought in a muddy attaché case and told Benjamin, "It's the Yankee Colonel's papers."

"Thank you, Lieutenant. I'll take them." and Benjamin emptied the contents on his desk and threw the case to the floor. He picked up the papers that appeared to be Dahlgren's marching orders and began to read them aloud oblivious to the fact that New was still in the room.

In desperation, New's mind was racing for ideas to save himself. He was now out of "protection" and didn't have a single friend to whom he could turn. He noticed the blank 3rd Cavalry stationery and, as he listened to the Secretary read, he got a flash of devious inspiration. New waited until Benjamin read the name of the general who signed the orders before he spoke.

"Mr. Secretary, I have an idea I think you'll like." New said enthusiastically.

Benjamin looked up startled, "You still here? What's your idea? Make it fast and then leave!" He said impatiently.

New took a deep breath and began. "We have been trying to get the major European countries to come into the war on our side. What if we could make them think that we are more civilized and worthy of support than the enemy? Might that not carry some weight and sway them to our side?"

"Yes, it might; but what's your idea?" Benjamin asked again.

"What if the orders you just read were changed a little? Instead of 'liberate the city' it was changed to 'sack and burn the city.' And instead of 'capture the Confederacy's leaders' to 'capture and kill Jeff Davis and his cabinet;' that sort of stuff. Wouldn't that make the North look barbaric?"

"Hmm, Yes. I see what you mean, but that would entail rewriting the entire order and forging the Colonel's signature. The Yankees would immediately deny and negate the forgery," Benjamin said, "and the egg would be on our faces."

"True, if we forged the Colonel's name; but how could a dead man deny signing it? Who could say, even in Washington, that Dahlgren didn't write them himself? He'll never talk, and he is a high-ranking representative of the Washington military establishment."

Getting more and more interested, Benjamin asked, "And who do you propose will write the orders and sign them?"

"I will. I've always been good at copying!" New said eagerly sensing Benjamin's favorable reaction.

"Let me think it over, and I'll test the idea out on a few trusted people. If I get the approval, I want you available at all time. This would have to be done with the strictest secrecy and dispatch. You must not now or ever discuss this matter with another living soul. Do you understand?"

"Yes, sir. I'll never breathe a word, and I'll be in my office awaiting your instructions."

CHAPTER 30

A Corpse & A Document

A fired-up Benjamin headed straight for the office of President Davis. Benjamin, a lawyer by profession, used his most persuasive "closing argument to the jury" technique. He tied the "Dahlgren Richmond Raid Orders Plan" into the Confederacy's current support-seeking propaganda efforts, which extended into Canada, including the area in and around the Great Lakes region of the United States, and spread across the Atlantic to England and the rest of the European community.

Davis played "devil's advocate" at first, but the plan had such appeal that Benjamin eventually won him over. Benjamin reasoned that even if the North were to refute the document's authenticity and institute damage control measures, their credibility, at best, would be irreparably tarnished or, at the least, suspect.

New didn't have to wait very long. He was summoned back to Benjamin's office at seven o'clock that night. A guard was posted outside the door with strict orders that no one was to enter under any circumstances.

New was then given the blank 3rd Division Cavalry stationery and told to copy the style as closely as possible and not to make any mistakes, because they had a very limited supply of the blank stationery. New worked carefully and diligently, with Benjamin dictating the changes of wording he wanted. He finished in just over an hour, signing it:

"U. Dalhgren, Col. Comd."

Benjamin examined the wording of the document carefully, and, although New's copy was not identical in style, he rated the work as "a first-rate job, good enough to fool anyone who didn't have the original to compare it with."

Lucky for New that Benjamin was so concerned with the wording, as most

THE TRUE SIGNATURE

THE FORGED SIGNATURE

Dahlgren Signatures

lawyers would be; that he never noticed that Dahlgren's named was misspelled "Dalhgren."

Now, the original was torn into small pieces, burned, and the ashes beat into dust, to forever eradicate any evidence, or possible proof, of their deception.

The excited and pleased Benjamin told New to report back to work in the morning, reinstated to his previous detective position, but at a higher salary, and that he would be receiving his orders directly from the Secretary in the future. He also assured New that he would never see Winder again, and reminded him that he "must never reveal any details relating to what transpired that evening. Never!"

Benjamin proceeded to have the bogus document photocopied for wide dissemination. As expected, the document created a tidal wave of Pro-Confederacy sentiment. Further north, the document caused heartburn and embarrassment despite the Federal Government's immediate renunciation of the forgery.

But, there was enough skepticism surrounding the document's wording, and doubt about the South's ability to win the war, to still prevent the European powers, who feared reprisals by the United States, to come into the war on the side of the Confederacy. Hence, no large-scale military troop aid came from the powers in Europe or Canada as a result of the document. For all the publicity, heated debate, and volatile rhetoric in the press, the document had almost no impact on the course of the war.

Among the Confederate military, including Lee, who was told that the document was authentic, there was some skepticism and only a mild reaction.

Elizabeth wrote her reaction later in her *Occasional Journal*:

"Does not the whole thing tell of Benjamin, Confederate Congressman Louis T. Wigfall and, in short, the 'Southern Confederacy?' If this paper was genuine, it would have been preserved as our richest treasure and used, even now, to the prejudice of the whole North, and damning murder to the name and fame of Colonel Dahlgren ...

The people who could put powder under a building filled with helpless prisoners with the intention of launching them into eternity in certain contingencies, in a part of the city, too, thickly populated at the time, would scarcely scruple to manufacture mental power from the pocket of a dead prisoner to inflame their own people."

In Richmond, where the pro-government papers swallowed the bait, "hook, line and sinker," the reaction was predictable. The Richmond Examiner called for reprisals; the Confederate Secretary of War, James A. Seddon favored executing at least some of the captured raiders; and the Chief of Ordnance, Josiah Gorgas, recommended killing all the prisoners.

However, General Lee opposed any violent retribution against the soldiers fearing it might trigger retaliatory hangings, and he sent a formal letter of inquiry to Union Major General, George Meade. Meade investigated the entire planning and execution of the raid with all the senior officers involved especially General Kilpatrick. Along with Meade's response assuring Lee that the "burning and murdering" objectives written in the alleged "Dahlgren papers" had no official sanction, he sent an additional repudiation statement signed by General Kilpatrick.

Dahlgren's body was ordered to be recovered from its initial grave, the sloppy mud hole at the fork of the road where he fell, put into a wooden coffin, and brought to the York River train station to be held in a boxcar for public viewing.

The people, outraged by the newspaper comments of "barbaric, bloodthirsty robbers, thugs and rapists," formed a mob and stormed the train station to spit on Dahlgren's body and coffin, "that monument of infamy" and to teach their children to despise the hateful Yankees in perpetuity. There was even talk of taking all of the raid's captives out of prison and hanging them all as "war criminals."

Satisfied with the publicity and reactions they desired from the public display of Dahlgren's body, the youngest Colonel in the Union Army was given a burial not much better than a dog's in an unmarked grave under the highest secrecy. The Confederate leaders feared that his death and grave might become a rallying point for Union loyalists who would turn him into a martyr for their cause.

Elizabeth got word from her network of collaborators of their outrage at the indignities and desecration of the body of the unfortunate soldier who gave his life for their cause. She was told that the heart of every person loyal to the Union was stirred to its depths, and they were committed to discover the hidden grave and remove his honored dust to friendly care. To that end, Elizabeth became tenacious in her efforts to learn its location.

At that same time in Washington, President Lincoln shuffled his military "deck" in order to engineer the final crushing blow to the armies of the Confederacy. Tired of the exasperating past three years of "trial and error," Lincoln was ready to go with proven generals who fought—and who won! On March 9th, 1864, he promoted Ulysses S. Grant to the newly revived three-star rank of Lieutenant General and put him in charge of all the United States' Armies. The solitary previous holder of the rank was George Washington. The promotion ceremony was held in the White House in the presence of the Cabinet. Lincoln and Grant met for several hours afterward in private to discuss strategy. Later that evening, a gala ball was given at the White House in Grant's honor.

The next day, Grant began the job of reorganizing the Army of the Potomac by meeting with General George Meade. He joined Meade in the field and ordered him to pursue Lee, "Wherever Lee goes, you go," and he stayed with Meade to ensure that he did.

On the 11th of March, at Admiral Dahlgren's request, General Butler wrote to Colonel Ould asking that the body of the Admiral's son be returned by way of the Flag of Truce boat. He included five twenty-dollar gold pieces provided by the father, to properly prepare the body for burial. Butler added that he learned from the Richmond newspapers that "some circumstances of indignity and outrage had accompanied the death."

Admiral John Dahlgren

Meanwhile, Elizabeth's persistent labors to learn the secret location of Dahlgren's grave were rewarded. She learned the grave's location from F.W.E. Lohmann, another loyalist, who had discreetly questioned a Negro gravedigger at Oakwood Cemetery. The gravedigger said he had seen a four-mule team government wagon led by a soldier on horseback looking to and fro for any possible witnesses, bringing a wooden coffin for burial a little before midnight. When he saw the soldiers, he hid behind a small rise and watched as Major John Wilder Atkinson supervised the burial. He watched them bury the body on the eastern side of the cemetery where thousands of other Federal soldiers were buried in grassless graves. He said that the government always specified that the Federals were to be buried outside the regular burial grounds so that they wouldn't desecrate the ground hallowed by the Confederate dead.

He swore that it must be Dahlgren's grave because the government used soldiers to handle the burial instead of the usual private contractors and cemetery personnel. And, it was done in the middle of the night! As further evidence, he pointed out that the grave was at a right angle to all the other graves, there was no marker on the grave and no identity card was put in the cemetery office alphabetical file.

The next night, convinced by the evidence, Elizabeth rode out to the cemetery with the gravedigger and marked the grave with a stick. The exact location was near the entrance road, one foot from a stump.

When Colonel Ould completed the work he had been arranging for the next prisoner exchange, he started to act on Butler's request so that Dahlgren's body could be made part of the exchange. Ould was told to see Major John Wilder Atkinson of the 19th Artillery, who had led the secret burial detail on direct orders from Jeff Davis. Upon questioning, Atkinson told Ould that he was under strict orders never to reveal the grave's location. Ould was told to see the President, because he was the only one who could grant such permission.

However, before Ould got to see Davis and obtain his consent, and being unaware of Admiral Dahlgren's petition, Elizabeth and her loyalists took the matter into their own hands.

Once Elizabeth had confirmation of the Dahlgren's gravesite, she concocted a daring plan for his body's removal and relocation.

As the first step, one of the Lohmann brothers, Frederick W. E. Lohmann, a local builder and one of Elizabeth's ring of loyalists, walked into the office of Martin Meredith Lipscomb, a civilian burial contractor for both the Confederate and Federal dead in Richmond. Lohmann told Lipscomb what he planned to do and asked for his help. A cold shiver ran up and down Lipscomb's spine upon hearing of the plan to disinter the body and carry it through the Rebel lines. His fear was so great that he refused, but Lohmann persisted. He pleaded with Lipscomb to assist "for humanity's sake," insisting repeatedly that he would be performing a noble act.

Lohmann wasn't aware that Lipscomb was still angered that Dahlgren's burial had not been entrusted to him but was carried out by the government. The combination of hurt professional pride and Lohmann's humanitarian pleas overcame his fear of the extreme danger, and he agreed to assist.

Ten o'clock on the cold, gloomy, and rainy evening of April 5th found four men in a heavy wagon heading for Richmond's Oakwood Cemetery. The squish of the wagon's wheels in the mud and raindrops on the empty, creaky wagon were the only sounds heard through the low ground mist that blanketed the cemetery.

The men sat silent, alert, and nervous. The Negro man pointed to Elizabeth's "grave marker" and the wagon pulled up alongside. The two Lohmann brothers jumped off and began to dig. Lipscomb watched as the Negro stood to one side holding a lantern.

Repeatedly, the shovels pierced the wet earth and took away small amounts of the terrestrial barrier. In the distance, the barking of a dog could be heard. While nearby could be heard only the mumbling of prayers by the provider of the shaking light and the sucking sounds of the shovels pulling the soggy earth free. They had dug less than two feet when one of the shovels struck wood.

"This is it," they whispered.

"Keep digging," Lipscomb said nervously.

The pace of the digging quickened, and the coffin was fully exposed. "Lawd sav' me!" the Negro wailed.

Now, with the use of ropes, they pulled the coffin out of the grave and placed it on top of the dirt mound they had created.

"Pass me the light!" Lohmann whispered. On the lid, in black stenciled letters, they read "Ulric Dahlgren." Using a chisel, they pried it open and gasped as the face of the corpse stared at them.

"Look at his leg," Lipscomb directed. Lohmann ran his hand down under the blue military blanket and felt the amputated right leg "wanting below the knee." Assured that it was Dahlgren, they resealed the coffin and passed the light back to the Negro whose teeth had been chattering since the body was exposed. Dahlgren's wooden coffin was then loaded onto the wagon, covered with burlap sacks, and the empty hole refilled. They all climbed aboard and drove silently through the dismal night over rutted back roads near Chelsea Hill to the home of farmer William C. Rowley.

William C. Rowley

The thin, heavily bearded Rowley, lantern in hand, greeted the creaky wagon as it entered his front yard. "Miss Van Lew is in the seed house. You can take the coffin right in," he said calmly.

They carried the coffin in to Elizabeth, who rose from the wooden box she was sitting on. The lid was again pried open and the remains examined with gentle hands and tearful eyes. The body was in a perfect state of preservation except for the head. Here and there was a spot of mildew. The comeliness of the face was gone, but the features had a look of firmness and energy stamped on them.

Elizabeth clipped a lock of hair, which she would send to the young man's father, from the once handsome head. She then instructed the men to shave the body hairless to make it hard to recognize. When the poor job of barbering was completed, Lipscomb left to get the metal casket that Elizabeth had purchased. The Lohmanns escorted Elizabeth home while

Rowley sat alone through the night with the corpse. "A brave and honorable deed," Elizabeth called it.

With the metal casket safely hidden in the back of his wagon, Lipscomb returned to Rowley's home. The body was transferred to the metal coffin and sealed by Lipscomb with a substitute composition made by Lohmann, since putty was no longer available in Richmond. It was Lipscomb's suggestion that a layer of dirt be used to cover the coffin in the wagon, which was then surrounded and covered with twelve peach trees, packed in typical nursery fashion.

His necessary part of the plot safely completed, Lipscomb left, saying he was not willing to risk any further participation. Now, the body had to be taken on the last leg of its perilous journey through enemy pickets. The punishment for all the guilty parties in this escapade would be swift and severe, considering all the passion that had been aroused in Richmond over the "Dahlgren Document."

It was farmer Rowley who volunteered to make the journey alone. He would have to take the body over eleven heavily patrolled miles and through several Confederate picket lines, one of which was on the Brook Turnpike, the main road from Washington to Richmond. For that reason, it was the strongest and most secure post surrounding Richmond. The destination selected was Robert Orrick's farm, the home of another trusted loyalist, where, in accordance with Elizabeth's instructions, the body was to be safely buried until the war was over.

After the brief handshakes and "Godspeeds," Rowley jumped into the driver's seat ready to carry Dahlgren's body over some of the same ground on which he and his men had fought so valiantly the day before Dahlgren was killed. The Lohmann brothers were to go by way of another route and meet Rowley a mile beyond the barriers, assuming that he made it through and was not on his way to the city prison and its gallows.

Rowley headed west toward the picket lines. As he approached the toughest one, he broke out in a cold sweat, his hands trembled, and he found it hard to breathe as he realized the danger he was in. There was no turning back now. His very life depended on his actions and the pickets. As he got closer, he saw that the patrols were stopping and thoroughly checking everybody and everything.

He pulled up in front of one of the tents pitched alongside the road and dropped the reins indifferently. A lieutenant came out of the tent, eyed the wagon, and gave the order to "Search this wagon." All that would have been necessary was for one guard to run his bayonet just a few inches into the wagon, and death would have been Rowley's reward.

A team approached the checkpoint from the opposite direction, and a guard perceiving that Rowley was in no rush, thoroughly searched it from end to end.

The Lieutenant in charge of the post returned inside his tent. Another guard, who had been staring at Rowley, approached him.

"I know you; you're farmer Rowley," he said. At first, a chill ran up Rowley's spine till the guard got closer, and he recognized him. They proceeded to have a lively and friendly conversation.

The Lieutenant came to the doorway as another cart approached, and he saw that Rowley's wagon was still there. "Dammit, I said to inspect that wagon, soldier!" he barked irritably.

The guard then asked him what he had on the wagon. "Peach trees," Rowley said, fighting hard to keep his voice calm.

"Whose trees are they?" the guard continued.

"They belong to a German living in the country," Rowley answered casually.

"Isn't it late in the season to be planting peach trees? The guard checked.

"Well, all I know is the German wanted them," Rowley explained.

"I see," the guard said as he started toward the back of the wagon to begin his examination. Just then, another cart pulled up, and Rowley volunteered, "Go ahead and inspect him. He looks like he's in a rush, and I'm in no hurry."

The soldier thanked him and crossed the road to check the other wagon thoroughly. When he returned, the guard said, "I like peach trees. Who did you say they belong to?" as he headed for the back of the wagon.

"They're the German's," Rowley repeated, as he was now bathed in sweat, his hands clasped tightly so that the trembling didn't show. Another cart approached, and the guard left to inspect it very carefully and then returned.

The Lieutenant reappeared and shouted, "Goddamn you, didn't I tell you to search that wagon! Do as you're told, or I'll have your ass!"

As the soldier headed back to Rowley's wagon he repeated, "Yeah, I really like peach trees. It must be the smell of the ripe fruit, but it's a mistake to plant them in April."

"Well, they're not mine. The German can do what he likes with them," Rowley responded matter of factly.

"That's true enough," the guard agreed as he stepped back surveying the wagon, "It would be a pity to tear them all up since you have them packed so well."

Now Rowley's heart was pounding wildly, and he had to fight the urge to jump from the wagon and flee for his life.

"Yes, you're right. I packed them so that they'd survive the trip over these bumpy roads I didn't expect them to be disturbed. But, I know you have your duty to perform, and if I lose a few trees after your inspection, I know the consequences. The German will be furious with me and won't pay me for the damaged ones."

Another cart approached, entailing another thorough inspection. The soldier returned, came close to the side of the wagon, and looked carefully over the trees in silence. They both heard the Lieutenant moving about inside his tent, and the guard said, "I won't delay you any longer. I think everything's in order. Your honest face is guarantee enough for me. You may proceed to the German's."

Rowley, bathed in sweat, thanked the guard, picked up the reins, and drove by the Lieutenant's tent. Just then, the Lieutenant emerged expecting to see the wagon still there. He was prepared to blast the guard and check the wagon thoroughly himself. He eyed the wagon suspiciously, looked at the guard who was heading for another wagon, apparently dismissed his thought, and disappeared inside his tent. At the same time, Rowley was occupied with silent prayers to his maker.

About a mile beyond sight of the pickets, the Lohmann brothers, who had flanked the barrier by horseback, leaped out from the bushes, giving Rowley a start. He breathed a long sigh of relief as if he had just gotten a last-minute gallows' reprieve. Elizabeth had chosen well. Rowley proved to be a man of iron nerve and a consummate actor on the stage of life and death. He managed a faint smile to the friendly faces of the Lohmann brothers, knowing the journey was not over until he had safely made it through all the pickets.

At Yellow Tavern, they headed west for ten miles to Robert Orrick, the German farmer's home at Glen Allen, near Hungary Station. Two loyalist German women had already dug a grave in the western pasture. The men carefully placed Dahlgren's body, now in a metal coffin, in its third grave and covered it over. To mark the spot, they planted one of the peach trees that had shielded its precious cargo during the perilous journey.

The Lohmann brothers, along with Rowley, Orrick, and the two German women paused, heads bowed, hands held, in a circle around the grave. They offered a silent prayer as they paid their last respects to the young Colonel—who lost his leg while serving with the many other brave soldiers at Gettysburg—and who ultimately rendered—"His last full measure of devotion." They all hugged and quietly returned to their homes, content with having been a part of this humane undertaking.

By nightfall, Elizabeth had received the news that her plan had been safely and successfully completed. Relieved, she thought, "Every true Union heart that knew of this day's work felt happier for having taken charge of this precious dust." She immediately wrote a cipher report to Butler. Shortly thereafter, a messenger slipped away from the Van Lew home.

A few days later, the messenger arrived at Fortress Monroe with the report and a silver locket containing the lock of Dahlgren's hair, which was the color of gingerbread. The ciphered message requested Butler to notify Admiral Dahlgren that the body of his son was safely in the hands of loyal Unionists and that once this unhappy war was over, it would be turned over to him promptly.

Butler sent the following note to the Admiral:

"The remains are not so far within my control as to be able to remove them from Richmond, where every effort is being made by Confederate detectives to find them, but they are in the hands of devoted friends of the Union who have taken possession of them. I hardly dare suggest to Ould when he reports to me, as I know he will, that he cannot find them, and that I can put them into his possession, because that will show a correspondence with Richmond and will alarm them and will redouble their vigilance to detect their source of information."

In Richmond, Ould was armed with orders signed by President Davis instructing Major Atkinson to show him the secret burial spot, and they proceeded out to Oakwood Cemetery to locate the gravesite. Later that day, at Ould's request, Detective Sam McCubbin appeared at Major Turner's office in Libby Prison with orders to disinter Dahlgren's body. Turner sent McCubbin, along with a metal coffin in the back of a cart, to see Major Atkinson.

Atkinson accompanied McCubbin to the grave. They ordered two grave diggers to open the grave while they sat in the wagon smoking and wondering, "Why all the stink over one worthless Yankee dog's body?"

After digging for some time, the sweaty gravediggers announced that the grave was empty. Annoyed at the news, Atkinson jumped out of the cart to see for himself. Puzzled and amazed at the empty grave, he blurted, "Shit!"

McCubbin, not far behind, also verifying the absence of the wooden coffin asked Atkinson, "What's the meaning of this? Are you sure there's not a mistake? How could anyone have known where the body was, let alone take it away without someone knowing about it? What the hell is going on?"

The Richmond Dispatch's account of the scene at the muddy gravesite said:

"When Captain McCubbin demanded an explanation, Atkinson could provide none; all that he knew was that he had seen the body buried, and that was all." Further, they printed McCubbin's theory of what might have happened to the body. "Having a suspicion that certain citizens indignant over the orders found on Colonel Dahlgren's body, have found the grave, taken the body and chopped it into pieces."

Richmond buzzed over the disappearance with many theories debated and, for the Confederates, it remained an unsolved mystery.

CHAPTER 31

Belle Isle, Andersonville & A Shell Game

With the attempt to free the Federal prisoners in Richmond thwarted, the mass movement south proceeded in earnest with groups of from five to six hundred prisoners leaving from Belle Isle. They were brought into Richmond, herded into boxcars like cattle, and sent primarily to the Camp Sumter prison facility in Andersonville, Georgia.

Many of the men on Belle Isle who could walk into the prison wards were turned away, as only those unable to walk were permitted. Most, who were unable to walk, couldn't get to the wards and, therefore, perished where they lay. Although many deaths were attributed to typhoid, over sixty percent of those admitted died from the effects of diarrhea. The biggest culprit was the lack of flour. In order to stretch the meal used for the baking of cornbread, one of the meager staples, the cornhusks were also included in the grinding process. The husk was the leading cause of diarrhea and was becoming as lethal as the musket ball.

The Union prisoners who had suffered through the brutal cold weather on Belle Isle were now agonizing and dying by the scores daily from the oppressive heat, overcrowding, vermin, and malnutrition at the Camp Sumter—Andersonville Prison in Georgia. The prisoners were so emaciated that when they died they were carried out two at a time with one man under each arm.

With the high number of desertions, Lee petitioned President Davis for reinforcements. As part of the response to Lee, Company C, 18th Virginia Infantry, detailed to the Richmond defenses, was ordered to rejoin its regiment in the field. Elizabeth's brother, John, who had been saved by General Winder from going into battle, had been assigned to the 18th Virginia Infantry as its bookkeeper. Realizing that even Elizabeth's powers of persuasion could not save him now, John decided to desert.

Knowing all the defenses as well as he did, he took one of the more proven routes through the picket lines that many of Elizabeth's messengers used. After safely navigating through the Confederate lines, he reported to General Marsena R. Patrick, Provost Marshall of the Army of the Potomac.

Upon identifying himself, and relating his relationship to Elizabeth, John was further examined by Generals Meade and Grant. He told them everything he knew of the Confederate positions and dispositions. Grant, hearing about the extent and potential value to him of Elizabeth's network, decided that he wanted all of Elizabeth's intelligence to come directly to him in the future, instead of sending it through Butler at Fortress Monroe. John was then sent to Washington, where he safely remained until the Confederacy was defeated.

All Elizabeth's future ciphered intelligence would be directed to Colonel George H. Sharpe, Grant's Chief of the Military Information Bureau of the Army of the Potomac, who would decipher it and hand it on immediately to Grant.

Because of his skill and efficiency, John had been able to spend most of his time at the Van Lew hardware store and only nominally at his bookkeeping position at the 18th. Now, with John gone, the business withered and, consequently, an important source of Elizabeth's operating income was lost. This forced her to begin to sell off her silverware, piece-by-piece, in order to sustain her espionage activities.

Horses were also in short supply in the South. Lee had to disband an entire cavalry division for lack of mounts, so he urgently requested the government to re-supply him fresh mounts or he "would not be able to keep the enemy from Richmond's door."

Finally, comprehending the gravity of Lee's communication, the Confederate government started its quest from its least difficult source ... the citizens of Richmond. Carriages were stopped in the middle of the street, and the horses "appropriated for government use, to be returned when the emergency had subsided."

The Van Lews would also be forced to make their dutiful contribution to the war effort to pay for the many benefits that all the citizens of Richmond received, which at this time was "protection from the enemy." For several years, Elizabeth had been without the continually replaced, matched team of four beautiful snow-white horses that carried her family in style to social and recreational activities. All that was left in her stable was a trusty old mare that Elizabeth desperately needed for her nocturnal meetings and missions.

Cashmeyer learned of the order to impress horses from the citizenry and got word to Elizabeth to prepare for their visit. The next day, the "horse collectors" paid the Van Lew home a visit. Elizabeth told them that her stable was empty of horses, but they were free to see for themselves, which they did. After a thorough examination for horses, or "indications of their recent residence," they were satisfied that she had none, and they left. Elizabeth breathed a sigh of relief as she gave Nelson the word that it was safe to take the mare out of the smokehouse and return her to the stable.

Shortly thereafter, Elizabeth received another secret note from Cashmeyer. He told her that a neighbor reported seeing the animal being moved from the smokehouse to the stable. To her dismay, she was told that the collectors would be back to confiscate the animal.

The next day, the same men returned and examined first the stable, then the smokehouse. Once again, they found nothing. Perplexed and angry, they interrogated Elizabeth about the vanishing and reappearing horse. She told them, "You are the victims of a spiteful hoax," and asked them why they still thought she had a horse after their careful and unsuccessful search of the premises the day before. They told her that a neighbor saw an animal on the premises the previous day and they demanded to know its whereabouts.

Elizabeth explained that anyone could have brought in their horse to feed and told them they should now be assured, once and for all, that they were wasting their time looking for a horse on her property.

She added, "There are many people who would attempt to mislead you, trying to hide the fact that they themselves owned horses. They believe that by occupying your time on 'wild-goose' chases trying to find horses that aren't there, you won't have time to find the horses they are trying to protect."

Feeling like saps and angered that they had been played for fools, and still not being sure of who it was who has duped them, they left, not to return again. Hoping that it was to be their last visit, Elizabeth returned inside the house to the library where her trusty mare had been concealed and carefully fed to keep her quiet. The floor had been thickly covered with straw to protect it and to muffle the sound of shone hoofs on the wooden floor from divulging the presence of its temporary occupant.

General Winder, the Confederate Commissary-General of Prisoners, sensing the approach of Federal forces, who were determined to liberate their feeble, sick and dying comrades in uniform at Andersonville Prison, sent Order No. 13 to the prison officials at Andersonville:

"The Officer on Duty and in charge of the Battery of Florida Artillery at the time will, upon receiving notice that the enemy has approached within seven miles of the Post, open fire upon the stockade and its prisoners with grape shot, without reference to the situation beyond these lines of defense. It is better that the last Federal be exterminated than be permitted to burn and pillage the property of loyal citizens, as they do if allowed to make their escape from the prison."

By order of,   John H. Winder
Brigadier General

The steady stream of Federal prisoners from Grant's Army of the Potomac's relentless clashes with Confederates had kept Elizabeth occupied in her daily rounds ministering and collecting fresh information on the enemy. Her "Crazy Bet-harmless old biddy" persona helped her considerably in her work by giving her less supervision and more freedom to move about inside the prisons. However, she was unprepared for the surprise that occurred one day in late May.

Lying on a bunk, in one corner of the large second floor room, was an officer newly arrived from the prison hospital. As Elizabeth stared at the wounded prisoner, her heart began to pound and a rush of adrenaline surged through her body. An inner voice wondered, "Can it be? Oh Dear God, let it be." She took a circuitous route to the bunk, not wanting to give any special attention to her destination.

When she arrived beside the bunk, she was ecstatic with joy; "It is Paul! I thought so!" she whispered to herself. Paul's eyes were closed, and his handsome face was gaunt and pale from the ordeal of suffering from a shoulder wound and his battle with dysentery; an illness he picked up while recovering in the prison hospital. She looked with respect and admiration at his honest face, so filled with conviction, character, and goodness.

She placed her hand on his and said softly, "Hello Paul." Paul opened his eyes slightly, not sure if the voice he just heard was real or if he was dreaming. Seeing Elizabeth's face so close, he opened his eyes widely now, "Elizabeth, is it really you?"

"Yes, Paul. I can't express in words how glad I am to see you."

"Elizabeth, you don't know how much I've thought about seeing you again, but it wasn't under these circumstances."

Putting aside her personal feelings, Elizabeth responded, "If you feel up to it, I'd like you to fill me in on everything that's happened to you since I saw you last." Elizabeth listened attentively as Paul related the events of the past few months since the night she sent him seeking Colonel Dahlgren.

Elizabeth had learned, through confidential inquiries, that Paul was among the Kilpatrick-Dahlgren Raid prisoners brought to Libby. She knew of his wound and his illness but had been unable to see him in the prison hospital. All the captured raiders were "off limits," due to the initial unfavorable status and resentment, caused by the publishing of the controversial "Dahlgren Document."

Elizabeth saw Paul at every opportunity. She unselfishly brought him most of her portion of food from her table, medicine purchased from Dr. Parker, newspapers and books from her library. She sprinkled her graciousness with a long-dormant affection, which grew deeper with every visit.

Despite the extra time she was spending with Paul, Elizabeth did not neglect her intelligence collecting activities. When she had received instructions to re-route all her ciphered dispatches directly to General Grant, she immediately established a five-station communication link. It started at her house, proceeded to her farm out on the old Williamsburg Carriage Road, and continued to the homes of trusted Union loyalists who relayed the secret messages back and forth to Grant's headquarters.

Grant repeatedly asked for specific information, and Elizabeth promptly acquired and forwarded it to him. So efficient were her transmissions, that the freshly cut roses from her garden, sent along with the messages, arrived fresh, fragrant, and dewy on Grant's breakfast table. She had become the provider of the greatest portion of the information the Army of the Potomac was to receive.

Lee's outnumbered 55,000-man army manned a defensive twenty-five mile long entrenchment from White Oak Swamp east of Richmond, down to the Jerusalem Plank Road on the eastern side of Petersburg. The ensuing "trench warfare," he employed was unlike anything the world had never seen before. And, with the destructive march by Sherman toward Atlanta, the Confederacy was beginning to act like the "once powerful but now vulnerable lion," who was unable to do much more than fend off the attacks of the numerous annoying antagonists.

CHAPTER 32

Houses: One A Plea; One A Proposal

Although Grant's loss of 7000 men at Cold Harbor horrified the North, it didn't prevent the people from nominating Lincoln for a second term. However, the Republican Party chose to call itself, "The National Unity Party" for this election. The ticket of Abraham Lincoln and Andrew Johnson faced a familiar opponent. The Democratic Party's candidate was the "American Napoleon" himself, Lincoln's dismissed General-in-Chief of the Union Armies, George B. McClellan.

Further south, Richmond continued to suffer from the unrelenting, sweltering summer heat and humidity, shortage of foodstuffs and materials, increasing crime, deterioration in value of the Confederate currency, and the inflated prices on what little was available for purchase.

Elizabeth learned from Mary Bowser that peace envoys sent by General Grant would be meeting shortly with Colonel Ould and Jeff Davis in Richmond.

It was nearly two o'clock in the morning of the day that the peace envoys were to meet. A solitary figure scurried along the deserted city streets. It was Elizabeth in her countrywoman's disguise carrying a large basket of odorous fish. At a pre-arranged location, she met young Charles Phillips, the newspaper boy, who had been waiting with brushes and a bucket of white paint. Elizabeth took them and hid the items in a secret compartment in her basket under the fish. Elizabeth then gave Charles the last details of her plan, and together they headed for Capitol Square.

As they approached the Custom House, there was a solitary light on in the office of the Secretary of the Treasury's Office where he was struggling to resolve the chaos of the Confederacy's financial situation.

"Miss Liz, do you still want to do it here while someone's still in the building?" Charles asked.

"Yes. It'll be seen by more people especially Grant's envoys. That'll show them that all is not so well in the Confederacy."

"Whatever you say, Miss Liz; you know best," the newspaper boy chuckled mischievously.

"That wall there," Elizabeth indicated, pointing to the spot having the greatest visibility from the Square and which was now in complete shadow, as she handed him his materials from the basket. With youthful vigor, Charles proceeded with his task as Elizabeth sat watch on the top step to warn him if anyone approached from either inside or outside of the building. Luck was with them as no one approached during the twenty minutes it took to complete the painting dictated by Elizabeth.

The Custom House

"All finished, Miss Liz, what do you think?" Charles whispered proudly.

Elizabeth stood and admired his work. "It's beautiful, Charles. Too bad no one will know who painted it, or you might be able to get some work as a sign painter," she joked.

As a preventative measure, she had Charles clean his hands, leave all the incriminating evidence where it was, and then they hurriedly departed the scene.

They walked up the gravel path away from the Custom House and turned to take a final look at their night's work.

Welcome Peacemakers
Down with Davis and the Rebellion
Free us from Confederate bondage
Long live the Union!

The pair continued down Bank Street to Tenth, and they parted at Cary Street; Elizabeth to return to Church Hill, Charles to lose himself amongst the ships in the Kanawa Canal basin.

Elizabeth continued up Cary Street until she saw a man in civilian clothing approaching her from the direction of Libby Prison. He was the first pedestrian she has seen that night. As the man headed straight for her, she reached for the forged, outdated pass that allowed Freda Crouch, fishmonger, to be on the streets past the curfew. Fearing a confrontation, she decided to reduce the risk by turning up Seventeenth Street. Once around the corner, she picked up the pace to put as much distance as possible between herself and the man. Just before the man reached the corner, she ducked into the tree-shaded entrance of George's Blacksmith Shop and watched.

As the man approached the corner, he stopped beneath the streetlight to see where the woman had gone. A shiver ran through Elizabeth's body and her heart started to pound. It was Detective New!

New looked up Seventeenth Street for the woman with the basket and large brimmed hat. "Where the hell did she go?" he uttered as he started up Seventeenth to look for her. Elizabeth was out of sight from the corner, but if the man got to within twenty feet of her, he couldn't miss seeing and capturing her. New continued up the street and thought, "Hell, maybe the woman lives here and is now inside her house. I'm sure as hell not going to do a house-to-house search at this time of the night. Detectives must preserve their anonymity to be effective."

Elizabeth's eyes riveted on New as he got within fifty feet of her. Then for no apparent reason to her, he turned and headed back to his original route down Cary Street. She breathed a deep sigh of relief and said softly, "Thank you God for your 'Divine Intervention.'" She waited about ten minutes to make sure he did not come back and then headed for home along the darkest streets.

New proceeded down Cary Street and up Seventeenth thinking about the woman. There was something familiar about her walk. He turned briskly up Tenth Street toward Capitol Square. As he entered the square, he saw the solitary light coming from Memminger's Office. Not sure if it was the Secretary or someone else, his decided to check it out. He walked up Bank Street toward the Custom House still struggling to recollect the walk. Now he remembered, "That goddamn Van Lew woman! The countrywoman getup threw me off, but I knew that walk was familiar!"

"Horseshit! I should have searched the area better. She was probably hiding in the shadows, and I couldn't see her. The bitch was probably on some secret mission, and I could have wrapped her up for good right then. At least, I've learned how she's been able to move around the city undetected; I know her disguise. I'll have her house searched, and when I find the outfit, I'll have her ... even if it's just for violating the curfew!"

Just then, the lone light went out in the Custom House office window. A minute or so later, New saw Memminger exiting the building. New heard the white-haired Secretary curse as he tripped over something in the dark and then continued walking towards him. Surprised at meeting the detective on the street, Memminger asked New what he was doing out at this hour. New answered that he frequently walked before retiring; that it helped him get to sleep. Memminger grunted that he hadn't been able to sleep very well himself lately and headed for his residence. They walked together for a short distance, then New bade him "Good Night," and cut across the Square on the way to his rooming house.

By nine o'clock that same day, the entire city had either seen it first hand, or heard about the "outrageous deed" by word of mouth. It also did not escape the notice of Grant's envoys, although they diplomatically avoided any mention of seeing it during their meetings with Ould and Davis. The slogans had no direct impact on the outcome of the meeting. While the firmly expressed positions of each side were for "Peace," the North wanted Peace and "Union," the South Peace and "Independence!"

The Custom House "messages" did cause embarrassment to the Confederate government's leaders, stinging Davis, in particular, more than the Bread Riot of the year before. It also irritated some of the Rebellion's supporters while pleasing others who were fed up with the poor performance of their government and the deteriorating quality of life. The Union loyalists got a large boost from the bold, public expression of their sentiments.

Secretary Memminger summoned Detective New to his office to inquire what information he had about the traitorous act since the detective was in the vicinity at approximately the time that the deed must have been carried out. New told him that the only activity that he observed was a woman walking several blocks away and that an investigation was under way to get to the bottom of it.

Memminger explained that Davis was equally concerned about the fact that someone high up in the government had leaked information about the extremely closely held knowledge of the peace envoys' trip to Richmond. He explained that he, himself, was one of the handful of people who knew about it, and that fingers were being pointed in every direction. "Do you understand my message?" Memminger warned.

"Yes sir, very clearly," New responded dutifully.

Back in his office, Detective New ordered Captain Gibbs, along with some of his men, to search Elizabeth's wardrobe. He instructed them to look for the countrywoman's clothing, wide-brimmed sunbonnet, and a large basket; the disguise that was evidence of her complicity in the treachery. The Captain obliged with a thorough search of everyone's wardrobe in the house to no avail.

Upon returning home from the sign-painting mission, Elizabeth had taken the precaution to hide the disguise in the secret room upon realizing that New might put two and two together after the deed was discovered. New was furious to hear that they did not find the disguise. Now, he had no leads whatsoever to pursue, and he said nothing more to Memminger about seeing the suspicious woman on the street only moments after the deed. To protect his own precarious position, he hoped the whole episode would blow over quickly. It did, and the case remained another unsolved mystery along with the disappearance of Dahlgren's body.

With time and Elizabeth's care, Paul fully recovered and was impatient to gain freedom and rejoin his comrades in arms. Elizabeth decided to undertake this new challenge. She discussed the situation with Dr. Parker, who was now very much aware of her strong feelings for Paul, and she asked for his help with an escape plan. After discussing the feasibility and risks involved, they finally agreed on how the plan could be accomplished. Elizabeth consulted with Sergeant Erasmus Ross, a Confederate clerk at Libby Prison, who played his role as "the meanest anti-Yankee guard" to perfection. Ross was the nephew of Franklin Stearns, a rich Unionist and outspoken abolitionist; therefore, he needed to constantly demon-strate unusual "pro-Confederate loyalty" in order to remain above suspicion. He was such a good actor that he was written about by prisoners as being the most brutal of all their jailers. Little did the prisoners know how many prison escapes he had arranged at extraordinary personal peril. Ross said that the attempt should be made on Dr. Parker's next tour of duty, which would be in two days, at the Libby Prison hospital ward.

On the morning the doctor visited Libby, Elizabeth, who was already on her prison rounds, slipped Paul a potion given her by Dr. Parker, and then she promptly left. The "medicine" given Paul would intentionally make him violently ill. During his frequent rounds, the Senior Union officer, upon seeing the serious-ness of Paul's illness, called the guard to have the sick prisoner rushed to the hos-pital ward. As planned, Dr. Parker was on hand to attend to him. Being alone in the small examination room, William gave Paul a freshly laundered Confederate officer's jacket and trousers. The uniform had been acquired from Lipscomb who had "borrowed" them from a cadaver. Late that night, when Dr. Parker left Libby, a "Confederate officer" accompanied him. The plan to get Paul out of the prison had been a complete success.

The co-conspirators entered the doctor's carriage where Paul promptly changed into some of John Van Lew's civilian clothing, and the carriage moved along at a leisurely pace to avoid attracting any undue attention. The pause at the Twenty-Third Street side of the Van Lew residence was just long enough for Paul to shake hands, thank the doctor, and make an unsteady dash into the shadow of an acacia tree. Dr. Parker then drove by Lipscomb's residence to return the uniform that had unwittingly provided a humane service before its "retirement." The faithful Van Lew family servant and trusted collaborator, Nelson, met Paul in the garden and guided him into the back entrance where Elizabeth waited anxiously. She then silently assisted him up the back stairs, and he had his second "visit" into the secret room.

The women, Mrs. Van Lew, Mary, and Elizabeth took turns bringing Paul nourishment and medicine throughout the next few days. Mary and Mrs. Van Lew noticed, without comment, the happiness expressed on Elizabeth's face; the smiles, the humming—such eagerness to personally serve this latest "houseguest!"

Paul's health and strength returned quickly. All too quickly for Elizabeth, who realized how much pleasure his closeness had brought her. She knew how compelling his call was to return to his military unit and to serve again with his men during this final push to end the rebellion. She respected his zeal to leave to serve his country and, at the same time, dreaded it.

Late at night, the day before he was to leave, Paul came out from his cramped lodging to eat his final meal set on an old trunk being used as a temporary dinner table. He and Elizabeth sat across from each other. The candlelight gave the room an intimate and romantic atmosphere as they shared their thoughts about the war. They both agreed that the war could not last much longer and felt certain that the Union would prevail. On a more personal note, Paul commented on Elizabeth's missions. "The things you do are downright dangerous. You have to be one of the most fearless women I've ever met!"

"Paul, I'm far from fearless. It's just that my desire to succeed is greater than my fear of failure … or … maybe it's my fear of failure that drives my desire to succeed."

"Either way, I'll be happy to know that you are busy with less hazardous pursuits. And what exactly are your plans when it's over?" Paul asked.

"I don't know," Elizabeth responded honestly, "There was little meaning in my life before the first Union prisoners arrived in Richmond."

"Does that mean you don't have any plans?"

"It means that I haven't thought about what would make me both happy and fulfilled. Perhaps, working to assist the unfortunate Negroes in making new lives for themselves," Elizabeth pondered tentatively.

"But, what about yourself, Elizabeth? Wouldn't you think of getting married and settling down to a normal lifestyle."

"Paul, when I was of marrying age, it was something I dearly wanted, and a family too. But, now that my time has passed, I've given it little thought."

"Do you think of yourself now as unlovable or undesirable?" Paul asked earnestly.

Elizabeth blushed and started to speak, but was momentarily and strangely at a loss for words as she looked deeply into Paul's eyes. "Elizabeth," he continued, in a voice filled with ardor, which visibly affected his listener as she experienced a surge of passion, so unfamiliar to her body, "I can tell you, first hand, that you are lovable—in fact, very lovable!"

Overcome with this powerful avalanche of emotion-laden words, Elizabeth's eyes quickly filled with tears that overflowed down her flushed cheeks. So deeply moved by Elizabeth's reaction to his words, Paul rose, lifted her from her chair, and took her into his arms. He tenderly brushed away the tears and kissed her cheek saying, "Tears flowing that freely from your tender heart on being spoken to of love, are like a dam filled beyond its capacity." Elizabeth, finally free to release the many years of pent-up longing for a loving relationship, and finding a man she has come to love and may lose in battle, Elizabeth murmured softly, "Yes Paul, and they are just a small indication of the depth of my feelings for you."

"Oh, Elizabeth, I have been carrying you in my thoughts for such a long time, not daring to disclose my feelings. I've admired you … dreamed of you … loved you. In my darkest moments of despair, the vision of you sustained me and gave me the courage to carry on. Elizabeth Van Lew, I do love you!"

Now, alone in the privacy of the room, the unexpressed love they shared could no longer be denied, and they acted on their hearts' and minds' desire for each other. They embraced and kissed with the intensity of two lovers who realized that this might be their last time together. The kiss had all the sweetness of a first kiss, combined with the passion and intensity of a last kiss. They clung to each other, desperately holding on, wanting to preserve the rapture and bliss of this moment forever.

"Elizabeth, when this war is over, I'm coming back for you, and I'd be honored if you would become my wife."

"Oh Paul, I love you so deeply. Yes, a thousand times, Yes! I will be your wife, and I'll be the honored one!"

Suddenly, there was a soft knock on the attic room door. It was Mrs. Van Lew come to warn Elizabeth that she heard Captain Gibbs walking around downstairs. Mrs. Gibbs had a toothache, and the captain was looking around for something to ease her pain.

Paul and Elizabeth looked at Mrs. Van Lew, and then at each other realizing that it would be disastrous if Paul was found here. He would be severely punished upon his return to Libby. And they also knew what Elizabeth's and her mother's fate would be for their complicity in the escape and sheltering of a Union prisoner, added to the rest of the charges. All three realized that Paul must return to the safety of the secret room, and Elizabeth to her bedroom, at once.

Not wanting to embarrass either lady, Paul resisted the urge to kiss Elizabeth again and offered his hand in thanks to Elizabeth while bidding them both "Good Night."

Elizabeth, who planned to tell her mother of their love and new commitment, surprised both Paul and her mother by taking his hand in hers and kissing it. Looking deeply into his eyes, she whispered softly, "I love you with all my heart, Paul." He sighed, kissed her hand in return, and disappeared into the darkness of the secret room. After returning the room to its innocent appearance, Elizabeth took her mother's arm and escorted her to her bed where she revealed her feelings for Paul and her acceptance of his proposal of marriage.

The next day passed all too quickly. Instead of it being filled with a celebration breakfast coupled with wedding announcements and toasts, it was a solemn day occupied with prison visits and final preparations for Paul's journey to the north.

With escorts and routes carefully planned and explained, the hour had arrived for Paul to leave Richmond. Mrs. Van Lew left Elizabeth and Paul alone in the attic room to say their private "good byes." They stood locked in a tender embrace. Elizabeth's eyes were filled with tears. Paul broke the silence, "How I've come to love you Elizabeth. My body is leaving you to take part in finishing this terrible conflict, just as you are doing your part. But, my heart remains here with you, and it will always be with you. As tempting as it is to stay with you in the safety of your home and not return to duty, I would lose my self-respect, especially when I see you doing what you do daily, without it being your sworn duty," Paul explained.

"Paul, I understand what you are saying, but it doesn't make your leaving any less painful for me. I will miss you and pray daily for your safe journey and a quick victorious return to this city and my waiting arms." An ominous chill ran through her body at the thought of Paul going back into combat, and she added, "If it is God's will."

Their final kiss was a promise, indelibly etched in their minds and hearts to meet again. Reluctantly, Elizabeth took Paul's hand in hers and silently led him down the stairs and out into the garden where Nelson was waiting to take him to his first "guide," who would then take him out of the city limits.

"God speed Paul!" Elizabeth rallied softly; and to herself, "Until we meet again, I'll keep you in my heart and thoughts. I love you so."

"And the same to you, my love!" Paul replied, and to himself, "God, please watch over her and keep her safe during her dangerous missions!"

Then, in an instant, the two men were out of sight. Elizabeth stood alone under the huge tree, looking at the spot where Paul had spoken his final words. She stood motionless, reflecting on all that had transpired between them—the meetings—the escapes—the hours of conversation—the shared special moments that developed into love. Straining her imagination to picture Paul in the same spot, safely returning to her at the cessation of the fighting, that she uttered,

"Dear God, let this cursed war be over soon!" For hours, she sat on her favorite bench beside the south-facing garden walkway. As she looked over her beloved Richmond, she thought of what could be ahead in the post-war years.

The next few days, Elizabeth was overly busy with prison visits and fulfilling General Grant's requests. Thanks to Samuel Ruth, the Supervisor of the Richmond, Fredricksburg and Potomac Railroad, she had been able to pass on valuable information regarding the number and disposition of Confederate troops and material both north and south of Richmond. His intentional printing in the newspapers of the train schedules allowed that information to be easily available for passing along to the Union forces.

Elizabeth had also learned that General Lee had recruited and trained two young boys to collect information on Sheridan's troops while selling newspapers amongst them. Her notification arrived in time to warn Sheridan. He detained the two very intelligent and observant boys, releasing them only after his troops had safely crossed the Chickahominy River.

In addition, Elizabeth included information passed on to her from J. O. Kerbey, a telegrapher working for the Confederacy in Richmond, who was "listening in" on all of the telegraphic communications in and out of the city. Elizabeth was also collecting privileged information from Mary, who was extremely well established in the Jeff Davis household, Dr. Parker's insights and unique prospective, Cashmeyer's inside information, and the observations from the prisoners in Libby. Also of inestimable value to her efforts was her extensive Loyalist network of housewives, farmers, tradespeople, craftsmen, factory workers, entrepreneurs, newsboys, civil servants of the Confederacy and Negroes, both free and slave. Elizabeth's reports were invaluable and extremely trustworthy, and practically anything Grant requested, she provided. With Lee and his Army bottled up in and around Richmond, Grant's requests for information grew in scope and frequency.

Lincoln's huge reelection victory over McClellan was a vote for preserving the Union, despite the unhappiness with the bloodshed. The respect and adulation for General McClellan was not evident in the soldiers' vote, as they almost exclusively supported Lincoln. Even during a mock election held by the prisoners in Andersonville Prison in Georgia, Lincoln won by a landslide.

Meanwhile, Thanksgiving for the Federal troops, now well entrenched along the Richmond-Petersburg siege lines, was a time of plenty. Northern citizens responded generously to a call to "give the soldiers a grand Thanksgiving Dinner." They enjoyed turkey, chicken, dried beef, apples, preserves, doughnuts, pound cake, sponge cake, gingersnaps, tobacco, and cigars.

At the same time, Lee's underfed forces continued their miserable existence with foul beef, old bacon, and stale bread. They were not in a very thankful mood. The citizens in Richmond were in much the same spirits as the Confederate military, with little or nothing to be thankful for this holiday season.

CHAPTER 33

A Close Call & More Abuse

The loss of Savannah to General Sherman turned the festivities of the Christmas season in Richmond to one of mournful despondency except in the Van Lew residence. Savannah was thought to be impregnable and would never be taken. Now, the feeling in the Confederate capital was that if that stronghold could be taken, so could Richmond and a blanket of foreboding covered the city. Instead of the sumptuous banquet around which families gathered to feast, toast, laugh, and share gifts from their bounty, the majority of citizens sat down to a poverty-stricken meal. People went through the motions more from habit and tradition than from the spirit. The vacant chairs were counted with eyes nearly blinded by tears and the questions that were thought but not spoken, "How much more are we to bear?" "Is it worth the price," or "Has it all been for nothing?"

Elizabeth and her mother shared this Christmas with quiet reflection and prayer for the prospects of the New Year. Elizabeth had received a letter from Paul telling of his being attached to General Wilson's forces in the Deep South. While delighted to hear from him, she was, naturally, much concerned for his safety.

The New Year was ushered in with the prospect of incessant decline or, at best, a continuation of the evils that shrouded the land in sorrow, misery, and destruction. Day by day, the wants and deprivations increased as deliverance was prayed for. Besides food, there was also a shortage of fuel, both wood and coal. When the last stick or lump was consumed, there was no more at any price. Anyone having an ample amount of fuel was likely to be burglarized. Those who were unwilling to admit the failure of the Confederacy used rationalizing to justify rationing.

The fatality rate of the men in captivity on both sides continued to grow at an alarming rate. Of the approximately 50,000 Federal prisoners of War being held in the South, roughly 3000 were still in Richmond. General Winder, who had moved his Prison Command Post from Richmond to Andersonville, then to Augusta, Georgia, had set up new headquarters in Columbia, South Carolina.

For Elizabeth, the dramatic events of the past four years continued without letup in the climactic year 1865. The determination of the Rebel government to ferret out and punish anti-Confederate elements and activities persisted and accelerated, even as the Confederacy itself was unraveling. The noose tightened around the group in Richmond loyal to the Union.

Brave little Charles Phillips, the newsboy, was arrested and thrown into jail when the son of another neighborhood loyalist family betrayed him. The son had been "recruited" by one of New's detectives to be on the lookout for "anyone acting suspicious or who might be acting to hurt our dear country." When the young informer reported that, "Charlie was busy running strange errands at all times of the day and night," young Phillips was promptly picked up, locked in jail, and questioned unmercifully. Although he never admitted any wrongdoing, the Confederate authorities never released him because "he was one less link in the enemy's chain of conspirators."

Samuel Ruth, the Supervisor of the Richmond, Fredericksburg and Potomac Railroad, was also arrested and thrown in jail. Elizabeth had been incorporating Ruth's information in her reports to Grant, and she resolved to get him back into his valuable access position. Knowing that her house was under constant surveillance and that all visitors were noted and questioned, she called a secret meeting of her closest and most trusted loyalists at the home of Mrs. Rose on the following night.

It was a dark, stormy, mid-winter night with a howling, bitter wind, so cold that it took one's breath away when attempting to speak. It was the coldest winter in Richmond in many years. The windows of the Rose home had been shuttered, and the curtains were pinned together for additional privacy. The gaslights were lowered to further protect the attendees' identity as they cautiously arrived, one by one. Such secrecy and utmost caution were not only necessary they were imperative. Confederate spies were everywhere.

When all those invited had arrived safely, Elizabeth revealed that Samuel Ruth, who had been a valuable source of information to her, had been imprisoned. She explained that he must be freed as soon as possible and returned to his vital role at the railroad. A jailbreak was out of the question because Ruth would then be a fugitive and forced to remain out of sight, losing his unique access to important data relating to the rail movement of troops and military material.

After a period of brainstorming and discussion, the group agreed on a plan to start a careful word-of-mouth groundswell of public outrage at Ruth's arrest, hoping that it would irritate and embarrass government officials into releasing him.

Suddenly, the barking of a dog and a tapping at the door startled them. They all drew closer as a pallor came over their faces. Blood rushed to and from their pounding hearts as they considered that they might be breathing their last free breaths. The tapping persisted, and they all looked at each other trying to decide who would go to the door and what they would say once they got there. "What if the group's incriminating deliberations had been overheard?" "What would become of them and their families?"

Finally, one of the men stood and walked to a window, his trembling hand ever so slowly moved the curtain just enough to be able to see, through the small crack in the shutters, who was at the front door. He dropped his head, closed his eyes, and exhaled loudly. The group interpreted his reaction as one of finality, "their goose was cooked," and they would soon be on their way to Castle Thunder Prison—it was all over for them.

"The wind has broken off a large branch, and it landed next to the door. The callers tapping on our door, thank God, are only Mr. Wind and Mr. Branch!"

His revelation brought a huge collective sigh of relief and a measure of color back into the cheeks of the group as they managed a feeble smile at the man's nervous attempt at humor while describing the identity of the "callers."

Feeling they had pushed their luck enough for one night, they quickly reviewed what measures they would use and who would receive their initial verbal pressure tactics on behalf of "outstanding citizen Ruth." The meeting ended with a prayer for God's continued protection and blessing on their efforts, concluding with a request for the granting of a "… a speedy end to the war, the bloodshed, and the Confederacy."

The citizenry in Richmond picked up on the outrage directed upon one of its own and stirred up such a ruckus over "outstanding citizen Ruth's" arrest, without just cause, that he was released just one week later. The same day, the United States Congress passed the Thirteenth Amendment—the Abolition of Slavery!

At Hampton Roads, Virginia on February 3rd, 1865, President Lincoln and Secretary of War Seward secretly conferred with Confederate Vice-President Stephens, Confederate Senator Hunter, and Judge Campbell, the Assistant Confederate States Secretary of War in a last ditch attempt at a negotiated peace. The emissaries from the South still insisted on peace with independence for the South, based on their instructions from Davis. With the direction of the war now going heavily in the North's favor, Lincoln felt no pressure to agree to anything but an unconditional surrender, and he rejected their offer. Dejected, they returned back to Richmond empty handed. The Confederacy was now resigned to playing out the hand they had dealt themselves and the continuation of the bloodletting, suffering, and destruction.

Prisoners by the thousands were now being exchanged. Many of the Confederate prisoners refused to be exchanged, preferring their life in the prisons rather than returning to the ill-fed and ill-equipped killing fields of battle. Even they sensed the futility of continued combat. They felt the war would be over soon, and they would be paroled and sent home.

A Polish national of royal lineage posing as a Polish Count had previously conducted a successful intelligence gathering operation on behalf of the Union. Upon his arrival in Richmond, the "Count" was given the royal treatment, and he gained a valuable amount of insightful information on some of the top Confederate political and military leaders.

In an attempt to duplicate the feat, an Englishman, Mr. Pole, a skilled machinist and engineer, was escorted into Richmond by a Lemuel E. Babcock, formerly of Massachusetts, and one of General George Sharpe's best agents. Babcock and Pool took rooms at the Spotswood Hotel at 8th and Main Streets. However, once inside the volatile Confederate capital, Pole began to feel uneasy and developed cold feet.

Before Babcock left the hotel the next morning, he told Pool that he would take him to a meeting with William White, who was another trusted member of Elizabeth's spy network. Babcock also instructed Pool to stay put until he returned from another meeting, at which time they would have breakfast. Fearful that he was in over his head in this dangerous spy business and of its grave consequences here in the heart of the Confederacy, Pool allowed Babcock a five-minute head start, then set out from the hotel to turn himself in.

When Babcock arrived at his prearranged, secluded rendezvous location, Elizabeth was already conversing with White. White was expressing his fear of this foreigner and was questioning Elizabeth about Pool. He anguished that he would be in grave danger if this Englishman turned out to be untrustworthy. He said, "I don't know why my life is not as precious as the lives of others."

Elizabeth agreed, "It does look very hard for you. No one else in our group must know him, or he of them, until I bring you word."

Babcock immediately arranged a subsequent debriefing appointment between Elizabeth and Pool, to follow the meetings Pool was to have with the Confederate leadership. "I'm a little suspicious of this man Pool," Elizabeth told Babcock. "Please take special precautions when you are around him. Don't allow yourself to be put into any kind of compromising situations." Elizabeth felt very uncomfortable about this new entry into their network.

Pool meanwhile, suspicious that Babcock might have gone to betray him and fearful for his life, was not only revealing the true purpose of his mission to the Confederate authorities with his U. S. government documents but was positively identifying Babcock and White as Union spies. Pool even offered his services to the Confederates as an expert on torpedoes and gunboats, but the days of gunboats had passed for the South. He was sent to Castle Thunder—the normal destination for political prisoners.

Detective New was on the spot to arrest the unsuspecting Babcock upon his return to the Spotswood Hotel. New then located and arrested White. Pool was placed in a cell with other criminals, while Babcock and White were each put in solitary confinement. The loss of Babcock was a blow to General Sharpe, but not nearly as serious a blow to the Union as it might have been if Pool had met and identified Elizabeth as well.

It was a nervous Elizabeth who read of the arrests of Babcock and White, wondering if she had been, or would be, implicated.

Babcock stubbornly refused to give any information, so New proceeded to work on White. In order to break White, New put a pistol to the spy's head and ordered him to, "tell all you know or I'll blow your brains out!"

White, just as loyal as Babcock, responded calmly, "Blow away."

New continued to hammer away at White to learn the names of the rest of the spy ring. "Tell us, who are concerned in this thing?" he screamed over and over.

"Are they Yankees … Virginians … military … civilian … men … women … children? Just give me the name of the ring leader, and I'll do the rest!"

No matter the question or the force behind it, White refused to reveal the name of a single person. He knew the fate that awaited those named and the damage to the network, especially to its leader, Elizabeth Van Lew!

Several days passed, and with the Confederacy's inability to break Babcock or White, no positive connection could be made to Elizabeth.

Elizabeth knew all too well that if New had even the slightest evidence connecting her to anything improper, she would be under arrest within the hour. Another "close call," and both Elizabeth and General Sharpe breathed a grateful sigh of relief, hoping to continue their important mission to its completion. Elizabeth immediately changed her pseudonym from "Babcock" to "Romona."

The successful efforts to get Samuel Ruth released and returned to his railroad vantagepoint paid rich rewards. Shortly after his return, Ruth advised the Union, through Elizabeth and her dependable communication network, that the Confederacy was shipping 400,000 pounds of southern tobacco to Hamilton Landing, Virginia. The tobacco was to be illegally bartered with a Yankee merchant for much-needed bacon, worth over $300,000. The transmitted information allowed the Federal forces to intercept and confiscate the shipment, seize twenty-eight railroad cars, take 400 more prisoners, and destroy four railroad bridges.

While walking back home from observing some troop movements a week later, Elizabeth noticed that a new grocery store, whose proprietor had a heavy English accent, opened at the corner of 18th and Main Street. After some tactful questioning of a nearby merchant, she learned that the proprietor was an Englishman by the name of Pool. Immediately, she warned all of her loyalists who the proprietor was and advised them not to patronize the establishment. Since there was no evidence that Pool was guilty of any actual spying, and that he was instrumental in causing two actual spies to be put out of commission, Pool was allowed to buy his way out of prison with cash and a letter of repentance to the Confederate government.

Not daring to return north after his betrayal, Pool was attempting to survive by making a go of it with his ill-gotten rewards in Richmond. However, as things got progressively worse for the Confederacy, he did the most prudent thing. Having barely the money he needed for passage, he abandoned the store, cheating the owner of the month's rent due, and returned to England.

Later that night, a rock crashed through the front parlor window of the Van Lew home, waking the sleeping occupants. When they came down to see what caused the noise, they found a large rock, with a note tied around it, on the floor. The note read:

Mrs. Van Lough,

Look out for your fig bushes. There ain't much left of them now. White caps are around town. They are coming at night. Look out! Look out! Look out! Your house is going at last.

FIRE
WHITE CAPS
Please give me some of your blood to write letters with.

Also on the paper were crude drawings of a "skull and crossbones" and of a house being set on fire. The residents looked out the window and saw some young boys running down 23rd street. They glanced at each other with knowing looks that said, "We brought this upon ourselves by choosing our unpopular path of righteousness." Without a word being spoken, they all returned to their bedrooms for the night, somewhat shaken by the threat of the house being set on fire.

Early the next morning, Elizabeth surveyed the damage. Bushes had been trampled beyond revival; plants pulled out of the ground, branches from the painstakingly planted, cultivated, and pruned trees had been broken and dangled lifelessly.

The garden had always been a source of great pride and pleasure for the Van Lew family ever since John Van Lew bought the house and laid out the garden over forty years ago. It would take significant resources, energy, and time to restore the garden to its previous splendor; all things which Elizabeth had little of now. She felt a mixture of sadness and anger over this wasteful destruction of something so innocent and beautiful.

Then, a feeling of compassion overcame her initial reactions as she put the losses in perspective. "As unpleasant as it is for me to experience the loss of something so treasured, it pales beside the losses other people have suffered as a result of this hateful conflict—losses of crops, livestock, property, limbs, eyesight, homes, and loved ones. This damage is really a small price to pay for following my heart, my faith, and for doing what I know is right!"

February 6th, 1865 was a bitterly cold day. At the railroad depot in Columbus, South Carolina, General Winder and some of his staff boarded the train bound for Wilmington, North Carolina. The entourage was scheduled to make a stop at Florence, South Carolina, some 100 miles away to meet with prison officials to discuss evacuation contingency planning.

It was late in the day when the train pulled into the Front Street Station in Florence. Rather than going directly to the Gamble Hotel across the street to freshen up as he normally did, Winder seemed pressured to complete the urgent purpose of the trip. The officers walked briskly into the prison compound looking for its Commanding Officer, who was not in his office at that late hour. Suddenly, Winder clutched his chest and silently slumped to the cold ground, suffering, as later diagnosed a massive heart attack. The officers gathered around him; one of them removing his own coat and placing it around Winder to help keep him warm. But, it was to no avail. Without ever regaining consciousness, Winder suffered the same fate, as had so many thousands of men under his supervision. He died surrounded by his comrades in arms … not from a battlefield wound … but nevertheless … he lay dead on a miserable prison floor.

Captain Cashmeyer accompanied the body back to Columbia. Telegrams of his death were sent immediately to Richmond and other points within the prison system. Very late that night, when word was spread of Winder's death, one of the prisoners in the Columbia prison broke the silence by shouting for all to hear, "Hell has received reinforcements … Winder is dead!" To which all the prisoners let out a rousing cheer. The guards made no attempt to quiet the prisoners. This was the only event they had been able to vent their frustration on and lift their spirits over during their miserable existence while in captivity.

General Winder's body was returned to Columbia to lie in state in City Hall. After the service at Trinity Church, he was buried February 9th, 1865 in a temporary, unmarked grave for safety. Thirteen years later, his remains would be transferred to his home state of Maryland and re-interred in Greenmount Cemetery in Baltimore.

Elizabeth sent a letter of condolence to Mrs. Winder expressing her genuine sympathy over her loss and sincere gratitude for all that she and the General had done for the Van Lew Family.

Adjutant-General Samuel Cooper notified Brigadier General Gideon J. Pillow that he was to replace Winder as Confederate Commissary-General of Prisoners. Pillow was one of the two anti-heroes who stole away in the night at Fort Donelson to avoid capture and the embarrassment of having turned a possible Confederate rout into a defeat.

Anticipating Sherman's imminent arrival, Pillow ordered the transfer of 10,000 prisoners out of Florence Prison to Charlotte, North Carolina; nearly 2000 officers from Columbia, South Carolina, and another 600 prisoners from Hilton Head, South Carolina. There were now about 7000 survivors left out of the 10,000 prisoners they received in Salisbury Prison in North Carolina. Functioning without Winder's knowledge and iron-fisted direction of the Confederate prison system, the prisoner movement situation was filled with conflicting orders and communications and was in a state of total chaos.

On February 12th, his fifty-sixth birthday, the Electoral College officially notified Lincoln of his election by a vote of 212 to 21.

Meanwhile, there was little activity along the Richmond-Petersburg entrenchment line … Lee was pleading for more men, rations, and clothing; hoping for a miracle. While Grant was as determined as ever to wait and wear the enemy down. Lee's army was losing men by desertion at the rate of almost every other man. When they enlisted, they were motivated to fight to "defend their way of life" … "home and hearth." Now, with much of that destroyed, they found little reason to continue. They had little food and suffered from boredom, homesickness, and frostbite—many had inadequate clothing, including shoes. The

President Abraham Lincoln

tear-stained letters they received from home, begging them to return, were the deciding factors for many. It was more than enough reason to desert after receiving a letter pleading, "If you don't return home soon, there will be not only nothing, but no one to return to. We will all be in the grave besides the others for lack of food and adequate shelter." Some men took to shooting off a finger or thumb causing them to be discharged as unfit for duty. The first men to use this painful ploy were successful. As the practice became more prevalent, a court martial and prison became the reward, or worse … a return to duty as "cannon fodder."

Elizabeth kept Grant informed daily with details of the desperate situation in Richmond and of Lee's urgent requests. She also related the government's last ditch pleas for support from the citizens to donate that which they were unable or unwilling to give to prop up the collapsing rebellion, and of the dissension and opposition within the Confederate administration and military.

Despite the mix-ups, Grant opened the way for 15,000 Federal prisoners to be returned during the last week of February. The men, who somehow managed to make it back to their lines in their emaciated and sickened condition, got a hero's welcome from their comrades in arms. The prisoners cheered for General Grant, Sherman, and Lincoln, but, mostly … for "General Exchange."

Tears of joy and relief filled the eyes of the prisoners, while tears of compassion and disbelief filled the eyes of the witnesses of the parade of hobbling skeletons. They thought, "Most corpses on the battlefield looked healthier than these poor souls. What determination to survive … what wills to live!"

CHAPTER 34

Evacuation, Conflagration, & Confrontation

Late at night in Washington, a tired Lincoln had been occupied signing bills passed by the Congress at the last minute and preparing his Inaugural Address for the next day. He was also writing instructions to Grant on how to respond to Lee's request to discuss a peaceful conclusion between the top military leaders—since the politicians couldn't come up with one. Lincoln thought of his oath, which he would repeat the next day, March 4ᵗʰ, "To preserve, protect and defend the Constitution of the United States against all foes, foreign or domestic" as he corresponded to Grant. Unwilling to weaken Presidential authority, or risk "old West Point cronies" from making political deals or concessions that would negate all that he had worked and stood for, Lincoln forbade Grant from conducting peace talks. However, he did give Grant authority and encouragement to discuss with General Lee the terms of the surrender of Lee's Army.

The cold and rainy Inauguration Day in Washington did not restrict the huge throng of over 30,000 citizens outside the Capital from witnessing Lincoln's swearing-in ceremony and listening to his important, wartime address. One of the more intent listeners, no more than fifty feet away, was an angry man by the name of John Wilkes Booth.

Around mid-morning the rain stopped, but the sky remained dark and overcast with ominous clouds hanging over the outdoor swearing-in platform. However, just as Lincoln rose from his seat to receive a second ovation from the multitude, the sun's golden rays shone on him like a spotlight, as if commanded by a heavenly director as an indication of approval for all to see.

Lincoln's message to the nation and to the world was simple, short, and punctuated with his views about the war and his hopes for a healing peace.

"… Both parties deprecated war, but one of them would make war rather than let the Nation survive, and the other would accept war rather than let it perish … Fondly do we hope—fervently do we pray—that this mighty scourge of war may speedily pass away … with malice toward none; with charity for all; with firmness in the right, as God gives us to see the right, let us strive on to finish the work we are in; to bind up the Nation's wounds; to care for him who shall have borne the battle, and for his widow, and his orphan—to do all which may achieve and cherish a lasting peace among ourselves and with all nations."

"Amen," said Elizabeth as she read the full context of his eloquent sentiments in the newspaper, "We will strive to finish the work we are in ... and will cherish a lasting peace." More committed than ever, despite the numerous hardships and persecution, Elizabeth's tired body received a much needed jolt of energy from Lincoln's words.

Showing how desperate the situation had become, the Confederate Congress authorized the recruitment of blacks as soldiers. Aware that the North had already proven the battle worthiness of blacks, the South envisioned conscripting 300,000 black men to shore up their rapidly depleting ranks. The value of slaves had already dropped to one-tenth of their prewar value, while the Confederate currency had dropped to one-sixtieth of its value. In some Richmond markets, speculators would not even take 100 Confederate dollars in exchange for one dollar in gold. The currency simply was not worth the paper it was printed on.

Few Richmonders had reason to go out, and the streets seemed deserted. A few curious people ventured out to Capitol Square to view the training of the uniformed black companies to see what kind of soldiers they would make, but the people usually came away even more depressed at the state of affairs.

To add to the returning Confederate prisoners' woes, Special Order No. 53 dated March 4th commanded that:

"All furloughs granted to exchanged prisoners ... are hereby revoked, and all enlisted men who are exchanged will at once report for duty."

For many of the men who had not been home or seen their loved ones for months, or years, this was a demoralizing stab in the back, and any who could avoid reporting for duty, did so.

On Thursday, March 23rd, Lincoln met with Grant at his City Point headquarters for a first-hand look at the military activity. Grant conducted strategy briefings, after which Lincoln gave his personal thanks to Grant for accepting his son Robert as a captain on his staff. The meetings, held away from Washington and its hectic schedule, gave an exhausted President some much-needed rest.

Meanwhile, Elizabeth had received word from Samuel Ruth that Lee was about to make a last ditch attempt to break Grant's strangle hold. She immediately notified Grant to be prepared.

Lee had been counting on Grant not attacking until April, when the rain-soaked, muddy roads would be dried out. Lee hoped to make an early morning surprise assault on the line at Fort Stedman and, thereafter, taking the fort and seizing the military railroad. By splitting the Union army, it would provide an opening for his men to pass through safely and head south to join up with Johnston's forces.

Lee made his move at 4:30 in the morning on the 25th of March and captured Fort Stedman. His opponents, however, were seasoned veterans who, when reinforced by General Parke's Union troops, counterattacked and threw the Confederates back to their original position, taking some of their advance posts and inflicting thousands of casualties; a strategy Lee could ill afford to continue.

Lincoln, still aboard the River Queen at the City Point dock, was awakened by all the gunfire. Later, when Captain Robert Lincoln came aboard to join his parents for breakfast, he matter-of-factly informed them that there had been a "little rumpus up the line this morning, ending about where it began," sounding very much like General Grant's manner of speaking. Later that afternoon, the presidential party reviewed the troops near the battle scene.

This bold attack by the Confederates stirred Grant to action, and he decided to quickly end the siege, destroy Lee's army as a fighting unit, and with it—the Rebellion. His plan was to get south of Lee, cut off his one remaining rail line, and force him to capitulate.

On the 29th, Grant rolled into action with heavy troop movement on the Southside Railroad toward the Five Forks junction. More "checkerboard moves" by both Grant and Lee made Lee aware of the futility of his situation, and he promptly notified Confederate President Davis. Powerless to do anything to assist Lee, Davis returned home from his office and sent his reluctant wife, Varina, the children, a few servants, and some family friends out of the city on the evening train to Danville, Virginia.

April 2nd was a beautiful spring day in Richmond. There were yellow flowers in bloom, and the trees were showing signs of new life after a bitter winter of dormancy. The Passion Sunday service at the crowded St. Paul's Church was half over when a messenger went to pew 63 and handed Davis the fateful news. Lee's forces had been penetrated in three places, and he was forced to retreat from the entrenchment protecting Richmond and Petersburg. Grant's attack on Richmond was inevitable, the city must be evacuated and the government offices moved to Danville, 140 miles to the south.

A pale and grim-faced Davis quietly left the church, going straight to his office in the Treasury Building. Congress had adjourned, so it would not be necessary to notify them. He immediately summoned his Adjutant General and the Cabinet. They discussed and made arrangements for the shipping of the most valuable government records via the Richmond and Danville Railroad.

All the gold and silver bullion and coins that were left in the treasury were crated for shipment. It amounted to less than $500,000—the total meager wealth of the nation.

Orders were given and carried out to destroy the James River fleet. Banks were opened and depositors swarmed in to withdraw their money. Some of the city's Defense Battalion was sent to guard the government's warehouses. Confusion seemed to be the order of the day as cabinet members scurried about looking for the latest information and guidance. They packed personal belongings, papers, valuables, and, in the process, aroused panic amongst the citizenry. Porters, heavily laden with items of personal property, ferried back and forth between the homes of loyal Confederates anxious to leave and the docks of the Kanawa Canal with its west bound boats.

Predictably, Elizabeth was busy watching and noting everything. She was filled with anticipation at what clearly appeared to be the dying gasps of the Confederacy in Richmond.

With the official channels of communications out of operation, word of mouth had it that Lee had fled west in retreat. The people didn't know what would happen to the city, to them, their homes, their families, and to their livelihoods. They wondered what life under an occupying army would be like. The people, who had been told repeatedly that the Yankees were barbarians, were understandably nervous and fearful. The streets were filled with citizens going to the homes of friends and relatives and places of business trying to decide how best to protect their property, possessions, and loved ones.

Davis, his few possessions and weapons packed, headed for the train depot. It was bedlam as cabinet members, Gorgas and some of his ordinance workers, some wounded Presidential sentries, key government clerks, government-connected entrepreneurs, prominent citizens and their families fought to get on the eight-car passenger train. It was after dark before the trains were overloaded with people and the government's baggage. With a perfect calm on his resolute face, Davis waved his final farewell and boarded the train.

The engine struggled against its load; the wheels spun and then grabbed the steel rail, as the cavalcade started out of the depot. Elizabeth saw a familiar face in the train window at the same time that the face recognized hers. It was New!

He opened the window, shouting and pointing at her, "I knew all along what you were up to, you witch. You were responsible for every anti-Confederacy activity in Richmond. If I ever get the chance, I'll get even with you, one way or another, if it's the last thing I do!"

Elizabeth took a handkerchief from her sleeve, waved it, and gave him a sweet smile as she wished him a loud, "Bon Voyage!" Realizing that she had bested him again, even in their parting, New's face got redder at her, "sendoff" and he struggled for words, but all he could manage through clenched teeth was, "Witch! Witch!"

Elizabeth watched the train disappear into the darkness over the James River and out of sight. The feeling of enormous relief at the ending of New's persecution was mixed with a tinge of regret at having lost an opponent with whom to match wits.

Now the city, from Chimborazzo Hospital at the tip of Church Hill to Camp Lee on the old Fair Grounds, was darkened and deathly still. Windows were shuttered and doors barred. However, near the depot and around the government warehouses stretched along Thirteenth, Fourteenth, and Cary Streets, the crowds had swelled since the trains left. The word had spread amongst the people who were desperate for food and clothing that the military rations and supplies were going to be distributed and then the buildings destroyed.

The distribution went well at first. Then, the typical impatient and greedy few started to help themselves and order was replaced with pandemonium. The soldiers gave up and left the people to fend for themselves. They proceeded with their second responsibility, which was to burn the tobacco warehouses and other government facilities. Torches were lit and thrown into the buildings, which immediately burst into flames.

Now, the last assignment, to destroy the government's supply of multiple-use whiskey, stored in preparation for a siege. First, the soldiers filled their canteens, then their stomachs, after which they smashed the huge barrels.

The mob continued to grow. From out of the dives and brothels, bordering the warehouses, people came hurling garbage and obscenities at the soldiers. At the sight of the stream of whiskey, the mob scrambled with any form of container at hand to obtain this treasure, even to the point of sprawling face down and slurping it up. The horde, turned even rowdier now, joined in the burning and started breaking into nearby stores and began the looting. There was no one to stop them as all authority had vanished.

The Confederate arsenal, with its several hundred carloads of loaded shells, along with the laboratories were ablaze and punctuated the roar, hiss, and crackle of the flames with glass-shattering explosions. Fanned by an intensifying south wind, the flames began to jump to buildings not intended for the torch. Women and crying children rushed from their homes in a panic as the flames licked at the front doors and windows of their houses. Prison guards, fearing for their lives, ran out of the prisons and allowed felons, guilty of every crime against society, to break free and join the burning and looting drunken mob. A number of those incarcerated as spies also ran out and sought solace and protection at the Van Lew mansion.

The original "burning brigade" headed for the Tredegar Iron Works to continue their arson duties. However, the armed Tredegar Battalion, under the command of Brigadier Joseph R. Anderson, stopped them in their tracks from burning their foundry.

Explosions from the Gorgas ordinance works provided a pyrotechnics display over the city and more than enough light to guide the way for the Confederate soldiers moving in from the city's outer defenses. Exploding shells soared high into the night sky like an aerial fireworks display and then fell down on, and ignited, the homes of helpless citizens. People not at the scene could not tell if the noise, fire, shells, and explosions were from the deliberately set fire, or if Grant's forces were bombarding the city. Richmond was now experiencing one of the heaviest bombardments of the entire war. Neighbors of the Van Lews, who previously had treated them as lepers, now helped themselves to Van Lew wheelbarrows to carry away their personal belongings. Meanwhile, Elizabeth had been waiting for this moment for over four years. She rushed up to the secret room and removed a well-wrapped package. Like a child with a Christmas present, she tore wildly at the paper to get at the contents. Once exposed, she kissed the nine-by-twenty foot, thirty-four Star Spangled Banner she had requested from General Butler.

"Nelson! Nelson!" she shouted, "Come to the roof with me!" And up to the roof they scrambled and excitedly raised the first flag of the United States to fly over the former Confederate Capital. As they stared at the sight of the waving Stars and Stripes, tears of pride flooded their eyes, and they made no attempt to hide their emotions.

Elizabeth remembered the words of a poem that seemed as if they were written for this very moment:

> There's a flag hangs over my household,
> whose folds are more dear to me
> than the blood that thrills in my bosom
> its earnest of liberty;
> and dear are the stars it harbors
> in its sunny field of blue
> as the hope of a further heaven
> that lights all our dim lives through.

Their eyes were not the only ones to stare at the sight of the huge symbol of the Union. However, the other eyes were not filled with tears—but with contempt. These were eyes now blinded with rage at whoever was putting "salt in their wound."

"Who dared to put that flag up?" "Let's find out!" And up toward Church Hill they stormed. As they approached the Van Lew mansion someone hollered out, "I know who it is!"

"Who?"

"Who else?" "Crazy Bet, the Van Lew witch!"

"Goddamn the old hag! Let's burn the damn place down along with the flag!"

"Yah, it will serve the witch right for kissing up to the Yanks and niggers!"

"Burn it down!"

"What do you do with witches anyway? Ya' burn them! Burn her too!"

The men stomped up to the front door, trampling her beautiful garden—their torches ready to be thrown—to incinerate the home and its occupants. Suddenly, the door opened, and Elizabeth stepped out alone.

"Get ready to fry witch ... your home and that damn flag are going up in flames!"

"Oh really?' Elizabeth responded, "I know you, and you, and you ..." she screamed, her eyes blazing, her face contorted with rage, as she called out their names while pointing her finger at each of them. "General Grant will be in town within the hour! You do one thing to my home and all of yours will be burned before noon!"

A long and intense staring match followed between Elizabeth and the burly men. The trials and tribulations Elizabeth had endured had forged her resolve, and she was prepared to stand there all night, not giving one inch.

Stunned by her fearlessness and their inability to intimidate her, and stung by the force of her counter threats, they turned silent. In the back of their minds were the newspaper accounts of the destruction left behind in other vanquished Southern cities. Then, like a squad of soldiers given the command to "fall out," they dispersed into the night and returned to the burning and looting of Richmond.

By now, the entire lower section of the city was ablaze and out of control. Explosions continued. Smoke filled the air. Elizabeth stood alone observing the devastation and thought to herself, "Oh my beloved Richmond! Our beautiful flour mills, Haxall and Gallego, the largest in the world and the prize of the city, being destroyed." Before her eyes, square after square of stores, dwellings, factories, government buildings, theatres, banks, hotels, bridges, all wrapped in fire in a scene of wild grandeur.

Elizabeth thought, "The clouds of smoke enveloping the city are like incense rising up from the land asking for its deliverance! What a moment—avenging wrath appeased in flames! Civilization has advanced a century. Justice, truth, and humanity are vindicated. Labor is now without manacles—honored and respected. The walls of our houses sway, as the heart of our city has become an altar, like a votive candle to God's almighty work. This wonderful deliverance wrought out for the Negro. They feel but cannot tell you. When eternity shall unknot the records of time, however, their unpenned stories will be written for them by the Almighty then to be read before a listening universe. Bottled are their tears on His ear."

Just before dawn the next morning, April 3rd, the city of Richmond was awakened and rocked by a tremendous deep boom as if in the grip of a giant earthquake. A powder magazine near the poor house had exploded from the heat of the still spreading fire, killing a dozen innocent people.

As the last Confederate soldiers crossed the Fourteenth Street Bridge, they tarred and burned it behind them, adding to the holocaust. The roar of the flames now sounded like a deafening hurricane. Sparks flew in the wind from building to building, and the smoke blanketed the city like a black fog.

As the partially obscured sun rose around six o'clock that morning, the eighty-year old Richmond Mayor, Joseph Mayo, and his committee, carrying the City Seal for identification, rode out of the city. The anxious group waved a makeshift white flag as they raced to meet the Union commander. They officially surrendered Richmond to Major-General Godfrey Weitzel, and they pleaded with him to save the city from being totally destroyed by the fire and to restore law and order to the city. As opposed to most of Grant's other hard fought and, in human terms, high-priced victories, the incisive capture of Richmond became synonymous with a task easily accomplished, and the quote, "Like Grant took Richmond!" was born.

Union troops marched into the city, led by members of a black Cavalry unit. They were cheered and danced around by former slaves whose arms were filled with booty from the continual looting and who offered them whiskey. As the troops headed up Main Street approaching 9th, the tremendous heat from the adjacent burning buildings singed the soldiers' facial hairs.

The combat troops were followed into the city by troops commanded by Brigadier General Edward Hastings Ripley, of the 9th Vermont Volunteers, who was given two assignments. First, he had the difficult assignment of bringing law and order back to the city. The second task was equally monumental; putting out the voracious fire which had already destroyed hundreds of buildings in the heart of the commercial district and was now threatening the residential.

As the troops reached Capital Square, they saw the many homeless women, crying children, and old men huddled around the few pieces of personal belongings and furniture that they were able to salvage from their fire-ravaged homes.

Even more upsetting to the Union troops was the "Stars and Bars" they saw still flying over the Capital building. They rushed to haul it down and replaced it with the "Stars and Stripes." The honor of raising the Union flag went to Louis Grund. It will erroneously be called the first time "Old Glory" was flown publicly over the former Confederate Capital in over four years. Due to the thick smoke, they did not know that the true honor should have gone to Elizabeth Van Lew for raising the first flag, which still flew proudly over the Van Lew mansion.

General Grant was fearful for the safety of his "spymaster," and he sent his aide, Colonel Ely S. Parker, hurrying to Richmond "To see that Miss Van Lew was properly cared for."

Parker galloped to Richmond, entering with Weitzel's troops. Having been given directions to her home, he was astonished to see the huge star spangled banner flying over the Van Lew residence. The house was filled with many Union people including young, fearful Erasmus Ross. Ross had played his anti-Union role a little too well. Several former Libby prisoners had threatened to kill him on sight and were on the lookout for him. They never imagined he would be at the Van Lew home.

General Edward H. Ripley

The servants informed Colonel Parker that, "Miss Liz went down to the city when she saw the troops marching in."

The colonel mounted up and began his search in the burning, smoldering remains of Richmond. After making many inquiries and following many leads, Elizabeth was found in the War Department Building knee deep in scattered papers, records, ledgers, and documents. Parker identified himself and gave her General Grant's regards and gratitude for her long service to him. He then asked Elizabeth what work she was engaged in at the moment and if she would like "protection" until law and order was restored.

Elizabeth thanked the Colonel and explained that she was busy trying to find papers that might be of value to General Grant. She declined his kind offer of protection, saying, "I haven't felt this safe in Richmond in over four years."

Based on what little information Grant had told Parker about Elizabeth, he was surprised by neither her activity nor her refusal of protection. Elizabeth, anxious to return to her "work," She thanked the Colonel again and asked him to extend an open invitation to the General to call on her upon his arrival in Richmond. One of the documents she obviously hoped to find was the infamous "Dahlgren Document."

Assured of her safety and anxious to return to join Grant in his pursuit of Lee, Colonel Parker promised to pass her invitation along to the General and bade her a respectful "Good Morning."

On his way out of the city, Parker made one stop at General Weitzel's office in the Hall of the State Capitol, previously occupied by the Virginia House of Delegates. After explaining to the General the purpose of his trip to Richmond, Parker asked Weitzel if he would be so kind as to have someone check on the safety of the Van Lew family, from time to time, as a favor to General Grant. He told him that Grant was concerned about possible recriminations by the citizenry for the loyal support and service given by the Van Lews throughout the war. Weitzel made a note of the Van Lew name and address and gave Parker his word to comply with Grant's request. The Colonel thanked him and rushed off to catch up with Grant.

By late that afternoon, despite sporadic sniper fire, Ripley's men had restored law and order. Looters were arrested, snipers disposed of, and the fire was reduced to smoldering embers. Nearly 900 buildings had been totally destroyed and hundreds more badly damaged.

The citizens of Richmond were filled with apprehension, remembering the fate of other cities in the South occupied by Union forces where looting, destruction, and other evils befell the populace. In reality, they had more to fear from other evil-intentioned citizens than from the soldiers. Not one incident of violence was committed by the troops that occupied Richmond. On the contrary, the Union soldiers were directly responsible for saving the city from total destruction.

CHAPTER 35

Visits, Sad News, & A Return

The same day that Richmond fell victim to the torch, Captain Paul Silman was with General James Wilson's 2nd and 4th division forces approaching Selma, Alabama. He was attached to the 4th U.S. Cavalry. The forces under Wilson were pursuing and whittling away at the troops of the legendary General Nathan Bedford Forrest.

Forrest had retreated inside the fortifications around Selma, the most important city in the Confederate southwest, heretofore considered impregnable with its arsenals, workshops, and foundries. A stroke of luck occurred earlier that morning when Wilson's men came upon the English civil engineer that helped lay out Selma's fortifications. The engineer was easily "persuaded" to sketch out a complete map of the defenses. With careful study, Wilson was able to determine the most vulnerable points for the assault.

After a quick reconnaissance verified the accuracy of the drawing, Wilson assigned attack routes to his commanders. Paul's men were to dismount and join in with a large contingent of other cavalrymen and infantry soldiers who would attack the earthworks on foot.

To many of the troops, this seemed to be a suicidal assignment to be pitted against 7000 of Forrest's seasoned veterans. Experience had proven that a force behind an earthwork could withstand a far greater attacking force, and that Cavalry never attacked fortifications. The engagement would be a deadly test between the sword, in the hands of brave cavalrymen, and the pistol in the hands of those just as desperately brave foot soldiers.

The designated time for the two-pronged attack was "after dark." However, General Long's division, which included Paul's troops, went forward just after 5pm because their rear had come under attack from a newly-arrived Confederate contingent that was attempting to link up with Forrest inside the city.

Paul led his men directly onto the breastworks, which they peppered with their Spencer Repeaters. To their astonishment, they succeeded in surmounting each obstacle with incredible ease and engaged the Confederates in hand-to-hand combat. In less than thirty minutes they had scaled, scurried, scrambled, fought, and then chased the confused Confederates without faltering once. They captured 2700 men, 96 artillery pieces, and considerable other resources.

One sharpshooter of the group of snipers, safely positioned to assist in covering the retreating Confederates, fired his last shot before joining his hastily retreating comrades. That final shot hit Paul in the chest. He winced and fell back as the oozing blood turned his uniform crimson. From the expression on the faces of those of his men who rushed to assist him, it was clear that his wound was serious. Their countenance told him that his life would soon be over.

Paul attempted to speak, but no words came forth—only a feeble movement of his lips. In those last moments, he thought of Elizabeth, and how it might have been. He wanted to see her, to speak to her again, but knew it was too late. If only he was able, he would have told her that, "He was sorry that it turned out this way. That he would have made a truly loving and devoted husband. That he loved her and hoped and prayed that she would be watched over while carrying out her perilous tasks … and that the rest of her life would be a happier one … and that she would not forget him …"

He closed his eyes, weakened from the loss of blood, and breathed his last breath.

Paul never heard the accolades calling the successful attack, "One of the most remarkable achievements in the annals of cavalry!"

It would be some time before Elizabeth learned of the heartbreaking loss of her post-war dreams, joining the hundreds of thousands who mourned the life-altering loss of their dearly beloveds … the hopes … the plans … gone forever. Along with their broken hearts, they were left with the unforgettable memories of what was—and what might have been.

The loud cheering and shouting on the streets on the morning of April 4th shook many Richmonders out of their lethargy. The President of the United States, Abraham Lincoln, was in Richmond. Admiral David D. Porter, Captain Bell, a few marines, and his young son, Tad, escorted the President.

While there were almost no whites in close proximity, there were hundreds of blacks that surrounded Lincoln to get a look at him, to touch him, to hear his voice, and to either shake or kiss his hand. Their enthusiasm knew no limits. They cheered, laughed, cried, sang hymns of praise, and shouted their feelings. "Gowd bress Massa Linkum!" "Da lawd sav' Fader Abraham!"

Tears started to well up in the President's eyes, and his voice started to crack with emotion, so much so that he was barely able to acknowledge their heartfelt praise and words of thanks.

They followed him as he walked up 10th Street, past the still smoldering ruins of the half-burned city, to Capitol Square. Waiting there for him was a fine carriage and an escort of black cavalrymen. Just as he was seated and ready to ride on his tour of the points of interest in the city, General Weitzel, who was part of the welcoming committee at the dock, approached him.

"Mr. President, this very persuasive lady insisted on meeting you and shaking your hand. May I present Miss Elizabeth Van Lew,"

"Good morning, Miss Van Lew."

"It's a great pleasure to meet you, Mr. President," Elizabeth said with sincerity. She then pointed to the huge United States' flag flying over her home saying, "Being able to raise that honored flag over my home was one of the greatest moments of my life. For what you've had to endure to make it possible, I'm deeply grateful. God bless you, Mr. President."

"I'm glad I've lived long enough to see it myself," he replied.

As he held her tiny hand in his, he looked in her eyes and wondered if this could be the same "loyalist woman in Richmond" who was writing the secret dispatches to General Sharpe. His curiosity aroused, he asked, "Do you have a habit of sending red roses along with your letters?"

Realizing that he must have heard of her policy of sending roses with her dispatches to General Grant, Sharpe, or Butler, she smilingly admitted, "Only for special people—on special occasions."

With the confirmation of her identity, Lincoln laughed briefly, shook her hand with gusto saying, "And the country is grateful to you. God Bless you, Miss Van Lew!"

"Mr. President, our schedule," reminded Admiral Porter. Lincoln released her hand and managed a resigned, war-weary smile as the carriage lurched forward.

"Who was that lady?" Tad inquired. "She was one of our 'soldiers' not in uniform whose contributions and sacrifices for our country may never be fully known or appreciated."

His father's answer puzzled him, but when he added, "I'll tell you more about her later, son," the boy was satisfied for the moment. As the Presidential carriage headed for the former Davis residence, Elizabeth joined Nelson and Mary, who had accompanied her to see the President. Elizabeth had invited other loyalists from her circle to see the President. But, they declined for fear that they would be exposed as sympathizers, and therefore traitors, and subject to the same persecution from their friends and neighbors as Elizabeth had been and would continue to be as long as "Richmond" had a memory.

General Butler, reflecting on Elizabeth's service and the fact that her brother John was still in Washington, dispatched a memo to Colonel James A. Hardie, an aide to Secretary of War Stanton. He recommended that a pass be issued to John Van Lew allowing him to return to Richmond to be repatriated with his family.

"The sister of John Van Lew is my secret correspondent in Richmond and has furnished me with valuable information. Their family is most loyal.

Miss Van Lew is now the repository of the (location of the) secret burial place of Colonel Ulric Dahlgren's body, whose remains were taken by the Unionists of Richmond from a dishonored grave and put in a place of safety known but to her. She is mentioned with commendation in some of my dispatches to the War Department."

John was granted the pass and rushed back to Richmond. He was overwhelmed and disheartened to see all the open spaces in the city punctuated only by columns of standing bricks that once housed the center of commerce. Gone too, were the Van Lew & Taylor Hardware business buildings. His eyes turned toward Church Hill, and he spotted the giant flag still waving proudly over the Van Lew home. "That's got to be Elizabeth's work!" It was a happy reunion that followed at the Van Lews' after the servants rushed to tell Elizabeth that her brother John was coming up the rear, terraced-garden path to the house.

Things began to return to their pre-war normalcy at the Van Lew home. The large flag was taken down and carefully furled; notes, papers, and the "country-woman's" outfit were tied up and stored away in the secret room. The faithful mare, which had been shuffled between the library, wine cellar, smokehouse, and barn, to avoid detection, was finally returned to her stall in the barn. The major casualties were the books, which the mare had taken a fancy to nibbling on.

With the hardware business burned to the ground and no work to be had, the only Van Lew family income came from the adjacent properties they owned on the city block between 24th, 25th, Grace, and Franklin Streets.

Bitterness, resentment, and a burning desire for vengeance was eating away at many that were devoted to the Confederacy and its ideals. However, John Wilkes Booth and his circle of collaborators took it a step further. They planned to exact revenge on the men they held responsible for the demise of the Confederacy—the leaders in Washington. Booth was the only one successful in carrying out his unheroic act to its infamous end.

On April 14th, the President and Mrs. Lincoln were watching the comedy "Our American Cousin" at Ford 's Theatre in Washington. During the third act, Booth, a prominent actor, slipped into the President's box and fired a point-blank, single shot from his derringer to the back of Lincoln's head. The reverberation from that shot was felt throughout the country. The critically wounded Lincoln was carried across the street from the theatre where the doctors worked feverishly to save the President.

The news of the shooting of Lincoln stunned the nation and there was in the North, sadness and prayer for his recovery … in the South, there was fear and prayer for his recovery. Clearly, Lincoln was more moderate and humane than was Andrew Johnson, the Vice President, who would assume power if Lincoln died. Strangely, Johnson, who was also a Southerner, hated Jeff Davis.

Andrew Johnson

As President, Johnson would set harsh terms of surrender, and even harsher treatment after the surrender, since the South would be blamed for the assassination as part of the desperate plot to blow up the White House and kill the Cabinet members.

Because the bullet fired at Lincoln was at point-blank range, the physical damage was extensive and beyond human repair. When he died the following morning, with his wife and Cabinet members in attendance, Secretary Stanton gave him a simple and eloquent, Lincolnesque-style eulogy, "Now he belongs to the ages."

Meanwhile, surrounded, vastly outnumbered, and with little doubt about the outcome of continued hostilities, Confederate General Lee did the distasteful, but honorable, thing to prevent further, pointless bloodshed—he capitulated. At 3:30 in the afternoon of April 9th, 1865, at Appomattox Court House, Generals Lee and Grant signed the Terms of Surrender Agreement. Now, with the largest army of the Confederacy defeated, it would only be a matter of time before the other Confederate commanders in the field would have to make the same unpleasant, but realistic choice. Cannons fired by the occupying Union forces announced the news of Lee's surrender to the citizens of Richmond.

Further south, the Confederate government made a hasty retreat from Danville, Virginia, moving farther away to Greensborough, North Carolina. They were not very welcome in Greensborough because the townspeople felt the North would punish them for harboring them there. Generals' Johnston and Beauregard visited Davis there and told him that surrender was their choice and that they should ask for terms from Sherman. After hearing them out, Davis consented. The Generals left heading east to talk with Sherman. Davis and his entourage continued their flight, heading south to Charlotte, North Carolina.

When Davis got the news of Lincoln's death, he decided to head immediately for Florida and, if necessary, out of the country, as several others had done. His accompanying guard force had dwindled along with the "treasury," from thousands of loyal supporters to only a handful. And, the "Treasury" went from a relative prosperity of half a million to twenty-five thousand dollars. It seemed that every time one of his supporters left, they did so with a portion of the "treasury." Davis, his family, and the dwindling number of followers were welcome as patriotic heroes in some areas, and in others as lepers.

Jefferson Finis Davis

Finally, Davis was captured, just sixty-five miles from Florida in Irwinville, Georgia and taken to Fortress Monroe to await trial.

Back in Richmond, Elizabeth's continued interest and voracious appetite for news and information on the national military and political scenes keep her busy reading the newspapers. Of course, she had an ulterior motive. Her eyes flitted from page to page hoping to find some news about Captain Paul Silman or his regiment. There was significant news about the events in and around Washington but nothing concerning Captain Silman or the action in Selma Alabama.

Elizabeth had to know, so she immediately sent two letters that involved "unfinished business." The first was sent to General Grant revealing to him that she knew where the body of Colonel Ulric Dahlgren was safely buried. She asked him if he could notify Admiral Dahlgren to make the necessary transportation arrangements. She would meet the Admiral's authorized representatives in Richmond and escort them to the secret location for the disinterring of the body.

Grant immediately notified the Admiral and the body was removed from its third grave and shipped to Philadelphia aboard a special train draped with mourning. In Philadelphia, the young Colonel received a belated, but elaborate military funeral and an honorable final resting place in Philadelphia's North Hill Cemetery.

The grateful Admiral had offered Lipscomb, the Lohmann brothers and Rowley a reward for their "contributions to the protection of my son's remains." They all refused to take the money saying that they, "Did it for humanity and therefore couldn't see accepting money from the poor boy's father."

Later, when the full saga of Dahlgren's body disappearance made the news, Richmonders, and especially former Confederates, were amazed and shocked at the audacity and ingenuity of the escapade, but they were not at all surprised that Elizabeth was involved.

The second letter penned by Elizabeth went to General Benjamin Butler. The letter thanked the General for arranging the passage of her brother John back to Richmond. In addition, she asked if he could inform her of the post where Captain Paul Silman was assigned. Elizabeth explained that she wanted to communicate directly with the Captain to thank him for his support during the Richmond raid by Kilpatrick and Dahlgren. She was concerned about his health following the serious wound he had suffered and captivity in Libby, and stated that she has not heard from the Captain in over a month.

Butler assured Elizabeth that he would have the records checked immediately, sensing that Elizabeth had more than the health of the Captain at heart. The "wheels of motion" were set in place as Butler, appreciative of her service to him, decided to handle the investigation himself and privately report his findings to her.

Butler's response marked "Confidential and Private" came by special military courier. When Elizabeth received the official-looking envelope, her hands began to tremble in anticipation, but she held off opening it until she was alone upstairs in the sanctuary of her bedroom.

Dear Miss Van Lew,

In response to your inquiry regarding Captain Paul Silman, I regret to inform you that the Captain was one of our brave officers who fell during the successful attack on the City of Selma, Alabama April 2, 1865. The Captain died a hero's death while participating in one of the most remarkable achievements in the annals of Cavalry. I am sorry to bring you such unpleasant news, I wish it could have been otherwise. If I can be of any further service to you in the future, do not hesitate to notify me. I remain your obedient servant.

Benjamin F. Butler
Major-General

Elizabeth stared at the words "brave officers who fell." Stunned with disbelief, disappointed, and devastated, a feeling of numbness filled her body. She cried out "No! No! Not Paul! It can't be true!" And she burst into tears as she fell with her face into the pillow to muffle the sounds of her heart-wrenching wails of sorrow.

All the plans, all the hopes, all the dreams, all the waiting … all gone! Gone in an instant … gone on one of the very last battles … how close we came … we almost made it … now it's gone … it's over! And the crying and remorse continued until sleep, blessed sleep, brought its temporary relief.

The next day, Elizabeth showed the letter to her mother, and like most mothers, she consoled and comforted Elizabeth in her loss. After a lengthy heart-to-heart, woman-to-woman commiseration, Mrs. Van Lew gave Elizabeth some advice.

"You were invited to visit the Revere and Lee families after the War. Why don't you go up to Boston, get away from Richmond, and visit them now? Remember the last time we were disheartened. We went to Europe and we felt much better by the time we returned? You don't have either responsibilities or restrictions anymore." After reflecting on the advice, Elizabeth said, "You're right mother. Yes, I will go, if they'll have me."

Elizabeth penned a quick note to Mrs. Paul Revere. She identified herself and stated that she would be in the Boston area the first week of August. She added that it would please her greatly to see Mrs. Revere along with Colonel Lee and any of the other men who were prisoners with Paul in Richmond.

A quick response arrived, "Please come. We are all looking forward to your visit."

The welcoming committee of men, women, and children at the Canton Junction train depot southwest of Boston, Massachusetts, was fitting for a returned family member from war.

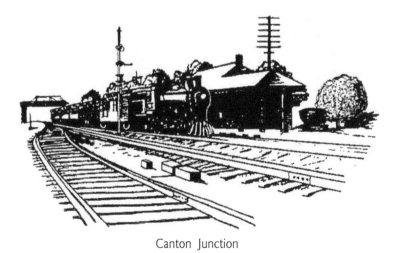

Canton Junction

There were introductions, handshakes, hugs, kisses and flowers. Elizabeth was overcome by the sincere display of affection for someone most of them had never met. For the first time, she fully realized the impact that her humanitarian kindness lavished on the prisoners in Richmond, had on the families of those unfortunate men.

The festivities continued at the Revere's Canton summer home a short carriage ride away.

Those attending consisted mainly of females who had all experienced the loss of a loved one in the War; Paul Revere at Gettysburg, Edward Revere at Antietam, Paul Silman at Selma—and they shared each other's grief.

After covering many facets of their lives before, during, and after the War's end, the topic of discussion turned to recollections and anecdotes of what each person was thinking and doing during the men's six months of imprisonment as hostages in Richmond. The women expressed their appreciation and stressed the value that Elizabeth's treatment, courtesies, funds and, most importantly, the flow of continual communication had on the spirit of the men while they were in such a wretched and hostile environment. It did a lot for them to know that someone was on the scene who cared, and who kept them informed. For them, the worst was "not knowing."

Paul's sister Pauline, Mrs. John Phillips Reynolds, and their little son, John Jr., took to Elizabeth, and they insisted that she stay with them the remainder of the visit. Elizabeth joyfully accepted the gracious offer.

A week passed all too quickly, and the bond of friendship that developed was a strong and lasting one. Elizabeth thanked the Reynolds for their wonderful hospitality and tour of the copper and steel factories and invited them to visit her when things got more settled in Richmond.

They thanked Elizabeth for coming and encouraged her to let them know if there was anything they could do for her to repay her kindness and generosity. She had left Richmond fatigued and heartbroken. She returned from Boston rested and rejuvenated. Besides the immediate mental and physical benefits, the trip will later prove to be one of the most important events in her life.

CHAPTER 36

A Four—Star Visit & An Appointment

Elizabeth was ecstatic when she received the letter announcing that General Ulysses Simpson and Mrs. Julia Dent Grant planned to visit Richmond and would very much like to meet with her.

"Get the 'McClellan Room' ready in case they want to stay over! Break out our best china! Polish the silver! Clean up the house! Do what you can with the garden! Clean up the barn! I want the best fish and meat you can get! Let's make lots of delicacies!" Elizabeth directed with glee. Her enthusiasm spilled over to the rest of the household, and they set about preparing with a fervor never before experienced at the Van Lew residence.

All eyes were focused on 2311 Grace Street as General and Mrs. Grant's carriage and military escort pulled up in front of the Van Lew home. Nelson rushed out, opened the gate, and looked to see if there was any luggage to bring in. There was none. Elizabeth, her mother, brother, and Mary waited in the opened doorway.

The introductions and greetings were warm and sincere, even though Mrs. Grant had never heard of the Van Lews before the visit. The general had told her only that there was a woman to whom the country was indebted for her valiant services during the war. He told her that they must pay her a call when they got to Richmond.

The general expressed his regrets at having only a few hours to spend with the Van Lews. He was on the last legs of a fact-finding tour of the South for President Johnson and had to complete and present the report to the Cabinet on December 15th.

"Yours was the only obligation I personally arranged, Miss Van Lew. I wanted to meet and thank the person who so courageously and devotedly provided the most valuable information from Richmond during the war."

"I felt it my duty to provide it, and I thank you for taking the time from your busy schedule to honor our household with the presence of both you and Mrs. Grant. And, let me add my congratulations on your 'fourth star.'"

The general nodded modestly as the group moved to the large room adjoining the rear portico with its magnificent south-facing view; the vista of which included reconstruction of the city's burned out commercial district.

"Besides the information, I wanted to thank you for the roses. As you can imagine, the smells of the battlefield are not the sweetest, so your roses were a refreshment in my quarters."

Elizabeth smiled and then remembered to thank him for taking care of notifying Admiral Dahlgren. The general responded, "It was our duty to care for that brave young officer. I want you to feel free to correspond any such requests to me personally and, if it is within my power, I'll grant it."

They both laughed at the unintentional play on words, then Grant followed with, "By the way, I heard you caused the Confederacy considerable embarrassment over that incident," he said still smiling.

"It wasn't nearly enough for the terrible way they treated that young hero," Elizabeth asserted, revealing her still smoldering upset over their disrespectful desecration of his body.

Grant responded, "And I heard all about the 'alleged' orders he was supposed to be carrying. I can't think of any senior officer, on either side, who would commit to paper and then transport such inflammatory and self-incriminating orders as those."

"I've heard that General Lee didn't believe they were authentic either," Elizabeth added.

With the topic of Dahlgren's burial and documents concluded, the general offered, "The small favor you asked of me was a military service that the government was obliged to honor. Miss Van Lew, I'll probably never know, nor will you ever relate, the full extent of your contributions on behalf of your country. However, for what I do know, I want you to feel free to ask any favor, in the future, that I can oblige."

"That's very kind General, and I will make the same offer to you."

The rest of the enjoyable visit was spent in questioning and listening to the general's views about the reunification and healing that lay ahead for the country. When his allotted time had expired and the Grants were about to head back to Washington, the general again expressed his gratitude and assured Elizabeth that he would never forget her many services to the country during its desperate days and would remain "her obedient servant."

Grant sent a follow-up "thank you" note to Elizabeth along with a signed photograph of himself. Unbeknown to Elizabeth, her brother John had quietly asked the general for the picture knowing how much Elizabeth would treasure it, but would never ask for it herself.

Throughout the year, Union soldiers for whom Elizabeth had performed some humanitarian service dropped by to thank her, and many gave her some small token of remembrance. Her "collection" included cards, buttons, photographs, drawings, letters, poems, and citations. She would cherish the calling card of Louis Grund who raised the second American Flag to fly over the former Confederate Capital, but her prize would always be the card and picture of General Ulysses S. Grant.

On June 16th, Congress passed the Civil Rights Act over the veto of President Johnson. It gave all males of every race or color born in the United States many rights previously denied to the "non-white" population. The right Elizabeth took issue with was the right of all males to vote. This was the first time that women were specifically excluded in the Constitution. Elizabeth was incensed at this injustice and began her support of Women's Suffrage. She initiated correspondence with her former schoolmate in Philadelphia, Susan B. Anthony.

The Civil Rights Act also incited a group formed in Pulaski, Tennessee by former Confederate General Nathan B. Forrest—the Ku Klux Klan. Forrest claimed the Klan was just a congenial, "good old boys" club of Confederate veterans. The U.S. Government argued that it was committed to the denial of the Negro's civil rights. The "white caps" in Virginia who tormented Elizabeth were willingly assimilated into the Klan as "brothers in purpose."

Charles Phillips, the former newsboy and secret courier for Elizabeth, had been given the opportunity to work in The Richmond Whig newspaper's office doing a variety of jobs after his release from prison. His goal was to become an apprentice reporter. One day while cleaning the office of the editor, who was at lunch, Charles saw a letter on the editor's desk that, because of the name on it, caught his attention. It was from someone in Washington asking questions about Elizabeth Van Lew. Since no one could see him in the office, he picked up the letter and read it.

The writer wanted to know if Elizabeth Van Lew had ever been interviewed, had voluntarily admitted, or had been identified by anyone concerning all of her anti-Confederacy activities during the war. The writer claimed to have learned of the existence of a file of evidence that indicated that she had been a secret agent of the Union. There was a suggestion made to the editor that if he were to interview the Van Lew woman, armed with proof of her secret work, that she might confess since there was no longer a Confederacy to fear. The writer theorized that it would be a perfect opportunity for Van Lew to feed her vanity, satisfying her craving for attention and recognition of her exploits; the editor would gain an "exclusive," and the writer would have the satisfaction of having his suspicions confirmed.

Unfortunately, the editor's practice was to conceal the names of writers dealing with "sensitive" issues, thereby protecting the identity of his sources. The name of the author of this communication had already been cut off the bottom of the letter.

Charles carefully placed the letter back on the desk and told the typesetter that he had to run a quick errand. He headed straight for the Van Lew residence. Elizabeth had always been good to him; in fact, she was the first one on the scene to vouch for him in order to gain his release from prison.

Elizabeth listened carefully as Charles recounted the letter's contents. She asked him to be as accurate as possible with the wording about the discovery of the "existence of a file of evidence." He assured her that the wording he gave her was exact. She complimented Charles on his alertness, thanked him for the prompt relaying of the information to her, and gave him a monetary token of appreciation when he left.

Elizabeth realized the seriousness of having unfriendly eyes sorting through the incriminating files of "evidence" and contemplated what to do about it.

"Oh, God, the names of people I used as couriers, people who escorted and sheltered escaped prisoners, sources of information inside and outside the Confederate government and military, decoded; if anyone sees them … damn! As for me, I don't give a hoot anymore. But the others … the hatred, the name—calling, the nasty treatment, the threats, the reprisals! I must get them back. I hope it's not too late!"

Remembering the words, "feel free to ask any favor in the future," Elizabeth grabbed a piece of stationery and wrote a letter to General Grant. She recalled that only George Washington had held the rank of full "General," and began by again congratulating him on being only the second man in American history to earn a fourth star from Congress. She ended the letter with a fervent plea to have all of her secret war-time correspondence returned to her, explaining that she had learned that someone knew about the file and was about to reveal its contents to the press. Elizabeth reasoned that if either the names or information that could lead someone to determine the names were made public, that it would pose a serious threat to the lives and livelihoods of the loyalists and her former Confederate accomplices in Richmond. She marked the envelope, "Urgent, Confidential and Highly Personal" and gave it to General Patrick to send directly to General Grant.

Living up to his reputation of not forgetting to help people who had helped him, Grant acted immediately. On December 12th, 1866, Elizabeth's secret file was returned to her. She had first decided that if Grant could get it released, she would bury it. However, once she received it and saw its magnitude, she changed her mind and burned the entire collection. It was a heavy load off of her mind knowing she had done everything possible not to betray the trust of those who helped her; not only with their "services," but with their very lives.

What Elizabeth did not know was that the clerk who was ordered to "immediately package and return the entire file," in his haste unknowingly dropped one document from the file. The document fell hidden between the desk and the wall. This one document, while it didn't give away the identity of any of her accomplices, did establish Elizabeth as a secret agent of the Union.

The post-war years had been financially difficult for the Van Lew family. Practically all of the family fortune had been spent helping the Union cause, both overtly and covertly. In particular, it had not been easy for John. With the loss of the family hardware business and the name of Van Lew being tainted by Elizabeth's activities, John had been unable to acquire a position in Richmond. Frustrated, he left and lived temporarily with sister Annie in Philadelphia, while seeking employment and a fresh start. The adjacent property was sold and the money used to pay taxes, sustain John while getting established in Philadelphia, assist several freed Negro families in relocating in the North, and to provide sustenance for the Van Lew household.

Shortly after John's departure, the Van Lew family had an opportunity to recoup a small portion of their war time benefaction. Aware of the extent and value of Elizabeth's dangerous and continuous intelligence gathering and reporting to his Bureau of Military Intelligence, Brevet Brigadier-General George Sharpe wrote to General Grant's aide-de-camp, Colonel Cyrus B. Comstock, urging him to do something for the Van Lew Family,

> "… For the military information steadily conveyed by Miss Van Lew to our officers, I refer to Major-General Benjamin Butler who ought to speak largely concerning it, while General Grant, General Rawlins, General Patrick, and other officers serving at headquarters during the winter of 1864-65 are more or less acquainted with the regular information obtained by our Bureau from the City of Richmond, the greater proportion of which in its transmission we owe to the intelligence and devotion of Miss E. L. Van Lew…. Though the sum may be made larger, I feel bound to recommend, from a very considerable knowledge of the matter that the sum of fifteen thousand dollars be paid to Miss Elizabeth L. Van Lew for the valuable information and services rendered to the United States government during the war. I do this now without waiting for future reference for what I believe to be the most meritorious case I have known during the war."

The "compensation" though only a fraction of what it might have been, was never forthcoming. Even if the check had been awarded, it's doubtful that Elizabeth would have accepted it strictly as "payment for services rendered." She might have accepted the money, as replenishment for that portion of the family wealth depleted for her clandestine operations, but not for her humanitarian services. No one had asked or recruited her to help and support the suffering Union prisoners; especially when doing so brought her every form of censure and revilement. Nor did anyone tell her to initiate and continue the dangerous intelligence gathering, assisting with prisoner escapes, harboring and transporting of prisoners on the way back north; recruiting for, and then managing a spy network at great personal peril. When asked why she took all these risks when she had a very comfortable existence, she said with all honesty, "I didn't do it for the money. I felt it my duty and privilege to serve my country in this way."

CHAPTER 37

Covert Activity Exposure & A Sad Departure

The summer of 1868 was a hot and busy one in Washington. It was the first election year after the War and the Republican Party had a "War Hero" to nominate for its Presidential Candidate, General Ulysses Simpson Grant.

It was also a time for some housecleaning in the War Department's offices. In one particular file room, a desk was moved and a single document fell to the floor. Now, Elizabeth Van Lew's role as a "covert operative of the Union" was confirmed. The information was immediately communicated to the editor of the Richmond Whig newspaper.

Elizabeth, proud of the outcome of her covert activities and feeling that she had protected all of her sources, refused to be interviewed, neither confirming nor denying the report. Publicly, she maintained the "Crazy Bet" persona because it helped to avoid the questions and perpetual verbal abuse. In the mind of the editor, by refusing to comment on it and not denying it, she had confirmed the report. Since it was supported by "official military intelligence evidence," the editor decided to print the story based on the meager evidence available, and a little imagination. Before long, Richmond was buzzing with comments such as:

"The old witch! We should have known. She was always coddling up with those goddamn Yankees!

The traitor!

What the hell could a lunatic like her have told them of any value?

If she did tell them anything of value, who the hell did she get the information from?

Who was in cahoots with her?"

To satisfy their zeal for vengeance, a "witch hunt" began. The people who knew that Mary had worked for both the Van Lew and Davis households, "put two and two together," and reasoned that she was the source of Elizabeth's information.

Now, everywhere Mary went she was badgered with questions, accusations, insults, threats, and ostracization. One day, after particularly abusive treatment, she came home with her clothes torn and covered with mud and spit. She was in tears when she told her father what happened. Later that evening, Nelson informed Elizabeth about Mary's treatment by the hostile crowds that appeared to be growing more and more dangerous. Upset and saddened by Mary's predicament, Elizabeth wanted to shield Mary from the kind of abusive treatment she had endured. Elizabeth asked Nelson to send Mary to her right away, and she began to think of ways to extricate Mary from the escalating hostility. When Mary arrived, Elizabeth remarked, "Mary, your father has told me about your mistreatment today. I am as concerned for your well being as he is. Were you hurt?"

"No, not yet, but they are getting more and more violent and physical."

"Can you tell me exactly what is being said," Elizabeth inquired.

"They are saying that I am the source of the information you reported to the Yankees, because I worked in the Davis household. They said I was in cahoots with you and just as big a traitor."

Elizabeth thought to herself, "Now they are using this poor girl as a scapegoat for the suffering, destruction, and humiliation brought on this city and its people. The fact that she is black must make the venting of their post-war frustration and anger even sweeter and more justifiable."

Mary, close to tears, was desperately in need of some relief from her torment. Elizabeth looked at her face. It was still young and beautiful, but now there were telltale signs of the trials and tribulations of the past six years since her return to Richmond. The pressure of having to constantly look over her shoulder every moment of the day, and the anxiety and frustration of waiting for "deliverance," was visible in the sadness in and around the eyes and the recently acquired pout that replaced her previously infectious smile.

"Miss Liz, I am so miserable. Now people are saying hateful things and getting meaner and nastier toward me. One woman swore at me and said that I was 'no better than a whore' for collaborating with you in your spying activities. Honest, Miss Liz, I have never told anyone anything about those years and never will."

"Mary, there is no one that I trust more in the world than you. You have performed a service to your country that, unfortunately, will probably forever remain unknown. At any time during those perilous years, you could have turned me in, and you would have been an instant hero. I put my trust and my very life in your hands, and you were so impeccably loyal and trustworthy. So, how could I possibly not believe you now?

"I can see how people are making assumptions about the possible connection between your strategic wartime position and my wartime need for such information. To deny any wrongdoing would be scoffed at and fan the flames of their resentment and hostility," Elizabeth reasoned.

"Then what am I to do, Miss Liz?"

"Look Mary, because the hurt is so fresh in the minds of this generation, I'm branded, labeled and maltreated. I'll have to live with it for a while. Hopefully, in time, they'll learn to forgive and forget. I alone chose the path that my heart had to follow, and I regret it not a lick!

"But you, Mary, are still young, and there is no reason for you to suffer for your part. You should be rewarded, not punished, for your contributions in helping to preserve the nation. I want you to know that I have received all of my correspondence back from Washington that would pinpoint any of the brave people who assisted me in any way. I immediately burned every scrap of it and buried the ashes. If people think you were my only source of information, that's good for all the other sources, but not for you. I must now protect you, my closest and most courageous friend."

Elizabeth continued, "I have heard of the talk about you and thought that, without any proof, it would pass, so I kept out of it. But now, I must step in. I have thought over several alternative plans and have decided on the one that is the most plausible to vindicate you. This will be my final request of you, and one of the hardest and saddest things I've ever had to do in my nearly fifty years on earth!

"Mary, I want you to openly and publicly denounce me. Tell people that I used you and betrayed your confidence and trust by passing on privileged information from the Davis household to assist the Union decision makers in helping to destroy the Confederacy. I want you to tell people that you hate me for this despicable betrayal and that you never want to see or speak to me again. And, Mary, you must do it for your own sake and safety; every bit of what I've said!"

"Oh, Miss Liz, I can't do that to you!" And all the years of pent-up emotions from gratitude for Elizabeth's generosity, their friendly and caring relationship, and their dangerous and supportive collaboration came to the surface in a rush of uncontrollable tears and crying.

Interspersed with the heartbreaking sobs, Mary wailed, "I've known you and grown to love you like you were the mother I never knew, and now you want me to say terrible things about you in public … to give up speaking to you … seeing you again? I can't … I won't!"

"Mary, because you are like the child I'll never have, I love you so much—and because you still have so much of life ahead of you, you must do as I ask!"

"Please don't ask me to do this!"

"Mary, I want you to know that you will always be in my heart and thoughts until my last breath. Knowing that doing this might erase some of the pain and suffering from your life, opening the hearts of the true Virginians … I know this is the right path for you to take."

"Miss Liz, If I do and say the things you ask, can't we still get together secretly?"

"If we do Mary, and anyone ever saw us together, you would never be believed again, and your life would become as miserable as mine. Now, what mother would wish that for her daughter?"

Mary knew it was futile to argue with Elizabeth once her mind was made up. She also realized that what Elizabeth was proposing was a practical solution that truly had Mary's best interest at heart. By saving herself in this way, however, she would be fueling the flames of bitter hatred toward Elizabeth, increasing the insults and threats of bodily harm. Having just experienced a taste of it personally, she knew this would further add to Miss Liz's lonely isolation and danger.

Torn between love and reason and the acceptance of what she was going to do, Mary broke into a soul-wrenching release of tears. Elizabeth held her in her arms for the last time and struggled to hold back her own tears. She lost the battle, saying, "To lose someone you love, who is an important part of your life, suddenly to death is tragic ... to lose that someone unexpectedly while you both live ... is devastating."

Her resistance drained by the emotional release, Mary sobbingly conceded, "Alright I'll do what you ask, Miss Liz, I only hope I can say those things that will break my heart and end our relationship in a convincing manner."

Elizabeth looked at the extraordinary young woman in her arms who had exemplified throughout her young life all that is good in humankind and said, "Mary, I loved you as a sweet little precocious girl. I love you even more as a sensitive, intelligent, and courageous woman. You have met every challenge in the past, and I know you won't let me down now. Our bond will never be broken. In fact, relationships never end they just change form. Even though we are physically separated, our relationship will live on in our hearts and minds throughout our lifetimes."

Mary looked up at the woman who was so influential in shaping her life and character ... for whom she had so much admiration and respect. She took a deep breath, smiled, and then they separated slowly. They looked at each other's face, drinking in the last look, as if to etch it indelibly in their minds. "I love you and I'll always carry you in my heart" was spoken silently with their eyes.

"Goodbye Miss Elizabeth Van Lew."

"Goodbye, Mary Elizabeth Bowser, and thank you for all you've done for me."

What Elizabeth felt, but didn't verbalize, was the unfulfilled void of a child of her own that Mary filled so perfectly.

Mary turned quickly and left the room, afraid that lingering any longer might change her mind, and closed the familiar door softly behind her for the last time.

The next day, Mary carried out Elizabeth's request. Her denunciation of Elizabeth was accepted by most of the people with glee, and the maltreatment of Mary was reduced but not eliminated. There were still the prejudiced and cynical few, who hated blacks and wanted to keep them down. And there were those who didn't trust anything others said, because they themselves were not trustworthy.

Even though the hostile treatment had diminished, it still bothered Mary, who was also having a tough time resisting the temptation to visit Elizabeth, knowing full well that it could negate her public denunciation. Nelson talked to Elizabeth about the precariousness of the situation and, after some discussion, Elizabeth recommended to him that Mary should leave Richmond. Nelson agreed with the idea, which included his accompanying Mary back to Philadelphia.

Although losing Mary pained her greatly, that pain was compounded with the loss of Nelson, who had cared for her in the absence of her father. After selling some silverware, Elizabeth gave Nelson enough money for both of them to travel to and get settled in Philadelphia. She gave them each a glowing letter of recommendation and also encouraged them to look up her sister and brother who could assist them in getting employment in the city. Nelson had tears in his eyes as he said "goodbye" to the Van Lew women and home in which he had served his entire life. His last words were, "God bless you and watch over you always." To which mother and daughter added, "The same to you and yours, and thank you for everything you've done for us for all these many years. We are very, very grateful."

As expected, Grant won by a landslide and was sworn in as the eighteenth President of the United States of America on March 4, 1869. Fifteen days later, he appointed Elizabeth Van Lew as Postmaster of Richmond, one of the few women to hold such a post in nineteenth-century America. While it was widely accepted as recognition for her wartime contributions, the United States' government denied it was the reason for the official appointment. Once out of office, Grant would admit that Elizabeth had earned the post because of her services during the war. It would be the only form of official public acknowledgement given by the United States' government for Elizabeth's loyalty, sacrifices, accomplishments, and contributions to the successful conclusion of the painful struggle.

The appointment angered the citizens of Richmond. They thought her unqualified and unworthy. They claimed she was only being rewarded for her spy work for Grant during the war. To them, this amounted to "adding salt to the wound!" Her appointment, at an annual salary of $4000, was desperately needed to return her finances to moderate stability. However, her continuous philanthropic habits consumed every spare cent of it. She continued to assist Negroes in "getting a start," and supported Susan B. Anthony's fight to gain the vote for women.

Although she was inexperienced in the running of a post office, her leadership and supervisory skills had been highly developed and honed while developing and managing her intelligence network. She was focused, efficient, and even earned the respect and trust of former Confederates.

While her appointment was not well received in some quarters, it was popular among the veterans to whom she had ministered during their imprisonment. The 79th Regiment of Highlanders, 4th Brigade, 1st Division, New York, during their Annual Reunion at the Regimental Armory, sent President Grant a large elaborately hand-engraved resolution approving of his appointment.

> "WHEREAS his Excellency the President of the United States of America has appointed MISS ELIZABETH L. VAN LEW Postmaster at Richmond, Virginia,
>
> We the undersigned officers and men of the 79th Regiment Highlanders, believe we express the sentiments not only of the officers and men of our Regiment, but of every prisoner of war during the period of their confinement in the Libby Prison in the following resolutions therefore,
>
> RESOLVED that our best thanks are due to President Grant for his acknowledgement of MISS ELIZABETH L. VAN LEW'S most disinterested self-sacrificing, humane and successful efforts in relieving the sufferings, and supplying the wants of the prisoners of war in the Libby and other prisons during the Rebellion,
>
> RESOLVED that these resolutions be entered at length in the minutes and a copy properly attested be sent to the President."

It was signed by all the officers of the 79th and sent to General Grant who thoughtfully forwarded it to Postmaster Elizabeth L. Van Lew in Richmond. By necessity, the Postmaster position brought Elizabeth into contact with some of her former circle of friends. Most of them still held onto their hatred toward her and to them, she didn't exist.

Acting within her Postmaster authority, she hired two women as clerks who were from very prominent ante-bellum families. She was then questioned, repeatedly attacked, and reported for her hiring practices. Attempts were even initiated to remove her from office. Grant's office would get a stream of letters of protest that the "Republican Party should have voters in these government positions."

Elizabeth related to her mother that, "So called 'chivalrous' men would come to the stamp window and upon seeing the women clerks I hired, would ask, 'What are these women doing here? We want voters!'"

In her typical "stand up for what you believe in" fashion, Elizabeth chastised the men with, "How can you hound a woman who does not vote because you won't let her?"

To one of the clerks who were delighted, but surprised, at the way that she stood up to the men, she replied, "I am not a politician, I am a salesman. I'll leave the politicking to them."

Grant, who was always true to his friends, refused all influences and assured Elizabeth that he would not remove her from her position without just cause and would always give her the opportunity to defend herself against any accusations. No credible accusations were ever made, and Grant rewarded her performance by re-appointing her upon his election to his second term.

During this time, Elizabeth's penchant for writing in support of "causes," widened her circle of correspondents during this period to include such prominent Americans as Oliver Wendell Holmes, Horace Greeley, Frederick Douglas, and Susan B. Anthony. She also penned numerous "Letters to the Editor" of both Northern and Southern newspapers.

CHAPTER 38

Loss Upon Loss

September 13, 1875, was a pleasant fall day in Richmond. Elizabeth was busy at her desk in the Richmond Post Office. Suddenly, a messenger burst through the door with an urgent request for Elizabeth to come home at once.

An extremely solemn faced Doctor Parker met her at the door. He walked her into the parlor holding her hands and sat beside her.

"Elizabeth, I'm sorry to have to tell you this ... your mother ... her weakened heart finally gave out. She fought a valiant fight ... right up to the end. But, even then, she knew that it was her 'time.' She was so far gone when I arrived that she didn't even recognize me—she thought I was you. Her last words were meant for you. They were barely audible, but they are etched in my mind. She whispered, 'I'm so proud of you ... I'll be waiting for you in Heaven, Elizabeth ... goodbye for now' ... she closed her eyes and went as peacefully as ever I've seen, with the sweetest smile on her face."

Elizabeth had listened intently to every word William spoke. Her lips had been quivering, fighting to hold back the emotion-filled sobs that were building up like a volcano. The tears had been falling ever since William said, "It's your mother." She heard every word spoken after it, but felt numb and unable to move or speak.

She knew it would happen someday, but not like this—without warning. She was not prepared for it. It was even more painful because she wasn't there at the end to thank her for the almost sixty years of unconditional love and companionship. It was thirty-two years ago that her father died, and it seemed so traumatic facing life without his guidance and protection. But, Mother was there to console the children through the initial pain of his sudden departure. Now, Elizabeth had to face this loss alone.

"Oh, William! William, my head says she's gone ... my heart says, No! No! Not Mother! I need her so! I've never been without her ... now I'm really all alone!" The overloaded dam of grief burst, and she broke down and cried uncontrollably. William held her in his arms until the beneficial outpouring of sorrow at her loss subsided. He offered her a sedative to comfort her. William knew the rest would do her good and help strengthen her for the difficult last rites' obligations that she had to fulfill.

Attendance at the funeral consisted of immediate family, a few servants, and almost all of the coloreds who had been employed, given their freedom, or assisted in some way by the Van Lew family's compassion and generosity, along with one family friend, Mr. Green. Elizabeth had sent a telegram to Philadelphia, and both John and her sister Anna arrived in time to attend the funeral. John, Mr. Green, and two former Negro servants served as pallbearers.

Now, mother and father Van Lew lay beside one another in the cemetery plot in Shockoe Cemetery. The solemn occasion was labeled a "nigger funeral," and Mr. Green was branded a "radical" for having participated in it.

Back in the almost empty house, Elizabeth persuaded John, who had lost his wife Mary three years earlier, to move back to Richmond with his two daughters. She convinced him that it would be good for all of them to be together at this time and that the girls would have the run of the house.

John had been barely able to make ends meet working as a butcher in Philadelphia, and he really wanted to get something more in line with his previous bookkeeping experience. He thought that if he moved back to Richmond, with Elizabeth's "connections," he might get a position working in his field for the occupying Federal military forces. So John moved back home, and Elizabeth was successful in gaining him a position. Elizabeth's salary sustained them all comfortably until John's employment began.

Elizabeth received a sympathy letter from Vice President Henry Wilson on behalf of the U. S. Government because of her official position in the government. President Grant was not aware of the death of Mrs. Van Lew. Despite being shunned by the citizenry like lepers, they had a comfortable and pleasant insular existence.

In 1876, John met "Gussie," with whom he fell in love and married, adding another bit of life to the household. Meanwhile, Elizabeth had her maternal instincts satisfied by playing "Auntie" to the two girls. She was especially fond of Kathy, who had been teased as being "Little Lizzie" because of her strong similarities to Elizabeth in both appearance and personality.

During the eight years of Grant's Presidency, many positive initiatives were begun or completed. The Fifteenth Amendment became law, the Department of Justice was established, the immigration laws were made more liberal, the Civil Service Commission was established, taxes were cut by $300,000,000, the national debt was reduced by $435,000,000 and many "pork barrel" appropriations by the Congress were slashed. Grant publicly admitted making many mistakes during his Presidency, explaining that they were "errors in judgement, not intent, due to his lack of political experience." However, the scandal-ridden administration he had appointed, tarnished his image and restricted his time in office to two terms. Grant's departure from office ended both Elizabeth's official connection with, and any appreciation from, the United States' Government in Washington.

On March 3rd, 1877, Rutherford Birchard Hayes was elected in a race decided by a special electoral commission. Samuel J. Tilden of New York, his opponent, had more popular and electoral votes, but was one electoral vote shy of election. In order to get the twenty votes needed for election, which were mostly from Southern states, Hayes promised the men from that voting block that, if elected, he would end the hated "Reconstruction" and remove all Federal forces from the South.

He got the votes and the Presidency.

Once in office, Hayes kept his promise. He ended Reconstruction and pulled the Federal troops out of the South. Because the Van Lew name was deeply connected with Federal forces and the Grant Administration, Elizabeth was promptly replaced by a former Confederate Officer, Colonel William W. Forbes as Postmaster. Her removal took some of the "salt out of the wound" of members of Congress from Virginia and almost all Richmonders. In addition, the departure of the Federal forces cost John his position as well, and the Van Lew Family's income dropped to zero. Elizabeth, never one to back off from a fight, didn't go quietly. She appealed to President Hayes to reinstate her. Failing that, she got a letter of recommendation from former Confederate General William Carter Wickham of the Fourth Virginia Cavalry:

> Dear Madam,
> Your management of the Richmond Post Office has, I believe, been eminently satisfactory to the community here. Certain it is that all my transactions with it, both as a receiver and transporter, have shown me that the office was well handled. Allow me to express the hope that nothing will occur to break your connection with it.
>
> Yours truly,
> W. C. Wickham

Elizabeth took the letter to Grant in Washington. He read the letter, and without speaking a word wrote on the back of the letter:

> Miss Van Lew was appointed by me as Postmaster of Richmond, Virginia soon after my entrance upon the duties of President from a knowledge of her entire loyalty during the Rebellion and her services to the cause. She has filled the office since with capacity and fidelity and is very deserving of continued confidence by a Republican Administration.
>
> U. S. Grant

Generals were not the only military personnel who were aware of Elizabeth's activities and who had great respect for her deeds. This letter was sent to President Hayes on April 18th from a former Confederate soldier, P.T. Atkinson:

"As a spectator over the great struggle for the job of Postmaster of the Richmond Post Office, observing by the daily papers the great annoyance given you by the candidates and their friends, I feel that if I could relieve you by any suggestions of mine, how gladly would I do so, but I am a stranger to you personally, and any suggestion that I may make would of course be absurd and probably too officious in me, a humble ex-soldier in the late Rebel army, but no less a loyal citizen to my country.

Miss Van Lew, one of the candidates for reappointment and the present incumbent, I have known for many years. She stood deservedly high with the people of this city until the breaking out of the late fratricidal war, during which she manifested strong Union sentiments and being so zealous a friend of the Constitution of her Common Country that she gave free expression to her sentiments, and by her own volition sought the furtherance of that cause against which, I with equal faith and earnestness had opposed. She was true to her Country, her whole Country, I was false to the Union but true to my State. She has been rewarded, and she deserved it. Again reward her by appointment. She is a good officer to all but the prejudiced and should not be cast off."

However, all of Elizabeth's actions and her supporters' efforts to regain her post were futile. She had been replaced as a "pawn of politics," a "political casualty," not because of any lack of performance. No matter how forceful, truthful or justified the appeals, Hayes had cut a political deal and would not budge, and she was "stonewalled."

CHAPTER 39

Rejection, Humiliation, & Closure

1880 was an election year, and Elizabeth had hoped that a new President might re-appoint her Postmaster of Richmond. She had hoped and prayed for the opportunity ever since she found out that Grant's name was placed in nomination, and she was crushed when he declined it. James Abram Garfield was nominated by the Republican Party on its 36th ballot and elected President, while his running mate, Chester A. Arthur, who had originally backed Grant for a third term, became the Vice-President.

Elizabeth immediately began to write for an appointment to see President Garfield. In February, and again in March, Elizabeth visited Washington but was denied an interview with Garfield on both occasions. The Washington Evening Star, in a March 25, 1881 editorial, condemned Elizabeth. She responded the following day with:

> "The purpose of my visit was to see the President. I was never once permitted an interview, hence my repeated visits. I thought I had won a right in times of peril, to courtesy and recognition there. The War which marched many loyalists North impoverished my family. Only the most resolute needs from the great depression of my property caused me to ask for the Richmond Post Office job, and with my record I believe if the question was left up to the Nation, it would be decided in my favor …"

On July 2nd, Garfield was shot and died two months later from the wound. She quickly had a new President to petition. President Arthur was as open and supportive to her request as he was to the Women's Suffrage march on the White House led by Susan B. Anthony—"request denied!"

In 1884, President Arthur lost the Republican Party's full support and James Blaine of Maine got the nomination. The Democrats nominated Stephen Grover Cleveland, and the Anti-Monopoly and National Greenback Labor Parties nominated Benjamin Franklin Butler. While she gave Butler little chance of becoming President, there was no question as to which Elizabeth would like to have seen elected. It would have meant the Postmaster position again! After a particularly nasty, mud-slinging campaign, Cleveland was victorious and was sworn in on March 4, 1885, as the 22nd President.

Now, Cleveland became the next recipient of Elizabeth's requests for an audience to ask for her coveted re-appointment, even to asking for a Postmaster position in another state.

Learning of Elizabeth's attempts to regain the Postmaster position, members of the Grand Army of the Republic, from privates to generals, registered their support for her and voiced their indignation against the White House for even considering anyone else.

The protests to the White House were strong, but not as bad as the publicity Cleveland received during the campaign about his fathering an illegitimate child, and he survived that. So, after reviewing the arguments pro and con, Cleveland asked his advisors to come up with a solution to the "Van Lew problem."

All the while, Elizabeth had been a regular contributor to both the Boston and Washington, D.C. newspapers. Her articles were substantial; in some cases, running two columns long. The Boston Herald would often print them in full. While they were politically astute, they were not always complimentary to the current Administration in Washington.

Having been informed that Elizabeth was willing to take a post away from Richmond, Cleveland's advisors proposed that she be offered a $1200 a year clerk's position in the Washington Post Office. They reasoned that the solution gave her a post office position, was far enough away from the Richmond area and all the conflicts with the citizenry, and just might silence her stinging newspaper articles. Cleveland approved the recommendation "off the record."

Desperately needing the money now for taxes and subsistence, and with no viable alternative, she swallowed her Southern pride and accepted the position. Elizabeth felt that it might be easier to get a Postmaster position once back in the post office system, and she would be closer to the President's "ear." She moved to Washington, taking a room in Mrs. Critchet's Boarding House on the corner of 6th and D Streets. Although she had a long walk to the Post Office, she took the room because it came "with meals" and helped her live within the budget of her meager wages. She still had the financial responsibility of paying the taxes and insurance on the house.

Meanwhile, back in Richmond, John's frustration got the best of him, and he took his wife, their new baby, George, and his youngest daughter back to Philadelphia.

On Elizabeth's third day on the job, a brawny Negro man who worked in the next office told her that he had been doing her job for the past five years, but that the heavy lifting had caused him a bad back. He said he had asked his supervisor for the past two years to arrange a transfer to a position that didn't require the heavy lifting of the mailbags all day. The supervisor, George A. Harvard from

Tennessee, a former slave owner, had never shown the man any compassion on any occasion and ignored his request for a transfer. The Negro man, in an attempt to help justify his incapacity to Elizabeth, added, "After all, I am fifty years old now!" Elizabeth never revealed to him that she was approaching seventy.

Then, one day, for no apparent reason, Harvard told the man that he was to be "transferred immediately because we have a 'hand-picked replacement.' That was when you arrived, Miss Van Lew."

He said he was surprised when he first saw Elizabeth in the job, and asked her, "What did you do to deserve that job?"

Elizabeth looked at the man, who was asking a valid, honest question and thought to herself, "What indeed!"

Several weeks went by, and Elizabeth was beginning to be badgered by Harvard. At first, he baited her with mildly insulting words, trying to get her to respond in an insubordinate manner. Then came accusations of laziness, followed by demands for more productivity. Finally, he claimed there were complaints about her work schedule and poor attitude that were purported to be causing morale problems amongst the other clerks.

To get some relief from his persecution, she brought him a piece of cake that he seemed to enjoy. She thought, "Aha, I see your stomach is the organ to cultivate." For weeks, she brought him a piece of cake daily, sometimes two and the complaints diminished. Then, for no apparent reason, he began to get feisty and rude again. She stopped giving him cake for a few days, but that only made him worse. He demanded more and more work although he did none himself.

Elizabeth asked him why he was being so antagonistic and unpleasant toward her. She stated that at age 67, she was doing the same amount of work that the man of 50 was doing before she arrived, and that she got along fine with everyone.

Harvard was not used to being questioned by his subordinates, especially by a woman; and worse yet, someone against whom he had a grudge due to her "traitorous support" during the War! He started to get red in the face and shouted, "Well, you don't get along with me!"

"I could if you'd let me," she responded politely.

"Look, it's bad enough I have to be around you eight hours a day. I wouldn't want to get too close and have anything rub off on me!" he smirked.

"What exactly are you worried about?" she asked innocently, baiting him.

"I wouldn't want any of that white covering over your black skin to come off," he laughed boisterously.

"Aren't you a little worried that I might report you for what you've just said?" she asked firmly.

"Not for one minute. I happen to know you need the job bad, so if you were to open your mouth, I'd run right up to Superintendent New," he bragged.

"Superintendent New!" she gasped, "That wouldn't be W. W. New would it?"

"That's the one!" he confirmed, "Does that name ring a bell?"

Elizabeth didn't answer—she just glared at him. "How do you think you got this particular clerk's job? It was Superintendent New's request to Postmaster General John Milton Niles for your services. You don't have Grant around to look out for you anymore.

Elizabeth's thoughts flashed back to July 26, 1885 when she heard of the death of Ulysses S. Grant, her dearest acquaintance, ally, and the antitheses of New. He died at the age of sixty-three, just after completing the work on his memoir … the only thing he had of value to leave to his heirs … he died penniless.

Harvard broke her reminiscence, "All I can say is, you are right where he wants you. So, you better do your job, keep your mouth shut, and forget about any more Postmaster jobs, or you'll be out on the streets!"

Elizabeth turned away from him as her eyes welled up with tears of despair and frustration at her dismal situation. She couldn't believe the turn of events … "New, an inspector over me … I thought he was gone out of my life for good … but he's back in it to get his revenge. How did he get that position? They're right though. I do need the job … but not the torment!"

The supervisor left laughing after seeing Elizabeth crying, knowing that she saw the hopelessness of her situation and that she wouldn't dare give him a hard time now. Harvard headed straight for New's office to report the incident. New ordered him to write a reprimand for "insubordination" against Miss Van Lew for speaking back to her supervisor and to put it into her file. He also instructed Elizabeth's supervisor to "Give Van Lew nothing higher than a 'barely adequate' performance rating, occasionally throw a reprimand for some transgression of Post Office policy into her file, and ensure that she is kept unaware of the reprimands." The supervisor, who saw eye to eye with New and wanted a promotion, was more than willing to oblige his superior.

From day to day, week to week, month to month, Elizabeth carried on for meager wages under the progressively miserable treatment from her gloating supervisor. She had also been constantly aggravated by a former member of the original Tennessee Ku Klux Klan staying at her boarding house due to her pro-black sentiments. Unwilling to put up with the persecution day and night, she took a room at 478 Pennsylvania Avenue for some needed peace of mind.

During this time, the main outlet for her innate capabilities was her after-work writing. She had become more of a firebrand than ever before. Her articles were even becoming popular among the newspapers' readership. Many an "amen" was spoken by women while reading her outpourings of frustration at the injustice of being denied the voting privileges that was supposed to go along with citizenship.

Cleveland, who was irritated by the accurate and politically damaging newspaper articles on his obstinate lack of support for women's suffrage, asked for her Post Office personnel file. Superintendent New was only too glad to provide Elizabeth's "doctored," highly negative file. When he saw the negative comments and reprimands, Cleveland again consulted with his advisors and ordered them to "come up with a damn-sight better solution this time."

Their new solution was to "leak" her personnel file's negative performance comments and reprimands to the press and, at the same time, reduce her to the lowest clerk's position available. They hoped the combination would both embarrass and insult her sufficiently, to cause her to resign and never again seek a post office position. Wanting her out of his thinning hair, Cleveland liked the chances of the plan's success and eagerly approved it … "unofficially of course."

New started the plan by leaking to the press some of the fabricated incidents the supervisor had planted in her file. Reprimands alleging that: "she is insubordinate," "comes and goes at will," "her peculiar temperament is a hindrance to the other clerks," "she owed her position to sentimental reasons," and other equally demeaning accusations were confidentially delivered to selected newspapers.

The press, always anxious to cover a newsworthy controversy or scandal, exploited the information without so much as checking its authenticity. New saw that they got enough damaging information to fill their columns. Based solely on the public disclosure of such negative work habits and characterizations, one northern newspaper printed a scornful editorial beginning with, "A troublesome relic," and ending with, "We draw the line at Miss Van Lew!"

The Washington Star, anticipating her resignation, commented that,

"Miss Van Lew will come no more. It seems as if another 'landmark' is gone."

That same day the paper came out, the Editor of the Star received a sharp note from the "departed landmark," apprising him that she was not "gone" and had no plans for leaving Washington.

Elizabeth was embarrassed, humiliated, angry, and deeply hurt by the widespread dissemination of misinformation. She knew exactly who was responsible for this vindictive and disgraceful act and his vengeful purpose.

At two o'clock on the afternoon of June 30, 1887, Elizabeth was about to leave the post office building when a messenger handed her an envelope. In it, was official notification that her pay had been reduced from $1200 to $720 per year—the same salary paid to the lowest-level clerk having no service time in the postal system. In addition, it stated that she was transferred immediately to the Dead Letter office. It claimed to have been ordered by Postmaster General Niles.

Both the shock of the unjustified punishment and the heartless and impersonal method of its communication stung Elizabeth. She showed it to one of her fellow clerks, Miss Best, who knew the quality of her work and to a friend, Mr. J. S. Smith, Esq. Mr. Smith also felt indignation at the cruel, insensitive treatment. He told Elizabeth that if he were in her place that he would not accept the insult—he would resign!

Elizabeth walked mechanically to her room to mull over her options and the precariousness of her situation. How much punishment and degradation should one endure? Surely now, the ashes of Elizabeth's long felt sympathy for, and empathy with, the slaves was rekindled as she experienced the same brand of humiliation and unprovoked suffering they endured during their lifetimes of bondage. New had won at last.

The next day, she packed up her meager belongings and gave up the rented rooms. She went straight to the post office to resign and return to Richmond. She had also decided to face New one last time.

Elizabeth marched straight to New's office where his secretary told her that he was busy working on an important report and that he was not to be disturbed. Ignoring her, Elizabeth pushed the door open. When it banged against the wall, New's arm jerked, knocking over the inkwell, spilling ink over the nearly completed carefully written papers.

"Goddammit, look what you've done!" he blasted. Then, looking up, he saw Elizabeth.

"Ah, so it's you, is it. What the hell do you want?"

"I just came to tell you that you are the most despicable, dishonest, and horrible man I've ever met. In fact, you're a disgrace to manhood. You're a perfect manifestation of the Anti-Christ!"

"How dare you speak to me that way? That's insubordination!" New charged.

"Why should I worry? You've publicly branded me with it already."

"So you know … good … I'm glad! That makes it twice as sweet!" New confirmed proudly.

"How did you sink so low that you are without scruples? Where did your parents go wrong?" Elizabeth goaded, probing to learn if he was totally devoid of feelings.

Sensing that she had crossed the line, gotten too personal, New decided that the moment was right. "That's it! You've gone too far. I'm not going to stand for any more of your insubordination! Traitor, you're fired!"

"As always, New, you're too late. I've already resigned," she said with calm dignity.

New was, at first, surprised that he couldn't continue his revenge, but then pleased that he could now inform Cleveland that he had "gotten rid of the nuisance." However, he couldn't resist the opportunity to say what was on his mind.

"You know, I was always wise to you. You never fooled me for one minute. I knew you were behind all the mischief and subversive activities in Richmond. If it hadn't been for that old fool Winder, I could have neutralized and eliminated you anytime I wanted!"

"Oh, really? And did you ever have one solid piece of evidence against me? I'm sure if you did, you would have produced it and used it to your advantage— maybe even given it to the newspapers!" she needled.

New stared at her, fuming, but not speaking, while he tried to recollect something besides hunches, indications, and suspicions. "I didn't need to have any 'solid proof.' All the signs of your dirty work were there; everything pointed to you alone!"

She said deferentially, "Now tell me, how could a crazy old relic of a woman like me put over anything on a man of such clearly superior intelligence like yourself?"

New was beginning to get the feeling that he was a "rat that's being toyed with by a cat" and he didn't like it, so he struck back. "Do you deny that you were a spy?" he blurted.

"How can anyone be called a spy who performs patriotic services for her country … within the confines of that same country?" she reasoned.

"You were in the Confederate States of America!" he corrected.

"I was in the United States of America! The 'Confederacy' was just a collection of states rebelling against their legal central government. Even though children get rebellious from time to time with their parents, the family unit still exists!"

Irked by her simplistic response, and unwilling to argue the point any further, he countered with, "You are truly crazy and so is your logic!" revealing his growing irritation and frustration.

Elizabeth persisted, "Have you noticed that whenever someone is losing an argument, and knows it, they switch to attacking the character of the party with whom they are arguing?"

New had about all he could stand. The open door had allowed people in the other room to hear the conversation, which he thought he would dominate, but had turned into an embarrassing besting by this lowly "clerk."

"If you don't work here anymore, get the hell out of my office right now!"

Elizabeth didn't budge; she just looked at him. Enraged by her resolute composure, he snapped, "Get out, 'former Postmaster!'"

She had enough of New as well and paid him a final "tribute." "Do you realize that you don't have a single redeeming quality?"

New glared at her as she started to leave the room. He could not let her get away with having the last word. To show her that he was the superior one, he vented his hatred by shouting, "Goodbye forever, traitor, to you and your delusions of grandeur!"

She turned, and with a smile said, "Goodbye forever, you lost soul with your delusions of adequacy."

With a smile on her face, her head erect, she left through the open doorway. As she walked by the people who had silently gathered unseen just outside the Superintendent's office, yet close enough to be able to overhear this unique confrontation, her steps seemed to gain a little bounce. She even noticed some smiles and signs of respect on some of the women's faces. Halfway down the hallway, she heard New shouting, "What in hell are you all standing around here for? Get back to work!" which was followed by the forceful slamming of a door.

CHAPTER 40
Poverty, Compassion, Support, & The Journal

Although she didn't admit it, Elizabeth was relieved to be home. In just a few days, the respite from the physical drudgery and verbal abuse gave her nearly seventy-year body a long overdue rest.

It was not long after Elizabeth's return that she wrote to her sister Anna Pauline Van Lew Klapp in Philadelphia that she was back home in the mansion. The response was warm and rapid. Anna felt that Elizabeth should not be alone and that her daughter, Elizabeth Louise Klapp, "Kathy" as she was called, would like to move in with her. Elizabeth was overjoyed to have a companion, especially Kathy, of whom she was so fond.

About the time Kathy arrived, Elizabeth's money had run out, and she was forced to sell more of the family heirloom silverware and Chippendale items to dealers in order to purchase food and other necessities.

Just as that money was running out, the property taxes came due. Anticipating the potential loss of her beloved and mortgage-free, home for "failure to pay its taxes," Elizabeth sadly put out a "For Sale" sign in front of the house.

A month passed without a single offer for the valuable, but stigmatized, unproductive property on which the taxes were now due. Elizabeth and Kathy scrambled to sell everything of value that they didn't absolutely need for their daily living. The money they raised paid only half the taxes and left them with no funds to buy food.

The residents of the Van Lew mansion were now at the most acute poverty level. They had no food, even though they had cut down to one meal a day for the past two weeks. Candles or the fireplace were used to cook what little food they had as the gas had been shut off for over a month due to lack of payment.

Elizabeth had borne the poverty in silence with all the pride of a Southern woman until it became indefensible. She was destitute and desperate. Kathy had become an invalid and needed a proper diet in order to maintain her health. Borrowing the money would be difficult because of a lack of means to pay it back.

While searching for options, she reflected, "I was a Postmaster for eight years, a clerk for two years and certainly was in the 'service of the United States' government' during the four years of the War. That's fourteen years of Federal Government service!" She then remembered one of her supervisor's many taunts,

"The South would not have forsaken you as the North has done had you espoused the Southern cause!"

A trace of warmth passed through her as she recalled Grant's acts of gratitude and support. But just as quickly, she cooled and thought, "I have stood the brunt alone of a persecution that I believe no other person in the country had endured who had not been 'Ku Kluxed.' I honestly think that the government should provide some form of sustenance."

Now, Elizabeth's thoughts went back to her visit to Boston just after the War and the offer to "let us know if we can do anything to repay your kindness and generosity." The thought of "begging" for money repulsed her and she agonized over the decision. Finally, she decided to send a letter to Mrs. Pauline Reynolds, Paul Revere's sister. It was not a "begging" letter. She simply told Mrs. Reynolds that she was in dire need, and that "Perhaps the family of a man for whom she had done so much might help her."

Now that the letter was written, she had to mail it, but she didn't have the three cents to buy a stamp. She was reduced to borrowing a stamp from a colored woman she had purchased for $1000 when the woman was a little girl. Elizabeth had bought the girl because she was the niece of one of her household servants. Once she owned her, she immediately freed her so that she could be reunited with her family.

Mrs. Reynolds responded swiftly by sending her son, John Jr., to Richmond. During his stay, John and Elizabeth discussed her current situation and ongoing needs. He gave her some "basic necessities" money to tide her over and promised to communicate with her again after he talked with his mother in Boston.

Upon his return to Boston, John explained Elizabeth's destitute predicament to his mother. At Mrs. Reynolds' request, surviving former prisoners, their families and friends, met, agreed on, and established a small annuity on which Elizabeth and her niece could live a comfortable existence. Some of the people who contributed were Mrs. Reynolds, Colonel William Raymond Lee, Colonel Henry Lee, Colonel Oliver W. Peabody, George Higginson, J. Ingersoll Bowditch, Frederick L. Ames, F. Gordon Dexter, Mrs. G. Howland Shaw, the Honorable John M. Forbes, and William Endicott.

The outpouring of compassion and support from Boston brought Elizabeth to tears. At the eleventh hour, her home—her very life—had been spared. The Union had forsaken her, but not the Union men or their loved ones. She gave thanks to God for answering her prayers and sent a letter of the most heartfelt thanks to her Boston benefactors.

Ironically, only a month later, she received two offers for her home. The first was from the Order of Monte Maria for $20,000. The Sisters wanted to transform the property into a Convent. The second offer was from a German tavern owner who offered her $25,000 for the property. He wanted to turn it into a German Beer Garden. Elizabeth politely turned down both offers now that she had the annuity which assured her of safe surroundings, care for Kathy, a garden to keep her pleasantly occupied and a place of refuge for homeless cats.

The Van Lew home might as well have been turned into a convent. Elizabeth and Kathy led a cloistered existence in nearly perfect isolation. They had virtually no visitors except an occasional pauper seeking a handout. Elizabeth was still shunned as a leper on the streets of Richmond. The dirty looks, snide comments, and mumbled curses followed her everywhere.

One day, a handsome, middle-aged man called at the home. Elizabeth answered the door but didn't recognize the man. When he handed her his card, it read: "Charles Phillips, City Editor." Elizabeth squealed with delight, "Charles! Look at you, all grown up and an editor! How very impressive!"

"Miss Elizabeth, I'm so glad to see you after all this time. I've read about you, but I don't believe a word of what I've read!"

"Well, you know how it is, whatever will sell newspapers," she kidded him, knowing that it was one of his responsibilities, "and to what do I owe this unexpected surprise?"

"Well, I've wanted to pay you a visit for some time, and I also had an idea that I wanted to try out on you, so I thought I'd mix pleasure with a little business," he admitted.

"Elizabeth, I'd like to do a piece on your life, with some interesting tales from your wartime years. I know it would increase our circulation because it is controversial. We could throw in the Dahlgren body snatch and …"

"Whoa!" Elizabeth said, "This is all pretty sudden. I don't want or need any more publicity, or the kind of attention that has dogged me for the past three decades."

"I can appreciate your reluctance, but it would make such fascinating reading and straighten out the record about all that you did for our country!" he pleaded.

"Here in Richmond, the North is not 'our country;' it is still the enemy. And, from the way I see the reunification going, the North and South are like oil and water—they don't seem capable of mixing."

"And whose fault would you say that is?" he continued.

"The South mostly. They don't seem to be able to accept what happened at Appomattox. The North has been more willing to forgive the disloyalty of the Rebels, but the Rebels are still not willing to accept my stand. If disloyalty can be forgiven, wouldn't you think loyalty might be?" she posed. Both knew the answer, so none was spoken.

"All right, Miss Elizabeth, but what you did has historical value. It is part of all that transpired during those eventful years. It had an impact—it influenced the outcome!" he implored.

"Charles, to even think of those days agitates me, so I've put them out of my mind. I'm sorry."

Knowing her esteem of Grant, he tried another tack. "Grant wrote his memoirs while he was sick and dying. You are still in good health. What if you just wrote your recollections and kept them to yourself for publishing only after your death?"

"I'd still rather not, because there are people and families whom I wouldn't want subjected to the abuse and ostracizing that I've had to endure. You know you could be included in that group" she explained.

"You're right. Well, just give events and details from your point of view and omit any references to the identity of others whose loyalty to the Union you want to conceal. Keep it vague and un-attributable for those persons, and name the others for the roles they played, large or small, for or against."

Charles' persistence was wearing down Elizabeth's resistance, and she began to relent. "Well, maybe I could write some kind of journal or anecdote or two of some of the events that happened—but not all!"

"Great, that's a start, Miss Elizabeth! Whether I get to print the story or not, I think it is important and should be told. Everything about it is so unique. The times, the causes, the contradictions of your social and political positions, the multiple roles and involvement you shouldered, your perspective and accomplishments!"

"Charles, please, enough! I agreed to write a little and to see how it goes. Maybe by writing about it, I may release some of my agitation. I thank you for coming today, Charles. You may have helped give purpose to some of my future lonely hours of isolation."

"There is one thing that's always bothered me Miss Elizabeth. You had such a dignified reputation in Richmond of being so well educated, intelligent, refined, and classy. Why did you take on the persona of a crazy woman with such bizarre behavior?"

She simply and calmly admitted, "It helped me in my work."

That evening, Elizabeth embarked on the task of writing a chronological journal. She hesitantly visited the secret room for the first time in many years. After sweeping away a path through the cobwebs she found the innocuous box she was looking for at the far end of the room. She picked it up and held it for a moment. "Do I really want to stir up all these memories?" She stood there for several minutes her eyes closed holding the box. She opened them still unsure of whether to proceed or not. This, she vowed would be the last time I will come in here. A slow look around the entire room that served so many purposes held such noble souls, and then she quietly latched the door for the very last time. She gathered and sifted through the well-hidden pages of previously written notes that she used when transferring them to coded messages.

At least the journal started out chronologically; then, as an event came to mind that she had forgotten, she digressed to tell of it, then leaped forward in time, leaving large gaps of information in between unreported. But, in the telling, she always sifted facts and identities through a filter of fear. She still dreaded the possibility of repercussions against her sources and allies. She gave only their rank, a pseudonym or the first initial of their last name in order to protect them. Her devout loyalty to them was unwavering. She neither embellished nor glorified her exploits. Often, she understated the value of her contributions and risks. To Elizabeth, whatever it took in time, money, energy or danger, "It was worth it for the cause." Then she burned many of the war time pages of notes used for the handwritten journal.

Ever since she returned to Richmond, Elizabeth had caused a mild commotion at the City Tax Office. Each year she paid her taxes and each year she sent an accompanying note of protest. She reasoned that because she could not vote, she had no "voice" in the Richmond City government and, therefore, should not have to pay any taxes to maintain it. On November 28, 1892 she sent, along with her taxes, a note to:

John K. Childrey
Treasurer, City of Richmond

I do hereby present my solemn protest against the right of any government, city, state or municipality, to collect taxes, or rather levy taxes, without representation, and I ask that my protest be recorded and published.

E. L. Van Lew

Her "taxation without representation is tyranny" notes brought a quiet reply from the tax authorities. They tried to justify her payments by explaining that her interpretation was not the way that the tax laws were written. Elizabeth was intensely committed to the continuance of the protests until women got the vote and was not that easily rebuffed. She knew it was just a matter of time, and public and political pressure, that would lead to the admission and correction of the injustice. Meanwhile, the City Hall tax collectors continued to look forward with amusement to receiving her taxes each year.

The protests did not make her any more popular with the male citizenry. In fact, the citizens' animosity toward Elizabeth had always been stronger for her long and continuous support on behalf of Negro causes than all of her other activities combined They characterized her humanitarian deeds as "pernicious social-equality doctrines and practices."

In 1895, Elizabeth had the body of her "dearly-departed brother John" returned from Philadelphia for burial next to his father in Shockoe Cemetery. He was seventy years old. At seventy-five, Elizabeth was the oldest surviving Van Lew. As she stood looking at the white marble headstone, she thought to herself, "I am the only one left of our immediate family, as those I love have gone to their long rest."

During one of her exercise walks along Grace Street, Elizabeth saw two ladies she knew walking with several sweet-looking young girls. She disliked little boys ever since the mean young boys had taunted her with their cruel insults and mud "brickbats," and later destroyed her prized fruit trees. Little girls, on the other hand, brought out her motherly instincts. She cheerfully invited them to bring the little girls to her house the following Sunday afternoon for cookies and ice cream. The girls squealed with delight; and the women accepted the invitation. The ladies tried hard not to show their excitement at the opportunity of being invited to see the inside of the fabled mansion.

When the two women, Miss Florence Peple and Mrs. R.D. Garcin, arrived that Sunday, they were accompanied by six excited and slightly nervous little girls. One of the girls told Miss Peple, while they were standing just outside the front, that she had been warned by her mother to, "Be careful of that Yankee witch! And now I'm afraid to go in. I don't know what that Yankee lady might do to me!"

"Hush, child. She won't harm you," Miss Peple assured her.

Suddenly, the door opened and there stood Elizabeth dressed in her Sunday best. She smiled at the welcomed guests and invited them in. As the frightened little girl entered, Elizabeth said to her, "And, I am not a Yankee!"

The girls enjoyed the ice cream and began to warm to Elizabeth's pleasant hospitality. Also feeling more comfortable with Elizabeth, Mrs. Garcin couldn't contain her curiosity any longer and asked, "Miss Van Lew, is it true that you hid Yankee soldiers here?"

Ever fearful of additional censure and maltreatment, she avoided a direct answer with, "Don't believe everything you hear, but I will show you one thing." She walked over to the fireplace and the tall brass andirons. She removed one of the brass couchant lion tops and showed them where she concealed secret dispatches. It was hard to tell who enjoyed the visit more, the guests or the hostess!

CHAPTER 41

The Final Days & A House Re-Honored

For Elizabeth, the next few years were devoted to caring for Kathy and her garden. When she felt so inclined, she sat and committed to paper her memories of incidents of displayed hostility, fearful conditions, humorous contradictions, and acts of shameful behavior, extreme audacity, and bravery.

The Christmas of 1899 found Elizabeth and Kathy going through the motions more from habit than from being filled with the Christmas spirit. The years of their social isolation had robbed them of the feeling of "community" with their fellow citizens and neighbors at this special holiday season. With no friends to share it with, Kathy had done her best to overcome their depression by sprucing up the house with Christmas decorations. Elizabeth's response to the gesture was noticeable. She acknowledged Kathy for her efforts. "Kathy, with our 'solitary confinement' here, it has not been easy for either one of us, but I want you to know that you have been my salvation these past ten or so years. I don't know how, or if, I would have survived them if you had not been here. I thank you for these years of companionship, I apologize to you for having to put up with a crotchety old aunt who created the miserable conditions that you tolerated without complaint. I love you dearly."

"I love you too," Kathy replied softly, "and I do appreciate all your looking out for me these many years. You have been my salvation too." And the two women sat in front of the fireplace sharing their thoughts, feelings, and recollections on this quiet and private holiday, neither one expecting it would be their last.

Soon after the holidays, in the year 1900, Kathy's health began to deteriorate, and Doctor Parker paid frequent calls on her behalf. He noticed that Elizabeth was also not well. The doctor told Elizabeth that Kathy was gravely ill and that her prognosis was not good.

It was a miserable spring evening outside the Van Lew home, but it was even more unpleasant inside. Kathy was in the final moments of her life, and Elizabeth was in a frenzy. "William, please don't let her die!" Save her! She's all I have!"

"Kathy ... Kathy, please don't leave me! Oh God, please don't take her from me!" she pleaded and begged through her heart-wrenching sobbing.

William tried to console her. She was as distraught as he had ever seen her. His heart was deeply touched by her open display of love and vulnerability. It was the first time he had ever seen her show fear, and he realized the full impact of the loss of her last close family member and companion. He worried how she would live without Kathy.

Parker looked back at Kathy and saw that her breathing had stopped. Elizabeth's eyes were so filled with tears that she was unaware of Kathy's peaceful departure. Filled with sympathy, William moved closer to Elizabeth, took her hands in his and said quietly, "She's in God's care now." Elizabeth cried softly on William's shoulder. Feeling the depth of her agonizing grief, William's eyes also filled.

The loss of Kathy was an extremely severe blow to Elizabeth. When someone, trying to be helpful, began to take down the Christmas decorations that Kathy had put up, Elizabeth shouted, "Leave them alone. I don't want them touched!" She was becoming more and more of a recluse, leaving the house only when absolutely necessary. In addition, she was beginning to show signs of the effects of edema—swelling of the feet and ankles—brought on by her physiologically and psychologically weakened heart.

An old neighbor, walking by her house one day, saw Elizabeth standing by the gate like a doorman waiting to open the gate for a visitor—any visitor. As she passed, Elizabeth whispered in a barely perceptible voice, "I have no friends—nobody loves me anymore. I am all alone. I am so lonely and so unhappy …"

Her spirit broken and her will to live gone, Elizabeth's illness worsened. The edema was causing fluid buildup in Elizabeth's lower legs and feet, making it painful to walk. Because of this, she was forced to spend much of her time propped up in a sitting position. Her favorite spot to be positioned was in the room overlooking her beloved Richmond. Judy Johnson, one of the Van Lew's former slaves who was given her freedom by Elizabeth and her mother, was now one of the people looking after her.

Around six o'clock on the evening of September 24, 1900, Elizabeth awakened from a brief spell of unconsciousness. She rallied wonderfully and, with assistance from Doctor Parker, she walked to her favorite spot and was comfortably propped up. They were alone, and they both knew the end was near. Elizabeth broke the silence.

"You know, I have always loved this view. Do you remember the first time I showed it to you?"

"As if it was yesterday," he responded fondly.

"You know, if things had gone differently, this view would have been ours," she reflected.

"Who says it isn't?" he said earnestly. "We've shared it on more than one occasion—some happier than others."

"Thank you, William. It makes this dying woman happy to think this view meant something to you as well."

"Elizabeth, I have treasured our friendship, respected you for the way you stood up for and supported your ideals, and then weathered the abuse you suffered for doing it. I know you will be received by God with open arms."

The last comment caused tears to well up in Elizabeth's eyes.

She asked, "William, how do you think people will remember me?"

"Well, I think we both know how Southerners will remember you. People in the North … probably as a spy. Whether or not that is a favorable impression, only time will tell," he answered honestly. There was a pause as his words were digested. William waited because he knew she was mulling it over and wanted to respond to his words. Then, she replied as if she had thought about it for some time, long before this night.

"For my loyalty to my country I have two ungracious names—here I am called 'traitor;' further north, a 'spy'—instead of the honored name of 'faithful.' If I am entitled to the name 'spy' because I was in the secret service, I accept it willingly; but it will hereafter have, to my mind, a high and honorable signification."

There was another period of silence as Elizabeth stared off toward the sunset on the James. William broke the silence with, "In response to that, is a question. If you had to do it all over again, would you have chosen to follow the same path?"

Without a second of hesitation, she responded, "I couldn't have lived with any other."

"Why did I know you would say that?" he smiled. "Well, I must attend to my granddaughter; her baby is due tomorrow. I'll check in on her, and I'll be right back. Remember now, do not let anyone lay you down flat. Your body must remain elevated."

"Yes, Doctor," Elizabeth said obediently, as he got up and left the room. Before he left the house, Doctor Parker cautioned the attending nurse not to let anyone lay her flat. The attending nurse looked in on her and asked if she needed or wanted anything. Elizabeth told her, "I'm fine, thank you."

Several hours later, the nurse went off duty, and the next shift nurse, looking in on Elizabeth, observed her sleeping peacefully. She asked Judy to help her get Elizabeth into bed, which they did and laid her flat. Elizabeth wakened sufficiently to say, "Doctor Parker said not to lay me flat!" Thinking her delirious, they verbally agreed with her, with a "Yes dear," but physically ignored her and kept her in a horizontal position. She was so weak and fell asleep immediately. Now the fluid began to back up into her lungs.

Doctor Parker, who had to admit his granddaughter into the hospital for care, decided to check on Elizabeth before heading for home. Upon his arrival, he became furious when he saw her lying flat. He immediately propped her up, and her eyes opened. She saw the concern on William's face and started to speak. She wanted to tell him not to worry, that she had faith that he had done everything possible for her, but she was ready to leave this life. He leaned close as he saw her lips attempting to speak. She whispered barely audibly, "Don't be concerned—rejoice. I am leaving to join those whom I love and who love me. Goodbye, dearest friend."

She closed her eyes, and her valiant and overworked heart beat one last faint throb—and no more. At precisely 4:10am, Doctor Parker announced, "It's over ... she is gone. She won't ever be lonely again. She was one of the most remarkable persons I have ever known ... Goodbye, Elizabeth Van Lew."

The sun was going down over the James when the undertaker wheeled Elizabeth's casket out onto the south-facing portico. Negro servants and former slaves who had been given their freedom by the Van Lews kept watch throughout the unusually balmy, moonlit night. The solemn scene was filled with the sounds of evening insects and the fluttering of the candles. Just out of range of the candles was a multitude of Negroes weeping and praying for "Miss Lizzie."

Because Elizabeth had outlived the rest of her family, and people feared repercussions by being seen at her funeral, hers was the least attended family funeral of all. Attendance consisted mostly of the few living Negroes she knew, or their descendants who were told of her genuine kindness and generosity toward them.

Elizabeth's death was front-page news in cities from Boston to Richmond:

> "Miss Van Lew Dead,"
> "Noted Woman Passes Away,"
> "Grant's Spy Succumbs,"
> "Crazy Bet Dead at 82,"
> "One of the Most Remarkable Personalities of the Century,"
> "She Contributed More Than The World Will Ever Know to the Salvation of the Union,"
> "For espousing her sympathies in support of the Union, she was ostracized by the people of Richmond, but she didn't care, her enthusiasm was fully equal to that of her opponents, and she never lost an opportunity to display it."

Since the cemetery plot was nearly full, Elizabeth was buried in a north-south direction, with her body facing north, coincidentally, the same as Colonel Dahlgren and all the rest of the Federal Soldiers who had been buried in Confederate cemeteries.

In her will, she named John Phillips Reynolds, Jr. as the executor of her estate and the beneficiary of her personal diary and manuscripts. He also kept the personal cipher that was found secreted in the back of her watch after her death. He followed her instructions to the letter. He began the task as red October closed by putting the house up for auction.

For the first time in over forty years, the doors of the Van Lew home swung open, and the Richmonders flooded in. The now gloomy great halls echoed with the whispered comments as people peered and peeked into nooks and crannies as if expecting to see the ghost of Elizabeth, some escaped Union prisoner, or a secret hiding place. Then, they would have confirmation of the rumors about her clandestine activities.

They handled the furniture and gazed at the cracked canvases of Van Lew and Baker family ancestors. Occasionally, a small piece of memorabilia was picked up and slipped stealthily inside a garment or pocket. The auction continued all day until the Virginia Club, a social organization, outbid everyone for the historical property. They wanted it for social and recreational purposes. Reynolds then shipped Elizabeth's personal belongings, memorabilia, and furnishings to Leonard's Auction House on Bromfield Street in Boston.

Once the Virginia Club took possession of the house, they upgraded it with electric lights, fresh paint, and turned the library and parlor into card and billiard game rooms. Even though the house had taken on an air of cheerful animation, the Negroes working for the Virginia Club believed it to be haunted by Elizabeth's ghost. Even the live-in Club President admitted hearing strange sounds and seeing mysterious apparitions. He attested to hearing footsteps on the creaky attic room stairs, the ringing sound of spurs, and Elizabeth's soft voice calling to her niece, and seeing candlelit shadows moving about in an otherwise empty room.

When the basement walls were being painted with calcimine to brighten the room for a buffet, there appeared on the wall a perfect outline of Elizabeth's face and figure. It terrified a Negro man who was busy shaving ice for the buffet. He threw aside the shaving utensil, fell on his knees, prayed for his life and said, "I gwine 'way f'om here. I don' hear Miss Lizzie walkin' 'bout—now I sees her. I knowed all 'long she was here!"

After relating this story to one of the members, the Club President was told, "The nicest thing about living in an old house is that you're never alone!" To which the President nodded his head vigorously in agreement.

The auction of Elizabeth's articles was held on November 22, 1900 at 3pm in Boston. It took just two hours to sell the 577 books, autographs, pictures of actors, statesmen and soldiers, glassware, Confederate bonds, silverware, flags, a bust of Lincoln, and assorted pieces of furniture. When required, John Reynolds would explain the historical significance of each piece.

Elizabeth's countrywoman's disguise sold for $4.50, a Cavalry saber for $2.75, letters from Horace Greeley, Charles Sumner, Henry Clay, Benjamin Butler, Oliver Wendell Holmes, President James A. Garfield, Vice-President Henry Wilson, Frederick Douglas, and others sold from $.80 to $4.25. A picture of Robert E. Lee went for $15.00, and a picture of Grant, on which he had signed on the back "To Elizabeth ..." went for $25.00. The thirty-four star flag that Elizabeth flew over her house April 2, 1865 sold for $75.00. The entire proceeds from the sale came to around $1000.00.

On July 29, 1902, a four-foot long, 2000-pound memorial headstone of gray conglomerate Massachusetts's stone arrived in Richmond. The composite nature of the memorial represented the multifaceted nature of the woman it memorialized.

THE ELIZABETH L. VAN LEW MEMORIAL

The stone was intentionally large and irregular in shape to make it stand apart from all those around it, calling attention to the uniqueness of the woman for whom the people on Capitol Hill in Boston had such high regard. As their final tribute and salute, they had a bronze plaque sculptured and mounted on one side with the inscription:

ELIZABETH L. VAN LEW
1818   1900

She risked everything that is dear to man—friends, fortune, comfort, health, life itself, all for the one absorbing desire of her heart—that slavery might be abolished and the Union preserved.

THIS BOULDER
From the Capitol Hill in Boston is a tribute from Massachusetts friends.

The memorial was sent to Otis H. Russell, himself a former Postmaster of Richmond, who promptly hired J. Henry Brown, a marble worker to place the stone in position. It was not certain if the memorial was placed in "reverence," facing the headstones of the rest of her family members, or in "revenge," facing the back of the cemetery away from public view.

Dr. Parker had such a love of medicine that he had refused to retire. His doctor ordered him to "slow down or suffer the consequences." After giving it much thought, he came up with a plan to do both. He would give up his regular medical practice and then establish, administer, and assist periodically with medical treatment in a sanatorium for the terminally ill.

Now, he had to find the right location. He mulled over several possible properties and then came up with the ideal location … the Virginia Club!" Excited at the solution, he headed for 2311 Grace Street. As he approached the building, his heart began to pound. "Still looks pretty good from the outside," he said to himself. When he was admitted and entered the building, he looked around at the drinking, gambling, and boisterous carrying on. He thought, "This is not a fitting use of this magnificent site. A sanatorium would be a more dignified and respectable use of the property. I think the humanitarianism in Elizabeth would approve of my intentions. The patients would love the view, the neighborhood is quiet, and it is just the right size to accommodate the amount of patients I want … and, I could move in myself—roll out of bed, and I'm in my office!" His mind made up, he was not willing to take "No" for an answer and made the Virginia Club an offer too good to be refused.

In 1908, Doctor William H. Parker became the last owner to live in the home. He had admired it as a young man, visited it often in a medical capacity throughout all of his adult life, and now he could live and work in it for the rest of his days. Day by day, his attachment and appreciation of the home grew. Now, he experienced first hand why Elizabeth loved the house and grounds and hated the thought of losing it. Not once did he ever hear any strange comings or goings. It was as if his presence in the house had approval—bringing peace to its "spiritual inhabitants."

One evening, however, he was baffled, then enchanted when he suddenly envisioned a mortar and pestle on the table of the rear portico. He liked to sit there every night admiring the sunsets over the James in the tradition of a former owner. The pestle was upside down in the mortar and along side was a freshly cut red rose. As he sat staring admiringly at the carefully arranged items on the table, he reached out to turn the pestle upright saying, "Yes, Elizabeth. Once again I got your message."

EPILOGUE

A House Dis-Honored

The most important agenda item on the Richmond City School Board's January 1911 meeting was to select a suitable site for the relocation of the Bellevue Elementary School. They had three possible locations to pick from. The first was the Jefferson Davis Home. The thought of destroying the home of such a "beloved historical personage" appalled everyone and was immediately rejected.

The next choice was the home of Supreme Court Justice Marshall, and the board was equally disturbed at the thought of demolishing the home of such a revered example of "high Constitutional authority," and it too was immediately rejected.

The last choice was the former home of Elizabeth Van Lew, Union spy and traitor to the South and its cause. A resounding "YES!" filled the chamber. The three options had been carefully selected to guarantee the outcome of their deliberations. There had never been any intention of destroying either of the first two properties.

But, before the votes were cast, a cautionary voice of a female member who had lived in Richmond for only twenty years spoke in dissent.

"You know we lost a lucrative tourist attraction when we gave up the Libby Prison. Now, we have another tourist attraction in the Van Lew property. People, especially from the North, would pay good money to tour the house. I bet the restoration money needed would be recouped in its first year of operation. After the first year, we could use the income to maintain our other historical Confederate attractions. In that way, Miss Van Lew would posthumously be supporting the cause she should have chosen from the beginning!"

While the suggestion was "applauded" by the nodding of many amused heads and smirks, the subtlety of the vengeance was insufficient to overcome the strong desire for a more punishing revenge. Now, the bitter counter arguments came like a tornado.

"To hell with the money. I say level the house!"

"We don't want to immortalize her; we want to wipe out every bloody memory of the traitor!"

"I agree. It would just be a Van Lew Memorial. I say build the school there!"

"Take down the house now, and ten years from now, no one will remember she ever existed!"

"Let's end the damned discussion and vote now!"

"I second the motion. Let's make it unanimous!"

Reading from a typed, prepared script, the Chairman of the Board rose and said, "All those in favor of declaring the old Van Lew home an unsafe building that should be condemned as unfit for human habitation, taken by eminent domain, and immediately destroyed for the safety and welfare of the community, and the grounds subsequently used to build a new elementary school, please signify by saying 'Aye.'"

Although there was one dissenting vote, a unanimous vote was entered into the minutes, and a round of applause, back slapping, and mischievous laughter sealed the fate of the historic residence.

It was a saddened and broken-spirited Doctor Parker who stood on the corner of 24th and Grace Streets. Behind him was St. John's Church. In front of him was the stately mansion he had loved ever since he first saw it—and even more for having lived in it. Like many things in this world approaching the century mark, the dwelling showed its age, but the stories it could tell!

Although it was only a structure, it was Elizabeth Van Lew who ennobled the edifice. It was her deeds that gave it an indelible identity of which it was proud and less noble detractors detested. So, by association, the building was also "guilty" and had to be punished. Destroying the building was redundant.

Elizabeth had already paid a heavy and cruel price for following her conscience. Her true legacy was in the human beings whose lives were saved and enriched by her caring and giving nature. The full knowledge of her efforts, Christian humanity, and largess may never be known to the world. However, the "ultimate judgement" is not of this world.

SELECTED READINGS

Arnold, James R. *"The Armies of U.S, Grant."* London: Arms and Armour Press, 1995

Blakey, Arch Frederic, *"General John Henry Winder C.S.A."* Gainesville: University of Florida Press, 1990

Bondurant, Agnes M., *"Poe's Richmond."* Richmond: Poe Associates, 1978

Bremer, Frederika, *"The Homes of the New World: Impressions of America."* University of Nebraska Press,

Brick, John, *"The Richmond Raid."* New York: Doubleday and Company, Inc., 1963

Carr, Caleb, *"Personal Memoirs: Ulysses S. Grant."* Toronto: Random House, Inc., 1999

Denney, Robert E., *"Civil War Prisons & Escapes: A Day-by-Day Chronicle."* New York: Sterling Publishing Company, 1993

Feis, William B., *"Grant's Secret Service."* Lincoln: University of Nebraska Press, 2002

Fichel, Edwin C., *"The Secret War for the Union: The Untold Story of Military Intelligence in the Civil War."* New York: Houghton Mifflin Company, 1996

Furgurson, Ernest B., *"Ashes of Glory: Richmond at War."* New York: Alfred A Knopf, 1996

Gindlesperger, James, *"Escape from Libby Prison."* Shippensburg, PA: Burd Street Press, 1996

Goss, Warren Lee, *"The Soldier's Story of His Captivity at Andersonville, Belle Isle, and other Rebel Prisons."* Boston: Lee and Shepard, 1868

Headland. Helen, *"The Swedish Nightingale: A Biography of Jenny Lind."* 2005

Lankford, Nelson, *"Richmond Burning."* New York: Viking Penguin Group, 2002

Leonard, Elizabeth D., *"All the Daring of a Soldier: Women of the Civil War Armies."* New York: Penguin Books, 1999

Livermore, Mary A., *"My Story of the War: A Woman's Narrative."* Hartford: A.D. Worthington and Company, 1889

Longacre, Edward G., *"Mounted Raids of the Civil War."* Lincoln: University of Nebraska Press, 1975

Markle, Donald E., *"Spies & Spymasters of the Civil War."* New York: Hippocrene Books, 1994

Moore, Frank, *"The Civil War in Song and Story."* New York: P. F. Collier, 1889

McPherson, James M., *"Battle Cry of Freedom: The Civil War Era."* New York: Ballantine Books, 1968

Pinkerton, Allan, *"The Spy of the Rebellion."* Hartford: M. A. Winter & Hatch, 1883

Poe, Edgar Allan, *"Complete stories and Poems of Edgar Allan Poe: The Gold Bug."* New York: "Doubleday Bantam

Ryan, David D., Edited by, *"A Yankee Spy in Richmond: The Civil War Diary of 'Crazy Bet' Van Lew."* Mechanicsburg: Stackpole Books, 1996

Schultz, Duane, *"The Dahlgren Affair: Terror and Conspiracy in the Civil War."* New York: W.W. Norton & Company, 1998

Scott, Mary Wingfield, *"Old Richmond Neighborhoods."* Richmond: William Byrd Press, Inc., 1950

Shaara, Michael, *"The Killer Angels."* New York: Ballantine Books, 1974

Smith, George Gardner, *"Spencer Kellogg Brown: His Life in Kansas and His Death as a Spy."* New York: D. Appleton and Company, 1903

Stern, Philip, Van Doren, *"Secret Missions of the Civil War."* New York: Wings Books, 1990

Weatherford, Doris, *"American Women's History: An A to Z of People, Organizations, Issues, and Events."* New York: Prentice Hall, 1994

CPSIA information can be obtained
at www.ICGtesting.com
Printed in the USA
JSHW020343190123
36307JS00003B/6

9 780595 466658